The Housewife's Handbook

The Housewife's Handbook

How to run the modern home

Rachel Simhon

BETTERWAY BOOKS

The Housewife's Handbook
Copyright © 2007 by Rachel Simhon

First published in North America (2008)
by Betterway Books
an imprint of F+W Publications, Inc.
4700 East Galbraith Rd.
Cincinnati, OH 45236
800-289-0963
www.fwpublications.com

The dictionary definition on p. vii is © Chambers Harrap Publishers Ltd 2003. Reproduced by permission of Chambers Harrap Publishers Ltd. • The extract on p. viii is from *The Second Sex* © Simone de Beauvoir 1953, published by Jonathan Cape. A new English translation is due to be published in 2008. Reproduced by permission of The Random House Group Ltd. • The extract on p. 4 is from *Cold Comfort Farm* © Stella Gibbons 1932. Reproduced by permission of Curtis Brown Group Ltd, London, on behalf of The Estate of Stella Gibbons. • The extract on p. 58 is from *The Lion, the Witch and the Wardrobe* © CS Lewis 1950. Reproduced by permission of CS Lewis Pte Ltd. • The extract on p. 104 is from *The Borrowers* © Mary Norton 1953. Reproduced by permission of Orion Children's Books. • The extract on p. 156 is from 'The Shrinking Song' © Ogden Nash 1938, as it appears in his collection *Candy is Dandy: The Best of Ogden Nash*, published by Andre Deutsch. Reproduced by permission of Carlton Publishing Group. • The phrase on p. 184 is from *The Tale of Mrs Tiggy Winkle* © Beatrix Potter 1905. Reproduced by permission of Frederick Warne & Co Ltd. • The extract on p. 198 is from *The Thirty-nine Steps* © John Buchan 1915. Reproduced by permission of AP Watt Ltd on behalf of The Lord Tweedsmuir and Jean, Lady Tweedsmuir. • Every reasonable effort has been made to trace the copyright holders of the other extracts in this book. The publisher would be glad to hear from them for subsequent printings.

First published in Great Britain 2007
The moral right of the author has been asserted
Bloomsbury Publishing Plc, 36 Soho Square, London W1D 3QY

CIP catalogue record for this book is available from the British Library

Illustrated and designed by Will Webb
Typeset by Hewer Text UK Ltd, Edinburgh
Printed in Singapore by Tien Wah Press

www.bloomsbury.com/rachelsimhon

ISBN-13: 978-1-55870-875-4
ISBN-10: 1-55870-875-8

For my mother, who hates housework

Introduction

Housewife (n): a married woman who looks after the house and family and does not have a paid job.'

Chambers Dictionary, 2003

What a world of meaning is invested in the word 'housewife' – and none of it particularly attractive. Because a housewife has no 'paid job', as the dictionary puts it, she is deemed not to work – in the eyes of governments, who pursue back-to-work policies to the point of obsession, in the eyes of the IRS and of the Social Services, and in the eyes of society. (How many women, when asked what they do by someone they have just met, have said, apologetically, 'Oh, I'm just a housewife'?)

Because a traditional housewife does not contribute to the national economy through taxes, or pay her way in a financial sense in the household, she is therefore also seen as a parasite, living off the money her husband earns in his 'real job'. The quid pro quo of being financed in this way is that she is expected to run the house, do the housework and look after the family. But, paradoxically, if she does her work well, far from being celebrated, she is accused of being an 'obsessive' or a 'drudge'. Either way, what she does seven days a week, 12 months a year is regarded as menial, unskilled and degrading.

Without someone to keep the house clean everyone would live in squalor and chaos, but those who keep the domestic show on the road are rewarded by being described as hysterics or zombies – the desperate housewives of television series and novels, cleaning and polishing their way to oblivion. 'That woman,' I once spitefully observed to a friend about an excessively house proud mutual friend, 'will be polishing her own gravestone.'

Simone de Beauvoir certainly believed that housework was a form of insanity and that housewives were complicit in perpetuating the madness. In her book, *The Second Sex*, she talks of the 'maniac housekeeper', a woman so busy with the Sisyphean task of housework that she loses her own existence: 'A household, in fact, with its meticulous and limitless tasks, permits to a women a sadomasochistic flight from herself as she contends madly with the things around her and with herself in a state of distraction and mental vacancy.'

It is tempting, on reading such unforgiving sentiments, to sniff and say that it's all very well for a free-thinking French bohemian, but I'd hate to have seen the state of Simone de Beauvoir's fridge. To be fair to her, de Beauvoir is not necessarily saying that houses should not be kept clean, though in the way of philosophers she is vague on the practicalities of how or by whom. Indeed, with her description of housework's 'meticulous and limitless tasks', she does comprehend the amount of work that is involved. She is saying instead that many of the women who have traditionally kept houses clean have used housework as an excuse for not engaging with the world and for shrinking from life in its widest sense.

Yet again, the housewife is put on the defensive – and yet what is actually wrong with housework? People have to live with and among other people; they have to bring up their children to be healthy; they have to be warm; they have to be fed and clothed, and they have to ensure that they can keep as free from disease as possible. To survive means washing, cooking, cleaning, nurturing – in other words, housework.

Taken at face value in this way, it is hard to see how housework and housewives have accrued so many layers of inference and subtext. Interestingly, the idea of housework as demeaning does not seem to attach to single women in the way that it does to married ones. The idea of the fussy spinster whose compulsive housekeeping is seen as a metaphor for a life unlived has disappeared. Single women can get on and clean or not as it suits without feeling that the state of their house is a reflection on them as a human being.

For married women, however, housework, or lack of it, came to be associated with virtue, or lack of it. In the 17th century, Dutch housewives were renowned across Europe for their cleanliness. Houses were cleaned according to a strict regime even to the point that cleaning the road in front of the house was a civic duty enforced by law. Contemporary travellers more familiar with the squalor and filth of other European cities commented on the clean, sweet-smelling houses of Amsterdam. The paintings of Dutch interiors of the period were not merely idealised interpretations, they were actual depictions of real life – hence their enduring popularity. To look at a Vermeer is to be transported back in time. But the Dutch did not just do housework because they liked it: cleanliness was a way of differentiating a proud Protestant nation from its neighbours. To be clean, as Margaret Horsfield says in her history of housework, *Biting the Dust*, was to be 'patriotic and vigilant, a militant defence of nation, religion and family ... Those who cleaned well and persistently were illustrating their virtue and righteousness.'

And down the years, this idea has persisted and waxed or waned according to the social mores of the time. For Dickens, who could always be relied upon to be utterly conventional when it came to portraying women, there was a strong correlation between housework and virtue. Thus, Mrs Jellyby in *Bleak House*, who is so preoccupied with the work of her African mission that she lets her household go to rack and ruin and allows her children to run wild and half-starved, is contrasted with Esther Summerson, who is always tripping round the house with her bunch of keys (the symbol of a housekeeper) at her waist, putting matters to rights in a way that tends to grate with modern readers.

Such depictions do housework a disservice. Strip away moral virtue from it and it is possible to see housework as something that has value in itself. From a purely mercenary point of view, our houses are the most expensive things we will ever own. Furniture and carpets also account for large chunks of our cash, as do clothes, shoes, electrical equipment and all the accoutrements of modern living. Though there are always swings in the housing market, the trend seems to be for staying put and improving houses rather than trading up. It therefore makes sense to know how to look after the biggest investment of your life.

Then there is the sense of ease that housework brings. Vestiges of the moral superiority of the good housekeeper still remain in that we are acutely embarrassed if an unexpected visitor turns up and the house is a mess. My mother was not a great housekeeper – in fact, we lived in anxiety-making chaos most of the time, except when visitors were expected. Then, my sister and I were dragooned into a frenzy of tidying and cleaning in a desperate attempt to make the house look respectable before they arrived. It does not take a psychoanalyst to work out that my own interest in housework is a rejection of that way of living. But there is more to it than that. I genuinely believe that domestic order is preferable to domestic chaos and that the aim of housework is not to tyrannise but to make life easier and more comfortable. Order enables us to establish rhythms so the house is ticking over. Housework allows us to create the space for living rather than being an end in itself.

In fact, in my twenties and early thirties, I followed my mother's example, doing no housework for weeks on end. This would be followed by an exhausting two-day blitz in which every surface was scrubbed and polished to within an inch of its life. Then it was back to squalor again. I had fond recollections of my grandmother's neat, tidy house in north London and my aunts' pristine houses nearby, but for years failed to spot the link between the feeling of warmth and comfort in those memories and the fact that those houses were clean and tidy.

It was only when I was sent to write a newspaper article on the work of the National Trust that I began to see the benefits and pleasures of housework applied in a consistent and professional manner. National Trust houses are actually museums but pull off the clever trick of making visitors feel they are stepping into a private house. As such, they have to look as clean and well cared for as they did when they were someone's home. At the same time, the fabric of the building and its contents have to be cleaned as gently as possible in order to preserve them.

I spent a week at the Trust's housekeeping conference and came back transformed. Surely these tried and tested, low-impact, environmentally sound techniques could be applied to a modern flat in London. That was when I discovered that housework can bring its own satisfactions and I set about learning as much as I could about it – not for its own sake, but because I was working full time and didn't have the time or the inclination to devote my whole life to my flat. So I had to learn the most efficient ways of cleaning and how quickly (or slowly) they could be done. As my knowledge increased, I came to view my mother's housekeeping shortcomings in a more forgiving light. She had, I now realised, instilled in me some good habits – how to cook and sew

(I suddenly remembered the exquisite clothes she made for my sister and me when we were little), and how to appreciate the value of things that have been handed down. It was my mother who taught me how to make a bed, how to fold sheets, how to sew a hem and put a button on a shirt, how to bake a cake and make pastry and jam. And now that she is old and frail and terribly forgetful, I am grateful for the memory of these small oases of calm and for the skills she passed on while I was eaten up with resentment that our house was so embarrassingly untidy that I couldn't invite friends back. When I went to a school reunion a few years ago and discussed this with my old friends, one of them said, 'We didn't mind, you know. We knew things were difficult and that was just how she was.' So the problem was really me and not my mother.

Coming to housework late and of my own free will, I had no trouble in approaching it in the same way as I would any job. No professional person starts a new job knowing everything – we expect to have to tackle new things, and we are expected to do them properly.

As with anything else, with housework it's as easy to do something the right way as it is to do it the wrong way. And the right way is always more efficient and safer than the wrong way, and – usually – saves time, its aim being not just to clean the object but to preserve its life. So, the right way to wash sharp knives is by hand, because the dishwasher will blunt the blades, and a blunt blade is not only useless but dangerous, because you use more force with it. The wrong way to polish a table is to spray it with silicone polish every time you dust – and not only because the silicone polish will ruin the table (although it will). Polishing every week is a waste of time: the right way to polish a table is with a beeswax polish, which takes longer, but only has to be done once a year.

The right way can save time, too – but not always. The right way to clean tarnished silver cutlery is by boiling it for ten minutes in a saucepan of water lined with aluminium foil. Knowing this definitely saves time – mind-numbing hours of work with silver polish and cloth. On the other hand, a piece of silver jewellery would be ruined by the foil-and-water technique. There's nothing for it but to polish it by hand, which will take as long as it takes. At least if you know that something is going to be a slow job, you can allow time to do it.

Many of the techniques described in this book show the way I clean my own things – methods that I have perfected over the years, or which have been the result of a brainwave, such as realising that the quickest way to clean a dusty

Venetian blind is to close the slats and vacuum it with the upholstery brush attachment. Others have been taught to me by the many experts who have shared their knowledge with me. All are tried and tested. Try them – you may be pleasantly surprised.

But while I suggest you give at least some of them a go, there are other sections of this book where I would be rather alarmed if someone followed them to the letter. Take, for example, the timetables suggested in Chapter 11. At first glance, they are terrifying, authoritarian and unrealistic. But they are not meant to be taken literally. I doubt if there is a single person in the world who cleans the house according to an unbending, rigid routine. And anyone who does has confused housework with tyranny. The schedules are there to point the way for the novice, to give hope to the disorganised and to give a few ideas to the experienced housewife. They are a framework for discussion. Adopt as much or as little of them as seems suitable for you and your family – or jettison them completely.

This book is not designed to be read from cover to cover. Treat it as a manual, to be dipped into as and when you need, like a cookery book. Neither is the aim to turn anyone into a perfect housewife. There is no such creature in existence – certainly not me. I am writing this in a study so untidy that the only way to walk across it is to pick a route through the piles of paper and books lying open, face down on the carpet. The desk is littered with dirty glasses and mugs, and so many more piles of paper that it is difficult to use the computer mouse properly. There is a thick layer of dust over every surface, the room has not been vacuumed for at least four months and I have no idea what is in most of the piles of paper. As I was editing Chapter 7 ('The Study'), the irony of my position struck me: here I was, full of good advice on how to organise and clean a home office, while my own study looked like a pigsty. It was far more important to finish working on this book than to do the housework (though housework is a well-known displacement activity: as anyone who works from home knows, there is nothing like a deadline to make one feel impelled to put the washing on).

At this point, then, I am as far from being a perfect housewife as it is possible to be. But who cares? Perfection is neither attainable nor desirable. It is cold, lifeless and bland, offering no hope or promise of change. Life is not perfect; houses are not perfect. They are like life – messy, unpredictable, sometimes chaotic, sometimes comfortable, sometimes the answer to a problem, sometimes the problem itself. This book is an attempt to help people create a sensible, positive way of running a home that will enable them to get on with what matters in life at whatever level they choose.

Housework becomes a source of resentment when a woman is expected to do it on top of a full-time job. The idea that it is demeaning came partly from the women 40 years ago who fought for the right to choose between home and a career. No one would dispute that women's lives and society in general have been hugely enriched by their entry into the workplace, and that they have grown in self-confidence as their earning power has increased. But at the same time, they feel resentful that they still do an average of 50 per cent more housework than men. They justifiably feel that the burden of housework should not fall entirely upon them. It is hardly surprising that money and housework are two of the major sources of dispute within families.

Until recently, men did not expect to do housework, nor were they expected to, nor were they taught to. Any man who did care or know about running a house was seen as a joke or an anomaly: Felix Unger in *The Odd Couple* fussing about coasters and cocktail napkins. For all that he was the least macho of men, Quentin Crisp's famous observation that 'there is no need to do any housework at all. After the first four years the dirt doesn't get any worse' was merely echoing the traditional male view of housework, albeit in a rather attention-seeking way. The conventional view is still that men are slobs.

To me, it is illogical as well as infuriating that a man can be fanatical about shining his shoes before going out to work and yet not see that the toilet needs cleaning. And yet there is more to it than a convenient blindness, allowing them to get out of housework; on the contrary, housework is seen as something mysterious and complicated and far beyond the comprehension of men. 'I love women and their airing cupboards and matching towels and things,' a boyfriend once said to me in tones verging on awe. 'Men just don't do that.'

And yet increasing numbers of men are having to learn to keep house, either through marriage in a household where both partners are working full time or because they live alone, voluntarily or as a result of divorce or bereavement. The cynic might take the view of American humorist Dave Barry as to how they might go about it: 'The obvious and fair solution to the housework problem is to let men do the housework for, say, the next six thousand years, to even things up,' he wrote. 'The trouble is that men, over the years, have developed an inflated notion of the importance of everything they do, so that before long they would turn housework into just as much of a charade as business is now. They would hire secretaries and buy computers and fly off to housework conferences in Bermuda, but they'd never clean anything.'

I take a more optimistic view. Men, even the most unreconstructed hairy clod, value the comfortable things in life as much as women, and one of the positive aspects of modern life is the loosening up of gender differences. Modern men, especially those who live in cities – metrosexuals as they are sometimes known – tend to have taken on board that a house will not look after itself and that nice things are better than poor-quality ones. A friend says that she knew her husband was the man for her when she went back to his flat and slept between his fine Egyptian cotton sheets. Whether they choose to address the problem by doing the housework themselves or by hiring a cleaner, they are still addressing it, and the fact that a man approaches housework in a different way from a woman does not mean that the way he approaches it has no value. In fact, women are often their worst enemies when it comes to the division of household labour, using it as a way of exercising power. 'I'd like to help,' a man once confided to me, 'but whenever I try to do something, she watches and criticises, so in the end I give up.'

For the most part, however, our homes are clean enough – 'clean enough to be healthy, and dirty enough to be happy'. We deserve a little credit for that.

It is interesting that 'housewife' is a word that has never been made gender non-specific by the politically correct, as some others have: it's not fireman, these days, but fire fighter; not chairman, but chair. Why not 'houseworker' instead of 'housewife'?

Perhaps it is time to broaden our idea of what it means to be a housewife. In the 21st century, housewives do not have to have a ring on their finger; they will more often than not have a job outside the home; they will often not do all the housework themselves, but may employ a cleaner; they could easily be men. So here is a new definition of an old word:

'Housewife (n): someone (male or female) who is valued because they care for a house, either full time or in conjunction with another job.'

Looking at it that way, we're all housewives now.

Contents

Part I
THE HOUSE

CHAPTER 1
The Kitchen

Flora watched him with interest while he turned the cold water on to the crusted plates, and began picking at the incrustations of porridge with his twig.

She bore it for as long she could, for she could hardly believe her own eyes, and then she said:

What on earth are you doing?

Cletterin' the dishes, Robert Poste's child.

Stella Gibbons, *Cold Comfort Farm*

4

I love my kitchen. It is my favourite room in the house, the source of warmth, of good smells and delicious things to eat. Whereas my mother loves pottering in the garden, I sometimes don't go outside all day, but I can potter for Britain in the kitchen – a bit of tidying up here, a bit of a wipe there, a quick check to see if there is anything we need.

If I am feeling a bit down, I will go to the kitchen and start cooking. If I cannot sleep, I will get up, go into the kitchen, make a cup of tea, turn on the radio and read recipe books until sleep overtakes me again. I have found some of my favourite recipes that way.

Like many people who work full time from Monday to Friday, the priority is to get dinner on the table as quickly as possible. The only opportunity I have to cook 'properly' is at the weekend. That is when I can make more complicated recipes, or those that require long, slow cooking. I make jam, I bake cakes, I make bread – because cooking is the one creative process that I understand and am good at. And I love cooking for other people. To my mind, there is nothing better than seeing friends round your table, eating food you have cooked and (one hopes) enjoying themselves.

My mother, grandmother, sister and all my aunts were and are good cooks. From my mother's side, I learnt the basics of good English cooking, and there is obviously a jam-making gene, because my grandmother, mother and I all make jam slightly obsessively.

Because my father's family is Jewish, I got used to the idea that special occasions demand special foods and that no substitutes are allowed – the matzos during Passover; the honey cake at Rosh Hashanah.

They are Sephardic Jews, who lived in Egypt until forced to leave after the Suez Crisis of 1956, so the 'Jewish' food I knew was not the tzimmes, latkes and chopped liver of European tradition, but the much more interesting flavours of the Middle East – clear chicken soup flavoured with lemon juice and celery; potatoes cooked with turmeric and lemon; rice cooked with almonds and sultanas; and delicious cakes – marbled chocolate and vanilla sponge cake and ma'amoul, little mouthfuls of mouth-wateringly rich and crumbly pastry stuffed with dates or pistachio nuts. Even now, when I make any of these, I am taken back to the kitchen of my aunt Renée, and its smells of baking, garlic and coffee.

The importance of the kitchen as the heart of the home is seen in the money we spend on it. The average cost of a kitchen is over $6,000, but many people spend considerably more. This willingness to spend cannot be put down just to consumer greed. For the fact is that people are very comfortable with the modern idea of a kitchen. It has become not just a room in which food is prepared, but also the room where the family eats; where guests are entertained; where homework is done; where friends come to sit and chat; where the neighbours pop in for a cup of tea. It is rather touching – considering that we are continually being told that 'no one' cooks any more – that when estate agents ask prospective buyers what they are looking for in a house, top of the wish list after such practicalities as the number of bedrooms is 'a large kitchen you can eat in'.

5

The essentials

Apart from the bathroom, no room in the house requires as much cleaning as the kitchen. Letting the kitchen get too dirty is not only unpleasant but, since this is where food is prepared and cooked, potentially unsafe. Bacteria and food are not a good combination. One bacterium sitting on a damp, dirty cloth can multiply 16 million times within eight hours. And there are reports of entire families being laid low by some lapse of kitchen hygiene, although admittedly this can normally be traced to undercooking the Christmas turkey. Hot spots are the waste bin, the sink, the floor, pets' accoutrements, such as feeding bowls and litter trays, food preparation areas and cleaning cloths.

The key to kitchen hygiene is therefore to clean little and often, which also has the benefit of keeping appliances in better working order and making for much less work in the long run. It takes only a minute to wipe a stove top. But leave the grease to build up for weeks or months, and it will take a whole morning to remove the grime.

The kitchen does not have to be clinically clean, nor is it necessary to have a plethora of disinfectants and anti-bacterial agents (there are many reasons not to use those – see 'Anti-bacterial cleaners', p. 234). Cleaning with standard household detergents and washing up in hot, soapy water or in the dishwasher will keep the kitchen quite clean enough under normal circumstances, as long as you bear in mind a few simple rules.

It is important to wash your hands thoroughly before cooking and preparing food, and to dry them well, too – but not on a tea towel.

When cooking, wash all fruits and vegetables before using them. If you keep fruit in a fruit bowl, do not let it get overripe, or it will attract fruit flies. Do not prepare any food on a chopping board that has been used for raw meat without cleaning it thoroughly. Better still, keep separate boards for meat, fish and vegetables. When it comes to kitchen hygiene, the problems stem from bad habits such as not washing hands before cooking, mixing raw and cooked foods, allowing pets to get on to surfaces where food is being prepared and not cooking food properly.

When cooking, clean as you go. As soon as I start cooking, I fill a large washing-up bowl with hot water, which means I can wash things up as they are used. Not only is this cleaner, but it also keeps the kitchen tidy.

Do not leave food uncovered in the kitchen. If food is left out for some specific purpose, such as bringing meat to room temperature before roasting, use a metal or nylon mesh food protector. Keep pets off worktops and other areas where food is being prepared.

Keep the fridge clean and follow the advice given on what to put where – and why – in the section of fridges and freezers.

After every meal, wash up (wash up pets' bowls separately). Clear all crumbs and other debris off surfaces before wiping them down thoroughly. For the same reason, sweep the kitchen floor, or clean it if there are food spills on it. Disinfect the sink once a week (see 'Drains', p. 49), and keep the top of the kitchen bin clean. Empty bins regularly – do not wait until they have begun to smell. Wash inside and out once a week. Replace washing-up brushes, dish mops and pan scourers frequently – every few months or so.

The stove

The type of stove you choose is a matter of personal preference. From the cook's point of view, gas is the first choice, but gas stoves can be fiddly to clean. Electric radiant stoves are easier to clean, but they don't have the instant adjustability of gas. Induction or halogen stoves are smart and convenient, because the cooking element is hidden beneath an easy-to-clean sheet of glass, but cooks dislike them because they don't cook as well as gas – and require ferrous pans to work correctly.

TO CLEAN GAS STOVES

Wipe quickly after every use, especially if something has been spilt during cooking, with a damp cloth and a little liquid cleaner, such as Mr. Clean. Remove burnt-on patches with a nylon scourer or – even better – a mark and stain eraser sponge, such as Mr. Clean Magic Eraser.

Tip: Sprinkle salt on to spills when they occur, to soak up grease.

Once a week, take the pan supports, burner caps and heads off the stove. If there is burnt-on food on the stove top, you can loosen it by leaving it covered with a cloth dipped in the soapy water while you clean the pan supports, etc. The pan supports can usually go in the dishwasher (but check the manufacturer's instructions). If not, wash them in hot, soapy water. Burner caps should generally not be immersed in water because of the danger of rusting the non-vitreous underside. Clean these and the aluminium stove rings with a Brillo pad.

For the burners to work safely, the slots in the burner head where the flames burn need to be kept clear of deposits. Clean with a nylon brush, rinse and dry thoroughly.

Once these are clean, wipe the stove top. The soaking will have loosened the dirt. At the same time, do the front of the oven and wipe the fascia and in between the knobs. Some free-standing gas stoves have a glass lid, which acts as a splashback. Wash it now. Rinse, wipe dry and put back pan supports etc. Take care to put back the burner caps and heads in the correct position, so that they sit squarely on the stove.

TO CLEAN ELECTRIC STOVES

After use, wipe the surface of the stove around the rings with a damp, soapy cloth

(a drop of dish soap will do).

Switch off the electricity. Clean sealed plates with a cream cleaner and a scouring pad, then apply a specialist stove polish, if available. Removable rings should be dismantled and the relevant parts washed in hot, soapy water. Consult the manufacturer's manual.

TO CLEAN GLASS-TOPPED STOVES
(i.e. all ceramic, halogen and induction stoves)

After use, wipe the stove with a damp, soapy cloth only. Stubborn stains and burnt-on deposits should be removed with a special scraper (normally supplied with the stove). If the spill is sugar-based, turn off the heat immediately, remove the pan and wipe the glass before continuing. Always consult the manufacturer's manual before cleaning these stoves, because some detergents can impair their ability to radiate heat.

Once a week, give the stove a more thorough clean, using a specialist stove cleaner, plus a special glass conditioner recommended for the make of stove, following the manufacturer's instructions.

TO CLEAN *AGA HOBS*

Wipe up spills as they happen with a damp, soapy cloth. Because the Aga is permanently on, use a thicker cloth than usual to protect your hands from the heat. Be particularly conscientious about wiping up any milk or fruit spills immediately, because they can permanently mark the enamel.

Once a week, clean the enamel parts with a mild cream cleanser (specialist cleaners are also available). Brush the hotplates with a wire brush to remove grit and crumbs. The hotplates do not need cleaning because their heat burns off food deposits. Clean the chrome lids and rail the same way, or use chrome cleaner to give a good shine. It is all a bit hair-raising and hot.

When the appliance is turned off for its annual service, tackle any particularly bad burnt-on bits, but in general I like an Aga to look as if it has seen a bit of life.

> *Tip: You can keep all stoves clean by cooking at moderate temperatures. Splatter guards are also available. These are wire meshes that you rest on top of a pan to catch spluttering fat, but in my experience they are not very effective.*

TO CLEAN COOKER HOODS

Once a week, kill the power and wipe with a cloth wrung out in hot water and a liquid cleaner such as Mr. Clean. About twice a year, dismantle the hood, clean the cover thoroughly inside and out and replace the filter. Some makes have a light to show when the filter needs replacing.

The oven

An oven is essentially a box with a heating element in it — usually either an electric element or a gas flame. Cleaning it is simplicity itself and takes a matter of minutes if done regularly, and yet cleaning the oven is one of the most neglected kitchen jobs. It is a pity, because a dirty oven is one of the trickiest things to clean, as well as being unpleasant and time-consuming.

More pertinently, a clean oven is a green oven, because no toxic chemicals are required to clean it, while a dirty oven is environmentally unsound because oven cleaners are some of the most toxic, un-green chemicals around.

There are a couple of tricks that will stop the oven getting dirty in the first place.

> Note: Before using any chemicals in the oven, check the manufacturer's handbook for what can and can't be used. For example, easy-clean panels (see below) can be damaged by chemicals.

A traditional, environmentally friendly method is to make a solution of baking soda (½ tbsp soda to 1 pint water). Swab this mixture over the oven and shelves (not easy-clean panels). It will dry to a white-streaked, powdery finish. Next time the oven is used, any grease will be absorbed and will wipe off easily.

Or:

Line the bottom of the oven with a specialist liner. This is a thick, plastic material than can be cut to size to fit the bottom of a clean oven. It catches all drips and can be taken out, washed and reused. Ensure that it is not covering elements or burners.

> Note: Lining the bottom of the oven and the bottom of a grill pan with aluminium foil is not generally recommended these days because of the danger of fire. Check the manufacturer's manual before doing so.

TO CLEAN CONVENTIONAL OVENS
(gas and electric ovens)

By far the best way to prevent an oven from turning into a black hole of horror is to wipe it clean every time it is used. Let the oven cool down and then wipe it with a damp, soapy cloth. Remember to wipe the oven shelves as well.

Many ovens these days have 'easy-clean' panels at the sides and back of the oven. The idea is that any spills or splashes will be burnt off. However, remember that even these do need to be wiped once a week, especially if you do a lot of roasting at high temperatures.

Wipe off any big splashes with a damp cloth and a little dish soap. Most detergents will damage the surfaces, so if there are any large, burnt-on patches, remove them with a nylon pan scourer (not a Brillo pad), water and dish soap.

Ovens that are not very dirty can be cleaned with baking soda. Wipe the surface and sprinkle with soda. Let it sit for a while, then rub with a nylon or metal scourer. Wipe off with a damp cloth as you go. Rinse with clean water and wipe dry.

TO CLEAN A REALLY FILTHY OVEN

If you have not been as conscientious as you might have been, or have inherited a filthy oven, here is what to do:

Try to clean the oven on a day when you can open the kitchen windows, on account of fumes. Switch off the electricity, put on something to protect your clothes and wear rubber gloves.

Spread newspaper on the floor below the oven to catch any drips. If possible, remove the oven door for ease of cleaning (consult the manufacturer's manual to see if this is a feature of your oven). Remove all oven shelves and shelf runners and either put in the dishwasher on a hot cycle or put them to soak in a sink of hot water and biological detergent.

First attend to the easy-clean panels, if your oven has them.

To clean the rest of the oven, use a proprietary oven cleaner. These normally come in the form of a caustic cream in a sponge applicator or as an aerosol spray and are some of the nastiest chemicals you can use in the home. Opt for the sponges over the spray because at least you will not be breathing in the aerosol droplets. You may consider wearing a protective mask.

By their very nature, oven cleaners are not green. But there are a number of biodegradable products available now with no acrid fumes. You brush it on and leave it for a few minutes and then wipe off the residue.

Whichever you choose, apply following the instructions. Do not put cleaner on chrome, on the elements of electric ovens or on rubber seals, because it can damage them. Wipe off any obvious residue with paper towels, then wipe out the whole oven with a cloth wrung out in hot water (do not use detergent). Tackle any stubborn burnt-on bits with a nylon scourer or a mark and stain eraser sponge.

> Tip: You can normally use oven cleaner on the glass door, too, but, because it can be difficult to avoid getting the chemical on the rubber door seals, even better is a mark and stain eraser sponge.

11

If the oven has not been cleaned in a long time, one application of cleaner may not do the trick. In which case, repeat the whole operation until it is cleaned to your satisfaction.

Finally, wash the oven shelves and shelf runners, which have been soaking. Use Brillo pads to get off any stubborn marks. If the shelves have been in the dishwasher, take them out of the machine before the drying cycle and wipe off any encrusted bits that have not been removed – the drying cycle will just bake them on again.

Another way to clean a really filthy oven: The following definitely is not a green way to clean an oven, but is very effective.

Put 1 tbsp of household ammonia in a dish. Beware: this is powerful stuff and gives off toxic, choking fumes. Put the dish in a barely warm – not hot – oven. Immediately turn off the oven and leave overnight.

The ammonia turns into a gas that lifts the dirt off the shelves and sides. The next day, open the windows and let the kitchen air for a while, before wiping out the oven using hot water and a little soap (do not use detergent). This is not a method for the faint-hearted and on the green credibility scale scores about minus five. A last resort.

Or if you really can't face it: Call in the services of a specialist oven-cleaning firm. Typically, they will dismantle the cooker, dunk all the loose parts in a vat of something strong and clean the rest of the interior and elements using special cleaners to remove all traces of burnt-on grease and carbon. They can also clean the stove and exhaust, and microwave ovens. Check if the company uses non-caustic, environmentally friendly cleaners – many do.

> *Tip: Once the oven is clean, make a resolution to wipe it after every use. If the oven incorporates the grill, turn the grill on once a week at the highest setting, with the oven empty, and leave for about 15 minutes, to burn off any grease that has got behind the elements.*

TO CLEAN SELF-CLEANING OVENS

The oven heats to around 900°F, incinerating any drips, spatters or spills and reduces them to ash at the bottom of the oven, which can then be wiped off with a paper towel. The process is totally safe, because the oven door locks during the heating programme and will not unlock until the oven is cool. Sometimes the oven racks can be left in as well, but check the manufacturer's manual.

Self-cleaning ovens should never be cleaned with caustic oven cleaners, because they can damage the surfaces.

To clean Aga ovens: These count as self-cleaning because the heat within them burns off fat and splashes. All you have to do is brush them out occasionally.

TO CLEAN GRILL PANS

There really is no excuse – every time you use the grill, wash up the pan along with all the pots and pans. Use a pan scourer or Brillo pad to get off any burnt-on bits.

If you have been less than conscientious, or have inherited a filthy grill pan, the ammonia method of cleaning ovens, above, gave me an idea for tackling it. Put a couple of tablespoons of ammonia in a grill pan, and put the whole thing, rack and all, in a black plastic bin liner. Fasten the opening with string and leave the bag outside for a day. Working on a similar principle, the ammonia will lift the grease.

The next day, take the pan out of the bag and rinse it out very well with cold water (ideally using an outside tap or hose, rather than taking it into the house). Even if all the burnt-on bits do not come off, most of the dirt will have lifted and it can then be washed up as normal.

13

The fridge

Like most people, I cannot imagine life without a fridge. But it is only relatively recently that this has been the case. When my mother got married in the 1950s, her brother gave her a fridge as a wedding present. 'Even then it was quite something to have a fridge and they were expensive, so it was a very generous present,' she said. 'We were renting a flat in London and when we came to move out and people were viewing it, they were all terribly impressed that we had a fridge and wanted us to leave it there. It seems hard to believe now.'

The fridge is the modern store cupboard. We keep more and more things in it, with centrally heated homes often having nowhere cool for food, and with manufacturers now routinely recommending that products be stored in the fridge after opening.

If you have space, I would always recommend having a separate fridge and freezer, or a fridge-freezer. If this is not possible, and you have room only for a small fridge with an ice compartment, make sure it is big enough for your needs and that the ice compartment holds a temperature of 0°F, which will keep frozen food in good condition for around three months. American-style fridge-freezers are very fashionable. They are wider than standard models – indeed, some of them are large enough to stash a body – but appearances can be deceptive. Check carefully to see how much usable space there really is.

TO STORE FOOD IN THE FRIDGE

Many foods need to be kept in the fridge after opening. Check on the bottle/package and follow the instructions. Some of them may seem unnecessarily stringent (I do not, for example, refrigerate jams, which have already been preserved by their cooking process), but it pays to be careful.

Never leave food in an opened tin in the fridge, because the metal can corrode and spoil food. Always decant it into a plastic container with a lid. Anything in a plastic container, such as yogurt, cream and cream cheese should, however, be kept in its original container – most these days have a plastic lid too.

It is easier said than done, but try to avoid overcrowding the fridge, or the air that cools it will not be able to circulate. The ideal temperature is 34–37°F, certainly no more than 39°F. If your fridge is getting on a bit, invest in a fridge thermometer and, while you are about it, buy another one for the freezer (it should be at least 0°F).

Use the thermometer to check which parts of the fridge are coldest, if any. In modern fridges, which have a fan to circulate the air, the temperature is pretty uniform throughout. Generally, the coldest parts are the bottom shelf above the salad drawers (because heat rises), the back of the shelves and near the freezer section.

Stock the fridge in an orderly fashion. The general advice is to rotate foods, putting new foods behind old ones, so the oldest ones are used first. But this is illogical, when you consider that some foods need to be kept colder than others and the back of the fridge is one of the coldest areas. Instead, every time you open the fridge, get into the habit of checking the rest of the contents and throwing away anything that is beginning to look suspect, or that is way past its use-by date.

With respect to use-by dates, I have to confess that my attitude is pretty blasé. In my book, if it looks all right and smells all right, it probably is all right, but use your own judgement.

To avoid raising the temperature, try not to open and close the fridge door too often and never leave the door open for any length of time.

TO STORE MEAT, FISH AND POULTRY

These should go in the coldest areas. Always wrap before refrigerating. Most butchers do not recommend leaving meat or poultry in a plastic bag for any length of time, because it cannot breathe and goes slimy. Remove all wrappings and wrap meat in greaseproof paper, then put on a plate to prevent drips. Fresh fish, which needs to be eaten the day it is bought, can stay in its plastic bag because it will not be there for long.

Ensure that raw and cooked meat (in fact, raw and cooked anything) are kept apart. Raw food can contaminate cooked food and cause food poisoning, which is why, in professional kitchens, they are kept in separate fridges. Keep raw meat on the bottom shelf, so that it cannot drip on to food below.

TO STORE FRUIT AND VEGETABLES

These belong in the salad drawers. Some authorities suggest that fruit and vegetables should not be washed before refrigerating because they keep better. But, for convenience, I always wash everything apart from salad and soft fruits, and I cannot say I have noticed any difference. Remove the leafy tops of carrots, radishes, beetroot and so on to prevent them going limp. Store all fruit and vegetables in plastic bags. Keep soft fruits in their baskets.

TO STORE DAIRY FOOD AND EGGS

Store dairy food in the coldest part of the fridge (at the bottom or the back). But butter seems to keep well in the special compartments, which are normally in the door. Do not buy more butter than you need. Either buy it as you use it, or freeze it and transfer it to the fridge one packet at a time. Make sure all dairy food is

15

covered or wrapped at all times. It is very prone to contamination, while butter oxidises and becomes rancid. Keep dairy food away from raw meat and poultry.

I never used to refrigerate eggs – it was not deemed necessary – but since it became known that eggs could be contaminated with salmonella, I have become more careful. It is true that some recipes (meringues, mayonnaise) require eggs to be at room temperature, but this just means you have to be better organised. It is a small price to pay.

FOODS TO TREAT CAREFULLY

The air in fridges is very dry (this explains the mummified carrot one always seems to find at the bottom of the salad drawer), so always wrap food in plastic food wrap, foil or greaseproof paper to prevent it drying out. It is also more hygienic to wrap food and prevents strong-smelling food imposing itself on the rest of the contents of the fridge. The following seem to taint the fridge more than most:

> Broccoli, Brussels sprouts, cauliflower, cooked cabbage – though why anyone
> would keep old cooked cabbage beats me
> Cooked chicken and other poultry
> Ground coffee – store in an airtight tin. Whole coffee beans can be frozen
> Hard-boiled eggs (shelled)
> Onions, garlic
> Melons
> Strawberries
> Strong cheese, particularly Stilton and some French cheeses

Conversely, eggs, milk and other dairy produce seem to be particularly efficient at absorbing odours.

FOODS THAT SHOULD NOT GO IN THE FRIDGE

Tempting though it is to put everything in the fridge, there are some foods for which refrigeration does more harm than good. They include:

> Bananas – they go black
> Bread – did you know that bread stored in the refrigerator goes stale more
> quickly than if it is stored in a bread bin? Bread is not supposed to be a long-
> keeping product. If you want to keep bread for any length of time, freeze it
> Fruit that you want to ripen

16

*Mushrooms – store in a cool, dark place in a paper bag or in a cardboard
    basket covered with a damp paper towel*
Olive oil – it goes thick and cloudy, though it won't come to any harm
Potatoes (they start sprouting at low temperatures)
Tomatoes – they go woolly

Never put hot food in the refrigerator. There are two reasons for this. First, the steam rising from the food can cause condensation to form inside the fridge. Second, the heat will raise the temperature of the fridge. This matters because food poisoning organisms will grow and multiply rapidly at room temperature if they have a supply of food, moisture and suitable atmosphere. Given ideal conditions, they can double in number every 20 minutes. The temperature above which bacteria will start to multiply is 46°F.

The usual advice is that cooked food that is not going to be eaten straight away should be cooled as quickly as possible. To do this, put it somewhere cool, away from heat.

If the recipe allows it, slice or cut up the food into smaller pieces. Pour things like soups or stews into shallow containers to allow them to cool more quickly, and spread rice on a baking sheet. Aim to get the food cool enough to be put in the fridge within 1½ hours.

TO CLEAN THE FRIDGE

Wash the shelves and drawers either by hand in hot, soapy water or by putting them in the dishwasher. You are not strictly supposed to do this, but I have never had any problem with using a short cycle at a low temperature (95°F) in my machine.

Wash the interior of the fridge with warm water and baking soda (1 tbsp to 2 pints water). To remove dried-on bits of food, soften them first with water. Do not attempt to scrape them off because you might pierce the shell of the fridge. Rub stubborn marks with straight baking soda on a damp cloth.

Remember to clean the seals because they can harbour mould. If you do spot mould, wipe over with a very weak solution of household bleach (1 tsp to 1 pint water). Check the drainage-hole on automatic defrosting models and carefully remove any blockages with a pencil or similar.

Baking soda is used because it cleans, disinfects and is odourless. It is also biodegradable and comparatively non-toxic, so it is the green option. Do not use perfumed detergents – it is amazing how they will linger and taint food. But if the fridge is really filthy, baking soda may not be strong enough. In this case, use warm water and a small amount of dish soap. Rinse with warm plain water and wipe dry with a cloth or paper towel.

> *Tip: To keep the fridge smelling sweet, tuck a fridge deodoriser into one corner. These contain activated charcoal or a special gel to absorb odours. They are extremely effective. Several are now made from temperature-sensitive plastic, which shows if the fridge is too warm. Replace every four months.*

After cleaning the interior, remove from the fridge door all novelty magnets, notices and pictures of yourself looking fat which are supposed to act as a deterrent when you fancy raiding the fridge at midnight. Wipe the outside with a damp cloth and a little detergent.

> *Counsel of perfection: polish the exterior of the fridge with a silicone spray polish, such as Pledge. Vacuum the coils at the back of the fridge occasionally (see 'To clean behind the fridge', below).*

18

If you go away for any length of time, empty the fridge, switch it off and leave the door open (wedged with a tea towel if it seems as if it might swing shut). This stops it smelling musty.

TO DEFROST THE FRIDGE

Most modern fridges defrost themselves automatically (when buying, look for one that is called 'frost-free'). But older fridges or those with an ice compartment will still need to be defrosted manually.

To do this, switch off the thermostat and unplug the fridge. Empty the fridge and transfer perishable goods to a cooler with some ice packs. Remove the shelves, open the fridge door and leave to defrost. To hasten the process, put a bowl of hot water on one of the shelves. Put newspaper or an old towel in the bottom of the fridge to soak up drips. Once the defrosting is complete, clean and the fridge and wipe as above.

TO CLEAN BEHIND THE FRIDGE

A woman I know cleans behind the fridge in her surgically clean kitchen once a month. For most of us a couple of times a year will do – maybe once every three months if you have lots of pets and/or children. Save time by doing it at the same time you were planning to clean the inside of the fridge (see above). First unplug the fridge, then pull it away from the wall. (That is one of those instructions that are so much easier to write than to carry out. 'Just pop the pill down the cat's throat' is another one.)

If you have not got a fridge with built-in casters (there is usually a lever at the side, which you lift up, thus engaging the casters), buy an appliance dolly, available from DIY stores for around $75; they can normally shift appliances weighing up to 700 pounds.

The amount of dirt, crumbs and pet hairs that accumulate behind the fridge is amazing. First, vacuum or sweep up the obvious debris. Then wash down the walls and floor with household detergent and hot water. Now spray the walls and floor with Pledge or a similar silicone spray polish. Spray only the bits that will be covered by the fridge. The idea is to give a protective coating so that cleaning is easier next time.

> Note: I would only use silicone spray polish for a job such as this.
> Do not use it on wooden furniture. (For more on care of wood, see
> 'Wooden furniture', p. 272.)

Finally, vacuum the coils at the back, using the upholstery nozzle. Cleaning off the layers of dust that accumulate on them will help the fridge work better and last longer – better for the environment and better for your pocket.

There is, of course, a way of avoiding all of the above, and that is to have fridges and freezers built in to your kitchen.

The freezer

Much of the advice on fridge care applies equally to freezers. Do not overload the freezer, and when planning to freeze a large amount of food, switch on fast-freeze, if the freezer has one, in good time (at least six hours). Open and close the door as little as possible and never leave the door open for any length of time. In any case, most models have an alarm buzzer to prevent this happening. The temperature in a good freezer should be at most 0°F; better freezers are colder. If you suspect your freezer is not cold enough, buy a freezer thermometer to check it. Always thaw frozen food in the fridge. Keep it wrapped and do not allow it to drip on to other foods.

TO STORE FOOD IN THE FREEZER

All food destined for the freezer should be well wrapped and sealed, otherwise the food will lose its flavour and dry out. Use Tupperware containers, freezer bags or heavy-duty aluminium foil. Separate chops, steaks, fillets of fish and so on and wrap in food wrap, then put in freezer bags. Freeze all meat, poultry and fish that you will not be eating immediately.

When freezing liquids, leave 1 inch at the top to allow for expansion. Freeze small quantities of liquid in ice-cube trays (useful for sauces, stocks, egg yolks and whites). Transfer the frozen cubes to freezer bags. Seal bags with tie closures or elastic bands, or use self-closing bags. Secure packages with freezer tape or freezer clips.

Label the contents using a freezer marker or a china marker (bags incorporating write-on labels make this easier). If there is a lot of food in the freezer, keep a stock book so you know what was frozen and when, and can rotate stock so you know what to eat first.

Refer to the maker's manual for detailed recommendations on what to freeze and for how long, and also for storage times. If you have, say, a lot of garden produce that you want to freeze, buy a freezer cookery book for detailed recommendations and instructions about how best to go about it.

FOODS THAT SHOULD NOT GO IN THE FREEZER

Just as there are some foods that are best kept out of the refrigerator, so some foods just will not freeze satisfactorily, either for hygiene reasons, or because they cannot withstand the changes that freezing causes. In general, do not freeze:

Salads and some other fruits and vegetables, including lettuce, radishes, cucumber, raw tomatoes, raw celery, chicory, raw cabbage, raw potatoes, raw onions, peppers, marrow, watermelon, melon. Strawberries can be frozen but will collapse on thawing

Whole eggs – the shell will burst if they are frozen whole. Break the eggs and beat lightly, adding a little salt or sugar (for use in savoury or sweet recipes – label,

*so you know which is which). Freeze in small quantities (freezing in ice-cube
trays is a good idea). Yolks and whites can be frozen separately.
Add a little salt to the yolk or it will thicken. Do not freeze hard-boiled eggs*

*Some dairy products, including sour cream, yogurt, cream cheese (unless the
pack states otherwise) ricotta, single cream and custard. Heavy whipping
cream can be frozen but coffee cream will curdle. Pasteurised milk can be
frozen*

Cake mixture

Milk-based sauces – they will curdle

Mayonnaise

*Thawed frozen food. Never refreeze once it has thawed out – not only will
the texture of the food be spoiled, there is also a danger of food poisoning.
However, if the food is first cooked through thoroughly, it can be refrozen*

*Anything else the manufacturers tell you not to freeze – refer to the package
instructions*

TO CLEAN AND DEFROST THE FREEZER

Many of today's freezers are frost-free (i.e., they do not need defrosting) but
older models will need defrosting. If you are scrupulous about not opening the
door unnecessarily, you should not need to defrost more than once or, at most,
twice a year. Do not wait until the ice is so thick that you have to send in a team
of huskies to find a packet of lamb chops. The time to defrost is when a modest
accumulation of ice has formed.

Defrost the fridge when stocks are low and try to choose a day when the
weather is not too hot. Remove all the contents and throw out anything that is
way past its use-by date (freezing halts the rate at which food deteriorates, but
cannot halt the deterioration indefinitely; eventually it will start to taste stale and
lose its flavour) or that you know you will never eat. Put the food in coolers with
some ice packs, or ask a kindly neighbour if you can put it in their freezer.

Switch off and unplug the freezer. Remove the drawers or shelves and wash
in hot, soapy water (or put in the dishwasher on a low temperature wash).
Rinse and leave to dry while the freezer is defrosting.

Make sure any drainage holes are not blocked and put a tray or other shallow
container under them to collect drips. Put thick bath towels in the bottom of
the freezer to soak up excess water and spread newspaper on the floor.

Remove chunks of ice as they loosen but do not try to scrape off ice with any sharp implements because you might pierce the shell. If you must scrape, use a rubber spatula. When all the ice has gone, wipe the inside of the freezer with warm water and baking soda (1 tbsp to 2 pints water) and wipe dry. Wipe the exterior with warm water and household detergent. You can also spray the outside with silicone spray polish. Periodically, vacuum the coils at the back of the appliance.

Other than that, defrosting is a curiously restful experience – one domestic chore that actually does itself.

Kitchen cupboards and the pantry

A cool, dark pantry, with a slate shelf, vegetable racks and lots of cupboards and shelves for dry and tinned goods is a lottery-winning fantasy of mine, along with the tall, thin house in Chelsea in which it is to be housed. We had a smaller version in the house I grew up in, on a north-facing wall so it kept cool, and with a tiled shelf rather than a slate one. It is only now that I realise that this was the perfect place to store food, as long as we could keep the cat out of it.

In fact, pantries are coming back into vogue again. Some property developers are beginning to include them in new houses, and upmarket kitchen designers are incorporating them when rebuilding kitchens.

Few of us, however, have this luxury. The next best thing to a pantry is a pantry cupboard, of the type included in most kitchen designers' repertoires. In the absence of either, most of us have to make do with kitchen cupboards.

TO STORE FOOD IN CUPBOARDS

When choosing cupboards to use for food storage, bear in mind that they should be cool, dark, dry, well ventilated and not sited too near a direct source of heat: if there are cupboards on a north-facing wall, these are the ones to keep food in.

Cupboards in which food is stored must be cool because food – even canned and packaged goods – will eventually deteriorate if kept at too high a temperature (the ideal is actually around 50°F). They need to be dark because many foods deteriorate in the light – particularly spices, oils and vegetables – which is why open shelves and glass-fronted cupboards are not a good idea. They need to be dry and well ventilated because humidity can cause some foods, such as cookies and cereals, to go soft; some, such as sugar, to cake; and others, such as dry goods, to grow moulds.

The key to hygienic, efficient kitchen storage is to not buy too much food at once. A pantry groaning with foodstuffs looks lovely and may make you think you are a perfect housewife, but you will end up throwing half the stuff away. Buy what you need when you need it and use it up before replacing it. This is not just a question of thrift: flour (particularly wholewheat varieties, which contain more fat), pulses and other grains can attract pests, such as weevils and pantry moths (see 'Household pests', p. 322). If you get an infestation, the only solution is to throw everything out, clean out the cupboards and start again.

Arrange the contents of the food cupboard in an orderly fashion, keeping like with like as much as possible – cans together, dry goods together, baking ingredients together and so on. Put newly bought cans or packets behind old ones, so that the older ones get used up first. Half-open bags of flour, sugar and so forth (but see below) should be folded over tightly. Many of them now incorporate sticky labels on the packet to keep them folded, but in my experience, they are never sticky enough. Use a rubber band, a freezer clip or – my tip – a clothespin to keep them closed.

23

TO STORE FOOD IN JARS

Once opened, dry goods should ideally go into storage jars, which should be airtight and preferably large enough to take a whole packet of sugar or bag of flour or whatever in one go.

Do not top up storage jars. Use up all the contents and wash them before refilling.

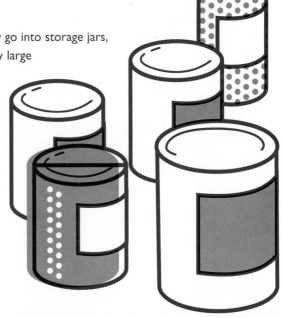

> Tip: If you are not sure how long to keep something, tear off the use-by date from the packet and put it in the jar as a reminder.

Buy for convenience rather than style. Pottery jars with 'sugar', 'flour' and so forth written on the side are to my mind rather corny and limit your options as to what to store. If you prefer opaque jars, choose a variety with a see-through lid, because you will never remember what was in each one. You could, of course, stick a label on the outside, but that defeats the point of their pure lines.

I prefer glass storage jars. They look elegant. You do not have to worry about matching them to a colour scheme and you can see what is in them at a glance. If storing them out in the open, there is the question of light deterioration, so use up the contents quickly.

My favourite jars look like old-fashioned candy jars. They have a glass knob stopper lid and were made by the now-defunct St Helens glass company, Ravenhead. They amply fulfill William Morris's dictum about beauty and utility, they are just the right size, they are solid, well-made and a pleasure to use – so naturally you cannot get them any more, except by scouring internet auction sites and antiques shops.

TO STORE FOOD IN PLASTIC BOXES

There was a story in the papers a few years ago about the Queen's breakfast cereal being decanted into Tupperware boxes. Apart from the fact that the Queen has thus presumably never had the pleasure of reading the back of the cereal packet, this seemed to me to be a bit unnecessary. Cereal keeps perfectly in its box if the inner wrapper is folded down tightly and the outer packet is closed.

It is useful to have a few Tupperware (or similar) boxes for storing food in the fridge and the freezer, and for keeping foods super airtight. Cakes, for example, keep much better in a plastic cake box than in a tin.

> *Tip: Never store cakes in the same container as cookies. The cake will make the cookies soggy, and the cookies will make the cake go dry.*

TO STORE KITCHEN UTENSILS

When deciding what to put where, keep like with like (e.g. all serving dishes and bowls together; all saucepans together). Put things that you use very frequently within easy reach.

> *China and glass should go in wall units near the sink. Some people also have a fine dinner service 'for best'. This should be kept separate from everyday china – in a sideboard in the dining-room, if you have one.*

Chopping boards go in a tray slot, if you have one. Otherwise, store upright on the worktop against a wall.

Cleaning materials go under the sink (if you have children, fit a lock to the door).

Cooking utensils (e.g. bowls, colanders, sieves, graters, lemon squeezers, measuring jugs) go in cupboards and drawers near the main food preparation area, close to the stove.

Cutlery goes in a drawer near the dishwasher or sink. Do not let it rattle around in the drawer. Buy a cutlery tray. Fine silver cutlery should be kept in a separate drawer, or in its chest, or in the sideboard in the dining-room.

Food mixers and food processors go on the worktop unless space is at a premium. If kept in a cupboard, they tend to get forgotten.

Instruction leaflets (for appliances) go in a drawer, which will probably also house rubber bands, a ball of string, miscellaneous screws and bits of plastic that you do not want to throw out in case they are important, pens, corks, etc, etc. This is the junk drawer, without which no kitchen is complete.

Knives go in a knife block (see 'Knives', p. 40).

Oven mitts go on a hook near the stove.

Pots and pans go in a low-level cupboard near the stove. Deep pan drawers are the most convenient method of storage.

Roasting tins and baking sheets go in an oven drawer (if there is one), or with pots and pans.

Scales go on top of the worktop in the area where you prepare most food.

Serving dishes go in a cupboard. Keep them all together.

Tea towels go on a hook near the sink.

Other table linens, such as napkins, placemats and the tea cosy, go in a drawer near the sink.

Tools (e.g. spatulas, whisks, scissors) go in a drawer near the stove. Keep those that are used most, such as wooden spoons, in a container on top of the worktop near the stove.

TO CLEAN CUPBOARDS

Once a week, wipe over the doors and drawer fronts with detergent and a damp cloth. Do not forget the handles.

Dust and crumbs in food cupboards encourage mould, attract pests and cause a characteristic stale smell. Every three months, empty everything out of them. Check that packages are not torn and that cans are not rusty or bulging. A small dent on the rim will not matter, but a bulging can shows that it has 'blown' and that the contents are spoilt. Throw it away immediately. Also throw out anything that is way past its use-by date.

Wipe shelves with a damp cloth to remove crumbs, then wash thoroughly with hot water and detergent. Wring out the cloth well before wiping the shelves: they should not get too wet. Even better is one of the mark and stain eraser sponges – they seem to be particularly good at cutting through that peculiarly tenacious mixture of baked-on grease and dust that afflicts kitchen surfaces. Rinse, if necessary, with plain water, then dry with a clean cloth and leave the cupboard doors open to allow them to get completely dry before putting everything back in.

Once the shelves are dry put back the contents, wiping tops of cans and packets with a barely damp cloth as you do so.

Cupboards containing china and glass should be washed during spring-cleaning. Empty everything out, clean the shelves as above, and wash anything that has not been used in a while before putting it away. If the kitchen is very greasy, it may be necessary to do this twice a year.

26

Washing dishes

When I was a student, one of my friends turned the avoidance of washing up into an art. It was not that he refused to do it. If anything, he was first at the sink. But then he would be so painfully slow – organising the dirty crockery on one side of the sink, meticulously washing one fork at a time – that eventually someone would seize the dish mop from his hand in frustration. Somehow, I noticed, the rest of us were always washing up and he was always watching television.

But his instinct was right. To wash up properly you need order, method and plenty of hot water.

TO WASH UP BY HAND

Try to get into the habit of washing up after every meal. When cooking, wash up as you go along as much as possible. That way, it is easier to deal with the inevitable last-minute items, such as roasting pans, which will have to wait until after the meal is finished. Soak dirty pans to make them easier to wash up later.

When ready to wash up, scrape the food off the plates into the bin. Do not let food scraps wash down the drain. Use a sink strainer, or consider installing a waste disposal unit (see p. 52).

Do not pour fat or oil down the sink (see 'To unblock a drain', p. 50). The blockage can be spectacular. Use an old tin or bottle.

After scraping the plates, stack items on one side of the sink in the order they are to be washed. Stand cutlery briefly in a jug of hot, soapy water until it is ready to be washed. This has a two-fold benefit. First it begins to clean the cutlery; second, it keeps all the cutlery together, so you do not end up fishing around for that last rogue teaspoon. It is particularly useful for bone- or wooden-handled cutlery, which should never be immersed in water or the handles will split. Make sure the water comes up to the handle and no further. (For more on care of cutlery, see 'Silver', p. 149, and 'Stainless steel', p. 285.)

> Note: Wash silver and stainless steel cutlery separately. A chemical reaction in the water can tarnish silver.

Always use a washing-up bowl – less chance of breakages. The water should be hot but not boiling. Some people wear rubber gloves so they can wash up in water that they could not put their bare hands in. Ceramics and glass, though tough, can suffer from thermal shock and can crack if a cold item is plunged into very hot water. Add a small squirt of dish soap. Literally 1 teaspoon of a standard dish soap is enough for the average-size washing-up bowl of averagely dirty crockery.

Wash in order: glasses; cutlery; less dirty items (e.g. teacups or saucepans that have only been used for boiling vegetables); dirty items; greasy pots and pans. Wash pets' dishes separately after you have washed and dried the rest of the washing up, and keep a special brush or cloth to clean them with.

Two tips to enhance washing up: Buy dish soap in industrial quantities from the cash and carry and then decant it into a more attractive glass bottle.

Buy an intensive hand cream that can be used with cotton gloves. Every time you do the washing up, or indeed anything that requires rubber gloves, smother your hands in the cream, put on the cotton gloves and the rubber ones on top. This works really well, because the hot water makes the hand cream more effective, but no one ever recommends it. Hand-cream manufacturers probably find the concept of combining their product with dirty dishes too unglamorous.

TO CLEAN A CHOPPING BOARD

Scrub wooden chopping boards after use with hot soapy water and a stiff brush. Do not leave to soak or the wood may distort. Dry well with a clean tea towel and store upright to prevent warping. Oil wooden boards regularly using butcher-block oil (available from kitchen shops). Oil once a week for a month after first buying, then once a month or whenever the surface seems dry.

> Tip: If you have been cutting raw meat on a wooden board and have deep knife cuts in it, sprinkle the board with table salt and scrub with the grain with a stiff brush to disinfect and clean. (See also 'Baking soda', p. 230.)

Polypropylene chopping boards are more robust and less likely to warp than plastic boards. Wash plastic boards as above. Wash polypropylene boards in the dishwasher.

28

TO CLEAN GLASS AND CUTLERY

Use a soft dish cloth. Even better is an old-fashioned string dish mop, available from the more traditional hardware outlets. It is an excellent tool, can go into all the crevices, through fork prongs and into deep glasses and mugs. (After use, rinse under the tap, squeeze it and give it a shake. Park it upright so it can dry. Once a week, stick it in the dishwasher – in the cutlery basket – on a low-temperature wash to deep-clean. This will not do the wooden handle much good but is not an issue.)

Rinse each item in clean water (a pull-out hose is brilliant for this, but is quite wasteful of water) and put to drain in a rack. Change the water as it gets dirty.

When washing glasses by hand, use even less detergent than usual – with fewer suds, you will be able to see the glasses more clearly in the bowl – less chance of breakages. Wash one glass at a time. Be particularly careful about faucets. It is easy to smash a glass against a faucet. Push swivel faucets out of the way or cover faucets with a cloth.

Detergent leaves a film on the glass, so always rinse glasses. A dash of vinegar in the rinsing water will make them sparkle. Put a clean tea towel on the draining board to pad it and leave the glasses to drain. If the water is hot enough, the glasses will virtually dry themselves. Finish by polishing them well with a clean, lint-free tea towel. This is particularly important in areas where the water is hard because it can leave water marks on the glasses.

TO CLEAN DECANTERS

Do not leave decanters to stand for a long time with alcohol in them. It can stain the glass and leave a ring mark. To remove stains, pour a little white vinegar into the decanter and add some dry rice. Swirl round – the rice acts as a gentle abrasive. Rinse out thoroughly, wash and rinse in plain water with a dash of vinegar in it. If the rice does not work, do the same thing with decanter beads, small metal balls that replicate the lead shot which used to be recommended to clean decanters. They can also be used on glass vases.

The problem with decanters is getting them dry. To do this safely, make the rinsing water a little hotter than usual so the heat will begin to evaporate the moisture. Then turn the decanter upside down in something like a plastic jug to finish off drying.

29

TO REMOVE STAINS FROM TEAPOTS

Fill with cold water, add a fizzy denture-cleaning tablet and leave for an hour or so. Before using the teapot, rinse thoroughly with cold water.

Or:

Fill with cold water and add sterilising fluid (the kind used for babies' bottles). Again, rinse thoroughly before using.

The above will also remove stains on vacuum flasks and coffee pots.

TO CLEAN VERY DIRTY DISHES

For dirty items, I like to use a brush. For tough, burnt-on bits use a scouring pad, but sparingly. Soaking items before washing is a gentler alternative. I prefer a plastic scourer to soap-filled pads, which I always forget about and find a week later in a rusty pile.

There are several sprays designed to tackle burnt-on bits on roasting pans and so forth. These work well, but it is far easier and cheaper to do the following:

Pour off excess fat from the roasting tin (note – not down the sink). Fill the tin with very hot water; add a couple of tablespoons of powder dishwasher detergent or biological detergent and leave to soak for at least 20 minutes.

Or:

Place on the stove and simmer until the burnt bits loosen (about 10 minutes), as if you are making gravy. In fact, if you have made gravy, you will not need to do this. One of the bonuses of making real gravy is that you are left with a roasting tin that is much easier to clean.

> Tip: To economise on soap-filled pads, cut in half. To prevent them rusting, wrap in aluminium foil.

To clean a pan after cooking eggs or milk: After cooking scrambled eggs in a non-stick pan, soak it in cold water. Hot water sets protein, and far from removing egg from a pan, will set it like concrete. The same principle applies to other protein-based washing-up problems, such as milk pans and saucepans in which porridge has been cooked.

30

To descale a saucepan: Washing up alone will not remove limescale deposits in saucepans, double boilers and steamers. To remove, boil half and half water and vinegar in the saucepan, for a minute or so. Rinse out and wash. To prevent limescale forming in the bottom of steamers or double boilers, add either a tablespoon of vinegar or lemon juice, or a squeezed-out lemon skin to the water.

DRYING DISHES

To dry or not to dry? I think dishes should be wiped and put away immediately after washing. In fact, if the rinsing water is hot, not much drying will be required, but wiping removes the last traces of water and means you can give a final polish to cutlery and crockery.

Leaving washing up in the rack looks slovenly. In hard-water areas the dishes will be marked with water spots, and it is unhygienic, especially in towns where there is so much dust in the atmosphere.

That said, a dirty tea towel is a health hazard. Always use a clean tea towel and replace it when it becomes damp. In any case, tea towels should be replaced every day along with dish cloths.

CLOTH CULTURE

Keep separate cloths for separate functions. Do not use the same cloth to wash up, wipe surfaces and wipe the floor. Do not dip a cloth in dirty washing-up water to clean it. In the same way, do not use tea towels to dry your hands – keep a separate hand towel for this purpose.

I find the best cloths for cleaning and washing dishes are the traditional loose-weave cotton dish cloths, which are sold everywhere, and are cheap, easy to clean, long-lasting and functional: the loose weave gives extra friction when rubbing off stubborn marks. Sponges are not a good idea because they are so difficult to get clean. I also find that they make too much lather, which can be a nuisance when cleaning.

After washing up and wiping down kitchen surfaces, fill a bowl with clean hot water and add a dash of dish soap. Soak the dish cloths for half an hour, along with the washing-up brush and/or dish mop. Remove, rinse them all in clean water, wring out the cloths and dish mop and leave to dry.

Use a clean dish cloth every day. Replace the tea towel every day, too, unless there has not been much washing-up, in which case, change it every 2–3 days.

If you have used a cloth to wipe a board or surface where you have been preparing raw meat, or have wiped up pet messes, replace it immediately with a clean cloth.

Wash dish cloths and tea towels on a hot wash and store separately from food.

The dishwasher

We have the Americans to thank for that blessing of modern living, the dishwasher. The forerunner of all modern machines was built by an Illinois woman, Josephine Cochrane, and unveiled at the 1893 World's Fair. The first electrically operated machines appeared in the 1920s, but it was not until the 1950s that dishwashers became cheap enough and small enough for domestic use.

The British were slow to catch on to the dishwasher – when a friend's parents got one in the 1970s, it was seen as impossibly sophisticated – but they are getting ever more popular. Now, 30 per cent of households in the UK have a dishwasher.

But how environmentally sound are they? There is some disagreement about this. On the minus side, a dishwasher uses a lot of energy and most commercial dishwasher detergents are environmentally unfriendly and non-biodegradable (unless you choose a 'green' brand). On the plus side, modern dishwashers are very efficient when it comes to using water, an average of 4 gallons per wash. Interestingly, washing up the equivalent load by hand can use far more water – up to 17 gallons – because of the habit of washing and rinsing dishes under running water.

So, common sense would seem to say use the dishwasher judiciously. Choose a model that has a low water consumption figure and has several different wash cycles, which means that if the dishes are not very dirty, they can be washed at a lower temperature. Run it only when it is full and at the lowest temperature practicable.

TO USE THE DISHWASHER

Scrape excess food off plates thoroughly. Excess food scraps can fly around inside the dishwasher and scratch china, glass and cutlery. It used to be necessary to rinse dishes before they went into the dishwasher, but modern models are designed to cope with scraps of food. If you are not planning to run the dishwasher straight away, however, run the rinse and hold cycle until you are ready to run the machine (dirty plates can get very smelly). Load the dishwasher according to the instruction manual. Apparently, only 10 per cent of people bother to read a manual, but it pays to spend a few minutes going through it.

Generally, delicate and least dirty items go in the top basket, and the dirtiest items go in the bottom. Do not load glasses (but see below) or plates so they are touching. Place items so that water can run off them easily – invert cups and so forth. Do not overload the cutlery basket, and mix up items of cutlery so that they do not nest inside each other, which means the water will not be able to get to them. Put knives with the blades pointing downwards. There was a terrible incident a few years ago where a teenage boy who was emptying the dishwasher for his mother was killed when the point of a knife went through his eye.

Ensure that the dispensers of detergent, rinse-aid (which helps reduce streaks as dishes dry) and salt (if your dishwasher uses it to soften the water in the dishwasher) are full. Always follow the manufacturer's instructions as to how much detergent to use, to prevent high levels of harmful chemicals entering the sewage system and harming the environment.

When it comes to choosing which detergent to use, powder is cheaper than liquids or tablets and you can vary the amount of detergent used. If the load is very dirty, sprinkle an extra 1 tbsp powder into the interior of the dishwasher, something that would be impossible with a tablet.

> Note: Dishwasher detergent is a heavy-duty chemical, containing phosphates. So, for preference choose an eco-friendly brand. Many more are becoming available, though Ecover and Seventh Generation are still the best-known brands.

Dishwashers run more economically when they are full. For small households this used to cause a problem, but now there are many models that include a small-load programme.

If you want to fill the dishwasher gradually throughout the day, be meticulous about scraping plates and use the rinse/hold cycle as mentioned above.

Empty the dishwasher promptly, tempting though it is to leave stuff in there. If this really seems like a chore too far, a recent addition to the market is a DishDrawer, a dishwasher with two drawers, which the manufacturers call 'storage that washes the dishes'. The idea is that you leave the crockery permanently in one drawer and then transfer the dirty ones to the other one as you use them. It is certainly worth considering if you are short of storage space.

> Tip: When emptying the dishwasher, unload the bottom tray first, to avoid drips from the upper tray falling on to the stuff below.

THINGS THAT SHOULD NOT GO IN THE DISHWASHER

Though the dishwasher is the housewife's handmaiden, there are certain things that can be damaged in it, either because they are too fragile or because they are made from materials that will be damaged by the action of the dishwasher or the detergents. They include:

Aluminium and pewter – they turn black

Antique china, or indeed any delicate china, especially if it is hand-painted, or if it has gilded decoration or an elaborate pattern, or if you value it and want it to last. This applies even if the china is marked 'dishwasher-proof'. Dishwashers are a great boon, but there is no denying that, with repeated use, they fade and scratch even tough ceramics. And dishwasher detergents are very harsh. Eventually they take off the glaze and therefore the decoration

Bone-handled cutlery (also wood or plastic) – the hot water will split and fade the handles. In addition, water can seep into the join between the blade and the handle, weakening the glue and possibly even causing the haft of the blade to rust and swell, again splitting the handles

Cast iron – it will rust

Glass – especially expensive, fine crystal or hand-painted glass. Repeatedly washing glasses in a dishwasher will cause them to cloud. What looks like a film of limescale is in fact erosion of the surface of the glass. This can happen very quickly – within a few months – and, believe me, absolutely nothing will get rid of the marks. Many modern dishwashers have a special low-temperature programme for glasses, and there are now dishwasher products specially formulated for glasses. For normal everyday, heavy-duty glasses, you can probably risk the dishwasher (you could also run it without any detergent at all if you are just washing glasses). But if in doubt, do not take the risk

Many plastics – unless they are marked dishwasher-proof, assume plastics will warp in the heat of a dishwasher. Some even melt

Microplane graters. These are American graters with razor-sharp blades. Even though the manufacturers claim they are dishwasher-proof, in my experience the plastic frames crack and break in the dishwasher

Non-stick pans, unless marked dishwasher-proof

Silver – will get scratched and worn. Silver plate can, in theory, be washed in the dishwasher, as long as it is not touching anything made of stainless steel. But I would not risk it

Sharp knives – they go blunt (for more on knife care, see 'Knives', p. 40)

Wood – eventually it will swell and split. I used to ignore this warning, until I opened the dishwasher door to find my best chopping board split in two

Anything else the manufacturers tell you not to – e.g. food processor parts

THINGS THAT CAN GO IN THE DISHWASHER THAT YOU MIGHT NOT HAVE THOUGHT OF

The dishwasher doesn't have to be just for dishes. Use it to clean other household objects, especially anything cumbersome, bulky or fiddly to clean. These include:

> *Oven racks – if there are burnt-on encrustations, remove the racks before they*
>   *have dried; otherwise, the burnt bits will be baked on in the heat*
> *Dish racks and cutlery holders – especially if made of metal*
> *Fridge and freezer shelves – on a low temperature*
> *Grill pans – follow the advice for oven racks, above*
> *The microwave turntable (but check the manufacturer's leaflet)*
> *Polypropylene chopping boards*
> *Some vases – especially if they are plain, not decorated and not your best*
>   *Wedgwood*
> *The washing-up brush and the dish mop – stand the handles up in the cutlery*
>   *basket*
> *Children's plastic toys – either put them in the cutlery basket or tie them to the*
>   *top rack with plastic ties*

35

TO CLEAN THE DISHWASHER

Once a week, wipe the interior seals with a damp cloth and wipe the outside as it needs it. Clean the filters regularly – at least once a week (Counsel of perfection: after every wash). Once a month remove the filter basket and wash in hot soapy water.

The spray arm can get clogged, especially in hard-water areas. Take it off occasionally and inspect it. If the holes are clogged, poke a toothpick or large needle into them to remove any deposits, including limescale. Afterwards, wash it in hot, soapy water.

To descale a dishwasher: Proprietary dishwasher cleaners will remove soap scum and limescale. They normally consist of a plastic bottle of detergent, which you up-end in the cutlery basket before running a full cycle with the machine empty. They are extremely efficient and leave the machine looking and smelling fresh and clean.

A cheaper alternative is to place a cup of white vinegar in the lower basket and run the (empty) machine. But if the machine is neglected, I recommend using a proprietary cleaner first and then using the vinegar – it is not strong enough to cope with a major build-up. Thereafter, use vinegar once a month.

Or:

Fill the powder dispenser with citric acid and run the full cycle with the machine empty. Citric acid can be obtained from pharmacies.

Appliances

Where once the term kitchen appliance might have been restricted to the stove, fridge and washing machine, now there is an electrical appliance to satisfy any whim – from the obvious (the toaster, the electric kettle and the microwave), to the slightly more rarefied (the food processor and the electric mixer) and to the inexpressibly fashionable (the espresso machine and the juicer). Whether you want or need any of these is a matter of personal preference and will depend on the size of your kitchen and your wallet. Looking after them, however, is much more straightforward.

TO CLEAN LARGE APPLIANCES
Once a week clean the exterior of the stove, the washing machine, the tumble-dryer, the fridge, the freezer and the dishwasher, using water and detergent. Any chrome bits will come up a treat if you rub them with a little baking soda and a damp cloth. And hard-to-remove marks will come off very easily with a mark and stain eraser sponge.

For more on washing machine and tumble-dryer maintenance, see 'The Laundry', p. 155.

Note: Turn appliances off and unplug (if possible) first.

TO CLEAN FOOD PROCESSORS, LIQUIDISERS/BLENDERS AND MIXERS
Clean immediately after using. Unplug the appliance and dismantle. The motor should not be immersed in water, so simply wipe over with a damp cloth and a little dish soap.

Put food-processor blades in a small bowl of soapy water until you are ready to wash them. Do not leave them in the main washing-up bowl, because you may forget they are there and plunge your hand into the water and get a nasty surprise. Wash one by one with a brush.

Do not put food processor parts in the dishwasher; even if they are marked 'dishwasher-proof', the lid and bowl will become crazed and clouded and the blades will blunt.

> Tip: Some foods such as carrots can stain food processor bowls. New stains can sometimes be removed by wiping the bowl with vegetable oil (use a paper towel). Rub until you have got as much of the stain off as possible, and then wash in hot, soapy water. Or try a mark and stain eraser sponge.

The blades on liquidisers/blenders are sometimes fixed. To wash the liquidiser goblet, fill about half full with water and run at full blast for about ten seconds. Then empty out and wash as usual. Do not put in the dishwasher.

Mixer bowl and beaters can normally go in the dishwasher. Otherwise, wash by hand.

37

TO CLEAN A JUICER

Before buying a juicer, make sure that it can be dismantled for easy cleaning. Otherwise, you will use it once and then never again. Clean immediately after using, or the fruit pulp will set to a cement-like hardness. Take it apart and scrape the debris out of the basket – most models supply a special spatula for this. Rinse the basket well under a running tap, using a brush. The basket can normally be washed in the dishwasher. The bowl, lid and pusher are best washed by hand, because the same caveats as for food processors apply. If the plastic bowl has stained, wipe with vegetable oil (see 'To clean food processors', above).

TO CLEAN THE MICROWAVE OVEN

Wipe the interior of the oven immediately after every use with a damp cloth and mild detergent solution. Pay particular attention to any food spills. If grease, fat and food splashes are allowed to build up inside the oven, they may overheat, smoke or even catch fire. At the very least, they will make the oven smell unpleasant.

Wipe and wash the glass turntable after every use, too (it can usually go in the dishwasher). Occasionally wipe the outside of the oven with a damp cloth.

> *Note: If the microwave is really neglected, bear in mind that professional oven-cleaning companies will often deep-clean microwaves too.*

To deodorise, put ¼ pint water and ¼ pint lemon juice in a microwave-proof dish. Heat in the microwave until the mixture is at a rolling boil. The steam will loosen dirt and remove odours. Wipe clean afterwards.

> *Note: When using a microwave, use only microwave dishes, rigid plastics and heatproof glass, such as Pyrex. Do not put fine bone china, fine glass, metal, wood or flexible plastics such as cream or yogurt pots in the microwave.*

TO CLEAN THE KETTLE

Wipe the outside with a damp cloth and polish metal kettles occasionally with an appropriate polish/cleaner. If you live in a hard-water area, descale frequently.

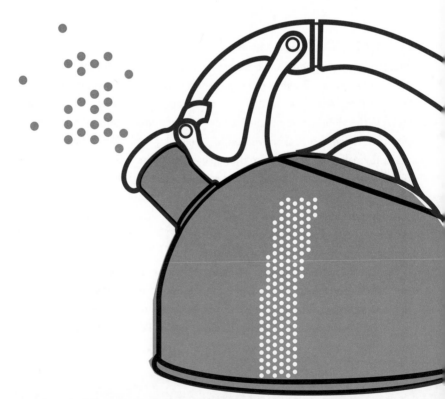

To descale a kettle: Boil a couple of inches of water in the kettle, then add the same amount of vinegar, and leave for several hours or overnight until the limescale has disappeared. Rinse the kettle out well, then fill, bring to the boil and discard the water. Do this a couple of times before using.

> *Note: Never boil up the vinegar and water mixture. It will boil over, sending jets of super-heated water all over the kitchen.*

Or:

Use powdered citric acid and treat the same way.

Or:

Use a vitamin C (ascorbic acid) tablet and treat the same way.

TO CLEAN A COFFEE MACHINE

Dismantle, following manufacturer's instructions, and wash parts in hot, soapy water. Rinse thoroughly to avoid tainting the coffee. If the frother gets blocked, poke a wooden cocktail stick into it to unblock and clean.

To descale a coffee machine: All coffee machines in hard water areas need descaling every other month, or according to manufacturer's instructions. Most coffee machines can be descaled only with suitable proprietary descalers and will be damaged by home-made descalers, such as vinegar.

> *Tip: Coffee machines that use ground coffee and resemble those found in coffee bars are often more fiddly to clean than cheaper models. Make sure when buying that the frother is removable – it is easier to clean than a fixed one. Newer models using coffee capsules are designed to be easy-clean.*

TO CLEAN THE TOASTER

Switch the toaster off if it has a switch, and unplug. Remove the crumb tray and empty it. Hold the toaster upside down over the sink to shake out any crumbs inside. Wipe the outside with a damp cloth.

39

Knives

You can do without most of the above appliances, but you cannot do without a set of decent knives. One professional I spoke to recommends a set of five knives that will cover most eventualities. They are: a chef's knife (8–9 in) for basic everyday use; a filleting knife with a slightly more flexible blade for fish; a boning knife with a rigid blade for meat; a paring knife for peeling and vegetables; and a carving knife with a scalloped blade for carving meat and slicing bread. All chefs have their own set of knives, jealously guarded and carefully tended.

It pays to buy the best knives you can afford if you are at all serious about cooking – or start with cheap knives and replace them with better ones as and when you can.

> Tip: Sharp knives are in fact less dangerous than blunt ones: it is much easier to cut yourself when hacking away at something with a blunt knife.

40

Good knives are forged in one piece, with the tang (shank) going all the way along the handle. The handle, which can be of wood, plastic or metal, should be riveted on, not glued.

There are many good makes available – some names to look out for are: Henckels, Sabatier, Victorinox and Global.

The best all-round material for knives is a good-quality stainless steel. It will need to be sharpened, and can be honed to a very sharp edge. Though it should be treated with care (see 'Stainless steel', p. 285), it will not rust. Steel is made from iron, to which carbon has been added. It becomes 'stainless' with the extra addition of chromium (minimum 10.5 per cent), which stops the iron from rusting. It does not in fact prevent staining, but if you follow the knife care tips below, this should not be too much of a problem.

Less widely available these days are carbon steel knives. Many people swear by them even though they require time and attention, and can turn some foods, such as onions and lemons, black. Although this looks alarming, it is not a problem, unless the appearance of the finished dish will be spoilt.

Carbon steel is softer than stainless steel. It can rust, which means it must be dried immediately after washing. If not, the metal can leave rusty marks on tea towels and on light-coloured foods such as apples. Carbon steel knives also seem to hold flavours, especially onions or garlic, which will inevitably be carried over to the next thing you cut. The smell can linger on the blade even after washing.

But because carbon steel is softer than stainless steel, it is easy to sharpen the blade to a razor-sharp edge, allowing you to cut through meat like butter, fillet fish in seconds and slice vegetables wafer-thin. It loses its sharpness quickly, so the blade needs sharpening frequently while you are using the knife.

Not worth buying are knives that never need sharpening (or so the manufacturers claim). These are made from low-carbon and hence very hard stainless steel. As a result, they become blunt less quickly than normal knives. But they will eventually lose their edge, and when they do, their hardness means they are difficult – if not virtually impossible – to sharpen.

In general, avoid serrated knives (apart from the carving knife mentioned above), too. By their very nature, they too cannot be sharpened.

> *Tip: If you feel you must have a serrated knife (useful for things like very soft tomatoes and the like), take advantage of the drawbacks of the above. Buy a cheap serrated knife of a kind that 'never needs sharpening' and be prepared to discard it when it becomes blunt. I realise this does not tally with my let's-be-thrifty philosophy, but sometimes one has to give oneself a break.*

41

TO CARE FOR KNIVES

Treat knives with respect. Always use a wooden or plastic chopping board. Marble or glass will blunt the blades. And use knives only for the purpose they were designed for – that is, cutting food. Do not use them to cut bits of string or tape, or to open letters, tighten screws, prise lids off jars, trim electric cord or anything else.

Many professional chefs store their knives in a drawer wrapped in a cloth. I prefer a wooden knife block. It is sometimes claimed that, with their deep holes, they are difficult to clean – though why anyone would be so obsessive as to want to clean inside a knife block beats me. In my experience virtually nothing gets into them and there is no problem.

Wall-mounted magnetic knife holders are not recommended, especially if there are children in the house. Even if there are not, these holders are not safe.

When you are busy it is easy to knock a knife accidentally. As one professional chef said to me, 'I've seen too many cut hands and knives sticking out of feet ever to have one of those.'

TO CLEAN KNIVES

Wash knives as soon as possible after using them. Vinegar, salt, tomatoes, eggs, fruit, even the mineral salts in hard tap water can damage stainless steel.

Always wash knives by hand, never in the dishwasher. Dishwasher detergents are very harsh and can pit and corrode stainless steel and cause 'rainbow' markings on the blade (carbon steel will rust). In addition the constant rattling around will blunt the blades and the heat will crack the handles.

Wash them one at a time in warm, soapy water. Do not leave them to soak. Apart from the fact that the handles can crack, prolonged contact with tap water can actually corrode stainless steel (see 'Stainless steel cutlery', p. 286). In any case, plunging your hands into a washing-up bowl full of knives is never a good idea.

Use a soft cloth or a dish mop rather than a brush. Do not use scourers or soap-filled metal pads. Minute fragments in the washing water can stick to the blades, causing indelible rust marks.

Rinse and dry immediately, polishing with a soft, dry cloth.

Light marks on stainless steel blades can be removed with vinegar or lemon juice (although vinegar and lemon juice can corrode stainless steel if left in contact with it for a long time). Rub the blade with vinegar and a soft cloth, or rub half a lemon along it. Rinse and dry with a soft cloth.

Other marks can be removed with a stainless steel cleaner.

> *Note: Do not use silver polish on stainless steel. It contains acids that can stain and ultimately etch the metal.*

To clean carbon steel knives: Wash and dry as above. Carbon steel must be dried immediately, or it will rust.

To remove marks from carbon steel blades, make a paste of salt and lemon juice and work it into the blade. Rinse off and dry.

Before putting carbon steel knives away, oil the blade to prevent rust, using neutral cooking oil, such as corn oil. Do not use olive oil, which is acidic and can corrode the metal.

TO SHARPEN A KNIFE

Every time you use a knife, sharpen it. If it feels as if it is getting blunt while you are working, stop and sharpen it again. There are many knife sharpeners on the market. The problem is that not many of them work. One good make is designed for sharpening Global knives. It consists of two small wheels made of a very hard stone material set in a small compartment, which you fill with water. The knife blades are run along the wheels, first to sharpen and then to hone the edge.

Better still, use a whetstone. Whetstones are available from cookware shops, hardware stores and DIY stores where they are normally sold for sharpening chisels or garden shears. There are two ways of using them:

Hold the knife horizontally along the length of the whetstone with the sharp edge of the blade facing away from you and almost flat. Then with your fingers on the flat of the blade, pull it towards you a few times. Sharpen the other side of the blade in the same way.

Or:

Hold the stone horizontally, then, holding the knife by the handle, position the blade against the stone so that only the cutting edge is against the stone. Then pull the knife towards you, keeping the same angle and point of contact along the length of the blade right to the top. To sharpen the other side of the blade, place the knife under the stone.

There really is no mystique to using a whetstone – worrying about sharpening at a magic angle of 45° or whatever. With a bit of practice, you can feel when the cutting edge is in contact with the stone and sharpening properly. The things to remember are to keep the whetstone well lubricated with water or oil (water is less messy) and to sharpen both sides of the blade an equal number of times.

Once you have got the edge back, finish off with a steel (available from cookware shops; or look in antiques markets). Do not clatter knife and steel together flashily in the manner of a waiter in a restaurant – a few firm strokes on either side of the blade will do.

If you use the steel before using knives, while you are cooking and after washing them, you will need to use the whetstone far less often.

Once the edge is dulled, no amount of sharpening will bring it back and you will probably have to have the knives sharpened professionally. To find a knife grinder, ask at a kitchen shop. It may well offer a knife-sharpening service.

43

I found a service in my area by asking in my local delicatessen. Butchers' shops and restaurants are other good sources.

The worktop

Worktops get a lot of hard wear, so have to be made of durable materials. The most popular choices are laminates, which have the advantage of being cheap and very hard-wearing, closely followed by wood. At the luxury end of the market are composites, such as Corian, which are made from acrylic resin and stone, and solid stone, such as granite and slate. Tiled worktops are now decidedly out of fashion, while popular modern choices are stainless steel and glass.

While there are specific cleaning techniques for each, what they all have in common is that they should be wiped frequently, especially in areas where food has been prepared, to prevent the transfer of bacteria. An anti-bacterial detergent is unnecessary: hot water and ordinary detergent will do the job perfectly adequately. When doing a more thorough clean remove everything from the worktop before starting.

TO CLEAN COMPOSITE (E.G. CORIAN) WORKTOPS
Wipe up spills as they occur. Fruit juices and oils can stain. Use dish soap and a damp cloth. Rinse and wipe dry to prevent water marks. If stains do appear, use a little abrasive cleaning powder, such as Bar Keepers Friend. Sprinkle on the surface, leave for a few minutes before cleaning with a soft cloth, using a circular motion. This will also deal with light scratches on the surface. Very deep scratches might need a nylon pan scourer, but go carefully and, if in doubt, consult the supplier.

With use, composite materials change in appearance, acquiring a lustrous sheen. To prevent this lustre developing unevenly, go over the whole surface with Bar Keepers Friend and a soft cloth once or twice a month in the first few months. Rub in a circular motion, rinse and dry.

To prevent damage, do not put a hot pan directly on the surface; use a pan stand or trivet.

TO CLEAN GLASS WORKTOPS

Clean with a soft cloth and mild detergent. Rinse by spraying with a mixture of vinegar and water and wipe dry to make the glass sparkle. (Always wipe dry to avoid water marks.)

To prevent damage, avoid banging anything down roughly on the glass. Always use a pan stand or trivet for hot saucepans. Always use a chopping board – you will not damage the worktop if you do not, but your knives will suffer.

TO CLEAN LAMINATE WORKTOPS

Use a damp cloth and any all-purpose cleaner, rinse and leave to dry. Alternatively, dip a damp cloth in baking soda and use to clean. Scouring powders are not a good idea because they can scratch shiny surfaces on cheaper makes, but if stains appear, use a cream cleaner.

To prevent damage, do not put hot pans directly on top of the worktop; use a pan stand or trivet. Do not cut food directly on top of the worktop: always use a chopping board.

TO CLEAN STAINLESS STEEL WORKTOPS

Wipe up spills thoroughly with a damp cloth and dish soap, rinse and dry to prevent water marks. Every now and again, polish with a specialist stainless steel cleaner, such as Bar Keepers Friend Liquid.

Stainless steel marks easily, but the scratches blend together over time. Stainless steel shows every greasy finger mark. To clean, put a drop or two of baby oil on a soft cloth and rub it over the stained area. Then put another drop or two of oil on the cloth and go over the whole worktop so that no smudges are left. You can use baby oil on all stainless steel appliances, such as fridges and cooker fronts.

> Note: Baby oil is the thing to use; cooking oils, especially olive oil, can corrode steel.

Alternatively, use a microfibre cloth. These use no chemicals, only water, but bring up stainless steel to a high, smudge-free shine.

To prevent damage, always use a chopping board to prevent scratching the surface and damaging knives. Do not let corrosive acids such as lemon juice or salt sit on the surface for any length of time.

TO CLEAN STONE WORKTOPS

Clean regularly with a damp cloth and all-purpose detergent, rinse and dry to prevent water marks. Acids, such as wine and fruit juices, and oils, particularly olive oil, can stain porous worktops such as granite if they are allowed to soak in.

To prevent damage, do not bang heavy pots down on stone worktops; although they are hard, they may chip. Use a chopping board, to protect knives.

TO CLEAN WOODEN WORKTOPS

Wipe up spills and food preparation areas with a damp cloth and dish soap. After much research, it has been concluded that wood has anti-bacterial properties. As long as it does not get deep scratches in it, you can safely prepare food on it (don't cut food on it, however, or it will get scratched).

To keep the worktop looking at its best, oil it regularly – every three to six months, or when the surface is beginning to look dull and flat. First, wash the surface all over with hot, soapy water using a cloth that's been well wrung out, then rinse and dry. When the wood is completely dry apply one or more thin coatings of worktop oil – several thin layers are better than one thick one.

Tip: A useful rule of thumb is to re-oil it when drops of water spilt on the worktop lie flat instead of forming beads on the surface. This is a sign that the oil has broken down.

If the worktop is damaged, badly scratched or very dirty, sand it down with fine sandpaper, working in the direction of the grain. Most small dents and scratches should disappear. If they are very deep, start with a coarser sandpaper, but finish with a fine grade. Then apply several coats of worktop oil.

To prevent damage, always use a chopping board. Never put hot pans down on a wooden worktop: always use a pan stand or trivet. If installing a new worktop, you might consider having a pan stand made of stone or tile built into the worktop at the side of the cooker. When cleaning do not saturate the worktop – a damp cloth is sufficient. Do not allow liquids to stand on it for any length of time. Pay particular attention to areas around the sink. Do not let wet crockery stand on the worktop and always dry it off after use. Iron and steel can mark wood if they stay in contact with it for a long time. So iron trivets or pan stands should not be left standing on the worktop because there is a danger that they may rust and mark the wood.

TO CLEAN TILED WORKTOPS

Clean as for any ceramic tiles, using a damp cloth and detergent. Wipe up spills as soon as they occur, especially potentially staining foods, such as curry, on the grout. Every now and then, clean the grout with a solution of bleach (three parts water to one part bleach) and an old toothbrush. You can also freshen up grout with a grout pen (available from DIY shops). If the tiles are very dirty, turn to 'How to clean really filthy tiles', p. 102.

To descale tiled worktops: Fill a spray bottle with half and half water and vinegar. Spray the surface, then wipe dry with a clean cloth. You can use this mixture as a daily final rinse for all tiles and worktops to take advantage of vinegar's antiseptic properties.

The sink

47

Dishwashers may be growing in popularity, but you will still need a sink – a double sink, or a one-and-a-half bowl sink would be even more convenient. Most sinks in this country are made from stainless steel, which is durable, good value for money and easy to clean. But ceramic sinks, especially the deep Belfast or butler's sink, are extremely popular because they not only look good, but are extremely durable. At the top end of the market, sinks made from composite, such as Corian, have the advantage of being extremely strong, durable and heat-resistant. And because they are moulded in one piece with the worktop, there are no joins to attract dirt.

One of the easiest ways to make a kitchen look immaculate is to have a shiny sink. Conversely, if the sink is dirty, the whole kitchen looks dirty.

TO CLEAN A STAINLESS STEEL SINK

After washing up or using the sink, empty it and then sluice it with very hot water, wiping it with a cloth as you do so, to loosen grease and dirt. Wipe again with a damp cloth and dish soap.

Although stainless steel is hard, it scratches easily, and eventually the scratches will dull the surface. Never use abrasive cleaning powders or harsh scourers. Never use Brillo pads. What you need are gentle cleaners and soft cloths. Bar Keepers Friend Liquid is an extremely effective cream cleaner, which brings up a shine on stainless steel that is a treat, so is also good for stainless steel appliances such as kettles.

Apply a small amount of cleaner and apply with a damp cloth, paying particular attention to the crevices around the taps. While you are at it, wipe the faucet and knobs, too. Rinse, then wipe dry.

It is important to wipe sinks dry to avoid water marks on the metal.

> *Tip: When you have washed up in the evening, use the tea towel to wipe the sink dry, put the tea towel in the wash and lay out a clean one for the next day.*

TO CLEAN A CERAMIC SINK

Turn to the bathroom chapter and see 'To clean baths and basins', p. 96.

TO CLEAN A COMPOSITE (E.G. CORIAN) SINK

Claims that Corian 'cleans itself' are not true. Wipe up spills as they occur. Clean the sink with a damp cloth and dish soap. Wipe well to get rid of any oils or fats, then rinse and dry. If there are any stains, use an abrasive powder such as Bar Keepers Friend. Sprinkle it on the damp surface and leave for a few minutes, then wipe off, using a circular motion. Rinse, then wipe dry. For more on the cleaning and care of Corian, see 'The Worktop', p. 44.

If necessary, deep-clean the sink occasionally. After wiping with a cloth, fill it with warm water, add 1–2 tsp bleach and leave overnight. In the morning, empty the sink and rinse.

> *Note: Hard water leaves marks on Corian, so always dry the sink after using. Aluminium pans can also leave marks, and some foods can discolour it.*

To descale a drainhole: Sometimes limescale builds up in crevices around the rim of the drainhole. To remove it, soak a cloth in vinegar and leave it on the drainhole for several hours until the deposits have softened. Then scrub them off with an old toothbrush.

Drains

It is difficult to comprehend that we enjoy standards of municipal cleanliness that would have been unimaginable to our ancestors. Even the most harrowing experiences in some of the less developed parts of the world today bear little comparison to the filthiness of towns and cities right up to the 20th century. Sanitation – or the lack of it – was a continual trial. In the 19th century, typhoid and cholera were a major threat. In 1853–4, 10,000 people died in one epidemic. Edwin Chadwick's inquiry into the sanitary conditions of the working classes in 1842 stressed the absolute necessity of clean water and adequate drainage to improve general health. And in 1854, Dr John Snow showed the link between one water pump in Soho and the number of deaths from cholera in the surrounding area, an observation that eventually led to the idea that germs – whether water-borne in the case of cholera, or otherwise – cause many diseases.

But it was not until the Great Stink of 1857, when the smell of the refuse and sewage rotting in the summer heat forced Londoners out of their homes and the Houses of Parliament to suspend the session, that anything was done. The result was the great sewer network built by Sir Joseph Bazalgette, which in a matter of eight years transformed the capital, and began a programme of civil sanitation works that eventually spread right across the country.

Nowadays it is out of sight, out of mind when it comes to drains, until they decide to remind you of their presence.

49

TO KEEP A DRAIN CLEAR AND PREVENT BLOCKAGES
To prevent a drain becoming blocked, always use a sink strainer to prevent bits of food clogging it. Never pour grease down the drain. Instead, pour it into an old tin or other disposable container, let it harden and throw it in the dustbin. Oils should go into empty bottles.

Coffee grounds can also block drains. Strain them into a sieve and put them in the dustbin.

Once a day, pour a kettleful of boiling water down the drain to dislodge any grease lurking inside it.

Once a week, disinfect the drain. All the following methods avoid using harsh, environmentally unfriendly chemicals. All will readily biodegrade. Try one of the following methods:

>*Pour a cup of baking soda down the plughole and slowly dribble warm water into it.*
>
>*Make a solution of soda crystals (sodium carbonate) (one teacup to a couple of pints of hot water). Flush the drain with hot water, pour down the soda solution, then flush with hot water again.*
>
>*Flush with very hot water, sprinkle 1 tbsp household borax down the drain, slowly pour through a teacup of hot water and leave for a couple of hours. Flush with plenty of hot water.*
>
>*Mix together 4 tbsp baking soda, 4 tbsp salt and 1 tbsp cream of tartar. Place in a jar with a lid, close it tightly and shake until the ingredients are well mixed. Pour down the drain, followed by a kettleful of boiling water. After one minute, rinse with warm or cold tap water.*
>
>*Use an enzyme-based drain disinfectant. Flush the drain with hot water, add a capful of the cleaner and leave for at least an hour. It fizzes dramatically but removes smells. These products contain a small amount of phosphates. The active ingredient is sodium percarbonate, a bleaching agent. Unlike chlorine bleaches, which leave chemical residues, it decomposes into oxygen, water and soda ash when it comes into contact with water.*

TO UNBLOCK A DRAIN

The commonest cause of blockages is food particles, followed by grease. Hair, fibres from clothes (if, say, you do a lot of washing by hand), limescale and soap scum can also block pipes. If you follow the maintenance tips, above, this should not occur, but if the drain does become blocked, here is what to do:

If the drain is clogged (water is running through, but slowly), first bail out any standing water. Slowly pour one cup of baking soda down the drain, then slowly add a cup of vinegar. The mixture will fizz in a satisfyingly dramatic manner. Cover the drainhole with the upturned cup and leave to fizz for about five minutes. Rinse the drain with boiling water. If the water is still running slow, treat again.

If the drain is totally blocked (water will not run out at all and collects in the sink), bail out the standing water and check to see if a wad of food or hair is blocking the drain. If this does not work, use a plunger to remove the blockage from farther down the pipe.

Tip: If you have a double sink, you will need to block the drainhole in the second sink to get a decent vacuum on the plunger.

If none of these methods work, use a chemical drain cleaner. The strongest ones are very caustic, dangerous to use and very environmentally unfriendly. Less startling are foaming drain cleaners. Use them as a last resort, only when all else has failed. The best way to avoid using them at all is to prevent blockages in the first place.

Waste

When I was a child, all our rubbish used to go into one dustbin for the whole family of four. The council supplied the bin; it was made of zinc and weighed a ton. Every Tuesday, after the dustmen had been, my mother had to line the bin with newspaper. Trash bags were a thing of the future.

Now I live in a London flat where the rubbish is collected and deposited in huge wheelie bins at the back of my block of flats. These bins are emptied several times a week, and they are always full. I am sure that I now produce the same amount of rubbish that four of us did 30 years ago. Despite my best efforts to recycle newspapers, glass and tins in the special separate bins that the council provides, there always seems to be something to throw away.

In this, I blame supermarkets. Quite apart from the 17.5 billion plastic bags that are given away by supermarkets each year, the amount of packaging for the simplest commodity is little short of scandalous. Why, for example, do four pears require a specially moulded polystyrene tray, a separate specially moulded plastic cover and plastic wrapping? Why aren't all bottles sold with a deposit, as they used to be, giving you the incentive to return them and get the money back?

In fact, my worries about the amount of rubbish we generate are well founded. We are in danger of drowning under it. The UK produces more than 434 million tonnes of rubbish a year and it is growing at a rate of three per cent per year.

In recent years, a form of social pressure has been building up about waste, how much we throw away and where it goes. Many local councils now require us to separate rubbish into separate bins for recyclable glass, plastic, paper and so on. But we still lag way behind many European countries, particularly Germany, Switzerland, Sweden and Denmark, where recycling is second nature.

TO REDUCE HOUSEHOLD WASTE

Before you think about how to dispose of rubbish, think about reducing the amount that comes into the house. Don't buy over-packaged goods or products, such as fruit in a polystyrene tray. Buy loose goods where you can. And buy refills where possible so you can decant into the original packaging.

Some eco-warrior types have started unpacking goods in the supermarket and leaving the packaging for the supermarket to get rid of. Once the problem becomes the supermarkets' and not ours, they might begin to think about reducing the amount of packaging they wrap food in. In a small way, I already do this with magazines, discarding the pointless leaflets and paper inserts with which they are stuffed before I pay for them.

When you go to the supermarket, bring used carrier bags with you instead of picking up new ones each time. Better still, invest in a shopping basket or bag.

Re-use where you can rather than just throwing away. Take used carrier bags to the supermarket, or give them to charity shops. If you buy eggs from a farmers' market, you can normally take the cartons back to be re-used. If you have the option, have milk delivered and put the glass bottles out for the milkman. Re-use envelopes where you can.

For cleaning, use cloths, which can be washed, rather than wipes which are used once and then thrown away. If you have a baby, you may also want to consider washable nappies instead of disposables. Use junk mail to write lists.

Do not automatically put all waste in the bin. Food scraps make up 25 per cent of household waste, so every kitchen should have a waste disposal fitted (see below). If you have a house with a garden, start a compost heap, into which any raw vegetable peelings can go (but no meat or cooked scraps).

THE WASTE DISPOSAL

Considering that the amount of household rubbish we produce is causing national and international alarm, it is astonishing that more homes are not fitted with a waste disposal unit. The amount of food we throw out in the UK amounts to 6.7 million tonnes a year. A third of this amount is inedible peelings, cores and so forth, and most of it ends up on landfill sites, where it rots and produces methane gas, one of the major contributors to greenhouse gases.

A waste disposal will enable you to cut down dramatically on the amount of food you throw away as rubbish. It grinds up virtually all household waste, apart from raw bones and very fibrous vegetables, such as globe artichoke leaves or corncobs. Most cooked food waste can go down a waste disposal, to be ground up to a pulp then washed away. Apart from reducing the amount of household rubbish, this also reduces smells.

TO CLEAN A WASTE DISPOSAL UNIT

Always use plenty of cold water when running a waste disposal unit to ensure that all the food waste is washed out of the machine (use cold water to keep particles of grease in suspension, so they will be washed away and not coat the inside of the machine).

Once a week, feed lemon rinds into the unit to keep it smelling sweet. An alternative is to freeze vinegar in ice-cube trays, then run the frozen cubes through the machine. Do not use harsh chemical drain cleaners, which can damage the units.

If the waste disposal becomes blocked, always turn it off at the main before attempting to unblock it.

RECYCLING

Although 65 per cent of us have access to recycling schemes, only 14.5 per cent of the contents of our dustbins are recycled each year. If there is a recycling scheme in your area, take advantage of it. Many municipalities now provide households with separate bins for glass, tins, paper, and even old clothes and shoes. Others have communal recycling bins. They are worth using, though they can have their drawbacks, particularly the rules and regulations about exactly what they will and will not take. Check with your local government (probably the waste management department) on what schemes operate in your area.

Squash cardboard boxes flat if you cannot recycle them. Tear up other papers. This should always be done anyway when throwing out confidential papers such as credit card bills or bank statements. Identity theft, although rare, is a real threat, and there is no harm in playing safe (for more on which papers to keep and for how long, see 'Paperwork', p. 202). Either tear into small pieces, or invest in a paper shredder (available from office suppliers and stationers).

Buy biodegradable plastics where you can. That said, most plastics cannot be recycled, so do your bit by crushing them as small as possible. Take the tops off plastic bottles, squash them as flat as you can, then put the top back on to keep them squashed. Wash bottles and tins before putting them in the bin, to prevent them smelling.

HAZARDOUS WASTE

Have you ever stopped to consider that much of your household waste might be hazardous?

There are environmental and safety implications for a startling number of substances, which we casually chuck away and then forget about.

They include all sorts of paint; hairspray; nail varnish; furniture and metal polishes; household cleaners such as ammonia, bleach and drain cleaners; aerosol sprays; hair dye; some moth killers and other insecticides; batteries containing lead, mercury or cadmium; some light bulbs; medicines; paint strippers and thinners.

Asks yourself if you really need a product before you buy it. There are often safer alternatives (for example, clean drains with baking soda instead of corrosive drain cleaner). If you do think you need it, buy the smallest amount possible and use it up.

TO DISPOSE OF WASTE SAFELY

Make sure products are used up. When it comes to disposal, read the manufacturer's label. Some local authorities have special facilities for the disposal of hazardous waste, such as large quantities of paints and varnishes. Contact your local waste management department. Otherwise, check whether metals or containers can be recycled.

Empty aerosol cans completely by turning upside down and pressing the nozzle so all the propellant is used up. Then put in the recycling bin or in the dustbin.

Rinse out empty bleach and disinfectant bottles and either put in the recycling bin, or wrap in newspaper and put in the dustbin. Small quantities of bleach or disinfectant can be poured down the drain, with plenty of water. However, never pour bleach down the drain with any other chemical.

Some pharmacies will take medicines for safe disposal. Otherwise, pour liquids down the toilet, flushing several times. Pills and capsules should be wrapped tightly and put in the dustbin.

> Note: Ensure that rubbish containing medicines is disposed of so that neither children nor animals can get hold of them.

Take the tops off old bottles of nail varnish and allow to dry. Close, then wrap in several sheets of newspaper and put in the dustbin.

Check whether there any facilities to recycle paint cans in your area. Otherwise, take the lid off the container and allow any leftover paint to dry. Put the can in the dustbin, leaving the lid off.

KITCHEN BIN HYGIENE

For the average-sized family, choose a bin that is at least 13 gallons in volume. For one- and two-person households, a smaller bin is adequate. A pedal bin is a hygienic option because you will not be touching the lid with your hands. Unless your kitchen is so small there is no alternative, avoid those bins that are attached to the inside of a cupboard door. They are usually too small for normal family use and are fiddly to clean. All kitchen bins should be lined. Ensure that the trash bags are big enough to fit it with a generous overlap. Use biodegradable trash bags as often as you can. They used to be a bit flimsy and fell apart, but modern makes are perfectly adequate for normal use.

Whatever its size, a bin should be emptied regularly – once a day. It astonishing how quickly a bin becomes smelly, especially in hot weather. Make it the last thing you do at night, or the first thing you do in the morning. Wash bins once a week, using hot water and detergent. Remember to clean inside the lid as well. Rinse with plain water, to which you may like to add a splash of disinfectant. A greener alternative is to use a solution of household borax (2 tbsp to 2 pints water). Borax is rather old-fashioned, but an extremely good disinfectant and deodoriser.

Make sure the bin is thoroughly dry before using it again. Mould and bacteria can thrive in wet conditions. Although the above should keep the bin from smelling, I sometimes put a fridge deodoriser (see 'To clean the fridge', p. 17) in the bottom of the bin as well.

THINGS TO AVOID

Think twice before pouring things down the drain as a way of discarding them. When in doubt, do not do it. Never put any inflammable product or a container that held one on a fire. This includes paints, solvents, aerosol cans and polishes. Some products will catch fire easily. Others will explode or give off toxic fumes. These include drain cleaners, ammonia and many plastics. In any case, there are strict rules about what you can and cannot burn.

Construction dumpsters are not designed for half-used containers of paint and so forth. Nor should you bury them in the garden, where they could easily corrode, pollute the surrounding earth or – in the worst case – actually leech into the water table.

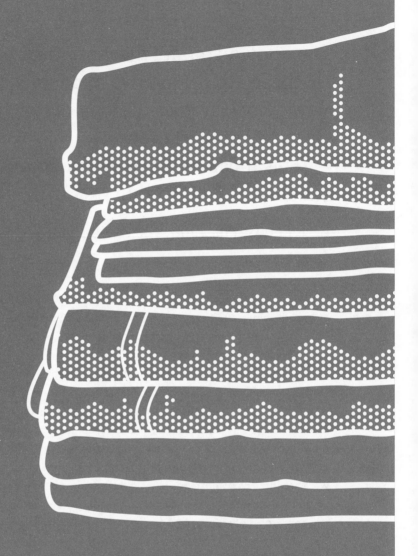

CHAPTER 2
The Bedroom

She took a step further in – then two
or three steps – always expecting to feel
woodwork against the tips of her fingers.
But she could not feel it.
  'This must be a simply enormous
wardrobe,' thought Lucy …

C.S. Lewis, The Lion, the Witch and the Wardrobe

I have noticed that when people show friends round a newly acquired house, the main bedroom is often passed over rather hurriedly and then the door is firmly shut. For this is the most private room in the house, where we are at our most vulnerable and intimate.

58

It is difficult to comprehend that this is a relatively recent phenomenon. Until the middle of the 19th century, it was common to share a bed with two, three or often more people, and in poorer households this practice continued for even longer. In royal palaces, the bedchamber was a public room, where the king or queen received visitors and petitioners while still in bed. Beds were primitive: mattresses stuffed with straw or feathers meant that assorted vermin were accepted as companions in even the grandest beds – a state of affairs that began to change only in the 18th century with the advent of cotton mattresses and cast-iron bedsteads. And bedrooms were not particularly comfortable. Apart from vermin, they were often cold – those heavy hangings around four-poster beds were for warmth rather than decoration.

So be thankful for modern comforts. Nowadays, bedrooms are not just clean, warm and comfortable; they can also reflect the most fanciful parts of our personalities. Walk into the bedding department of a large store and you will be assailed by infinite variations of colour-coordinated linen, beds piled high with dozens of cushions, beds dressed with complicated assortments of throws and coverlets in jewel colours – beds, in short, to suit your every mood.

It is all a far cry from my own childhood, when we were allowed a fire in the bedroom only when we were ill (no central heating) and a bed was just something you slept in. Like most households, we made do with a motley collection of mismatched sheets and pillowcases. Being of a frugal nature, my mother kept bed linen until it literally fell apart.

Bed essentials

By this, I refer not to what you do in your bed, but what you do to it, both day to day and in the long term, in order to sleep soundly and to keep the bed, bedding and mattress clean and to prolong their lives.

The four most important things are the following:

KEEP THE BEDROOM COOL AND WELL VENTILATED

If you cannot sleep, it is tempting to think that the bedroom is too cold. In fact, we fall asleep when our body temperature drops. Therefore, set the temperature in the bedrooms lower than in the rest of the house – around 60°F. And keep the room well ventilated, preferably by opening a window (although this may be a security problem if you live in a ground-floor flat or basement). This way, the room will be less stuffy at night and will also smell better in the morning.

AIR THE BED

Every morning, on getting up, open the window wide, pull back the duvet or blankets and top sheet on the beds, plump up the pillows and allow the sunlight and air to get to the bed for as long as possible – the optimum period is about an hour, but if you have to leave the house in a hurry, just do it for as long as you can.

Why is this important? Every night, while asleep, we breathe out quantities of carbon dioxide, which can leave the room feeling stuffy. This, combined with the sweat we produce, gives that characteristic musty morning smell. Airing the bed in the morning obviously makes the room smell fresher and keeps the bed linen sweet for longer. There is also some evidence that numbers of dust mites are reduced, though not eradicated, by sun and air.

Mites love a warm, humid atmosphere with plenty of food, so our beds – hot, sweaty and full of flakes of skin on which they can feast – are their idea of a dream home. Luckily, they hate sunlight, so it makes sense to get the bedding as dry as possible. For more on dust mites, see 'Household pests', p. 322.

MAKE THE BED

It is funny what is beyond the pale for some people. I would not leave the house without making the beds even if an invading army had parked its tanks on my lawn. To my mind, an unmade bed looks untidy; it makes a whole room look untidy even if it is, in fact, immaculate in all other respects; and it is depressing to come home to. Now that most people have duvets, it takes a matter of seconds to shake it out and smooth it over the bed, and just a few seconds more to plump up the pillows. If time is of the essence, forgo throws, cushions, bedspreads and other frills.

Though often derided as the sign of a control freak, the best way to keep bedclothes anchored to the bed, especially if you prefer blankets to duvets, is the hospital corner. To make a hospital corner, tuck the sheet or blanket under the mattress at the bottom of the bed. Pick up the sheet/blanket at the side and tuck in the overhanging corner. Let the side drop back, then tuck in at the side. You will have a neat, mitred finish.

CHANGE THE SHEETS

Sheets, pillowcases and duvet covers should be changed and washed once a week. I find it astonishing that young men, whose raison d'être is to lure young women into bed, do not understand how much clean sheets can help them in this aim.

Change sheets more regularly in hot weather, or if a member of the family has been ill. Crib sheets should be changed daily (or as frequently as necessary). Don't forget mattress and pillow protectors (for more on these, see 'Bed accessories', p. 69). Change and launder once a month.

Turning the mattress: Until recently, it was always considered necessary to turn a mattress, the reason being that mattresses settle and change as they age, according to the weight and shape of the people sleeping on them. And, frankly, mattresses being heavy and cumbersome, it was rather a chore. Thankfully, many modern mattresses are designed to be turned infrequently – or not at all. When buying a new mattress, therefore, it is important to follow the manufacturer's instructions on this.

With older mattresses, the general rule is to turn it once every three months.

Tip: Rotate the mattress on the bed base before turning. This way, you will turn it both side to side and end to end.

Bed linen

The enormous variations in price between different makes of bed linen depend as much on fashion (fancy names equal fancy prices) as on quality. A great deal of snobbery also attaches to the thread count of cotton sheets – that is, the number of threads per square inch. But the basic considerations are actually quite straightforward – comfort, fit, durability, price and how easy it is to look after.

When deciding how much to buy, a good rule of thumb is to have three sets of bed linen for each bed – that is, sheets, pillowcases, plus a duvet cover if you use a duvet.

Three sets gives one set on the bed, one in the wash and one spare. Having a spare set means less wear and tear and allows for mishaps, such as spilt cups of tea (my particular forte) or sick children. Having endless spare sets of sheets is no advantage. They will just sit in the linen cupboard, and go yellow or crack along the creases through lack of use.

Tip: After laundering bed linen, put the newly washed set at the bottom of the pile, so that each set is used an equal number of times.

Linen: The queen of sheets, and the fabric that gave 'bed linen' its name. Flax, from which linen is made, is a remarkably strong and hard-wearing fibre. It is smooth to the touch but launders very well and lasts for a long time. It also softens considerably with washing.

In its natural state, linen is cream or brown in colour. To make it whiter or to allow it to take a dye, it must be bleached, which weakens the fibres (deep-dyed linen sheets and pillowcases are therefore less durable than plain ones).

61

Linen's drawbacks are that it is expensive and wrinkles easily, which means that it has to be ironed. It can shrink badly, so be sure to buy a pre-shrunk brand (most are, these days, but it pays to check).

Cotton: The best all-rounder for bed linen. Like linen, cotton is absorbent, cool, smooth and strong. Cotton sheets are extremely hard-wearing, and can be laundered at high temperatures. Like linen, cotton wrinkles, but unlike linen, it takes dye very well.

Egyptian cotton, grown in the Nile valley, is one of the most sought-after types of cotton, producing exceptionally soft and fine bed linen at prices to match (when buying, check that it really is 100 per cent Egyptian cotton, and not mixed with cotton of an inferior type).

Some cottons have been treated to make ironing easier (or even unnecessary). They will be labelled 'easy care' or some such. They have their champions, but are not as hard-wearing as a plain, untreated sheet.

Brushed cotton or cotton flannel sheets are the ones to choose if you do not like the cold feel of smooth cotton sheets.

62

Polyester and/or poly-cotton: All-polyester sheets are not a good idea. They are harsh and scratchy on the skin and are not very absorbent, leading to a clammy night's sleep.

Poly-cotton blends are a better bet, but can still feel harsh on the skin. The reason people choose them is because they do not require ironing, but their reputation for being harder-wearing than cotton is misplaced. Once a poly-cotton sheet becomes worn and transparent, that means that the cotton has worn away and what you are left with is a polyester sheet.

Their main advantage is cost: they are considerably cheaper than cotton. When buying, look for blends of at least 50 per cent combed cotton, which means the fibres have been straightened, to give a smoother feel.

Whichever type you choose, check the washing instructions. You should be able to wash sheets and pillowcases at 140°F, the hottest cycle. It stands to reason that bed linen should be colourfast (for those who prefer coloured sheets) and hard-wearing, and should not need special treatment when laundering. Never buy everyday bed linen that needs dry-cleaning: satin sheets should remain a porn-film fantasy.

The case for all-white bed linen: There is so much beautifully coloured and patterned bed linen around that it is easy to be seduced into buying it. But consider what happens a few years down the line. Colours and patterns fade in the wash, however careful you are, though polyester blends fade less. If you don't wash all pieces of a set in the same load, they will fade at different rates. Sheets and pillowcases get worn and sometimes torn. You are left with a collection of mismatched, faded sheets, duvet covers and pillowcases.

All-white bed linen is the choice for the busy lives we all lead. It can stand many washings. You can just bung it all in the machine without having to worry about matching sheets with pillowcases and so on. White looks effortlessly cool and elegant, and you can always add colour with throws, cushions and so forth.

I make two exceptions. First, for children's bedrooms. An all-white children's bedroom can seem a little austere. There are plenty of cheerful, cheapish bed-linen designs for children. And if your ten-year-old son wants his Arsenal duvet cover, it seems a bit mean to impose cool good taste on him at that age. Second, if you are desperate for colour, have white pillowcases and duvet covers, but have a selection of different coloured bottom sheets.

> *Tip: The problem with all-white linen is that it is sometimes difficult to tell at a glance in a pile of sheets which size is which. The answer is to sew a small cross on an unobtrusive corner, using a different colour for each size. Special iron-on tags are also available for this purpose. Or use laundry markers, available from sewing suppliers.*

63

SHEETS

The choice is between flat sheets and fitted. Flat sheets are more versatile, because they can be used as a top or bottom sheet, but my preference is always for fitted bottom sheets. They give a smooth, wrinkle-free surface and, because they stretch over the mattress, they never need ironing. However, many modern mattresses are very deep and you may find that fitted sheets will not stretch over them, or that there is not enough overhang to tuck in a flat sheet. If this is the case, go up a size.

> *Tip: Look on the Internet for companies selling sheets and other bed linen for non-standard beds.*

TO CARE FOR SHEETS

The point of sheets is that they are hard-wearing and durable and able to withstand many washes. Ideally, you should be able to wash them on hot, although a warm wash will normally suffice, as well as being environmentally friendlier. For detailed instructions on the laundering and ironing of sheets, see 'The Laundry', p. 155.

Tip: If a fitted sheet has shrunk in the wash, when putting it on the bed, first fit one corner over the mattress, and then fit the corner diagonally opposite. This seems to make it go on more easily.

PILLOWS

Most pillows are filled with down, feathers – or a mixture of the two – or with a synthetic filling, such as foam or Hollowfibre. The pillow you buy is very much a matter of personal preference – although it is worth remembering that most chiropractors and physiotherapists recommend sleeping on only one pillow, at a height that keeps your head aligned with your spine.

Goose down is the softest and lightest filling, while synthetic fillings are the firmest and do not change shape under your head. Feather pillows are firmer than down, but have more give than those with synthetic fillings.

Asthma and allergy sufferers used to be advised not to use feather pillows, but recent research now seems to support the idea that synthetic fillings harbour more dust mites than natural fillings. The best advice would seem to be to use a good allergen-resistant pillow protector.

A standard pillowcase, sometimes called a housewife pillowcase, is a plain rectangle. An Oxford pillowcase is the same size but has a decorative edge. If you are into 'dressing' beds with piles of pillows, it is a good idea to put Oxford pillowcases on the bottom pillows and housewife cases on the top ones, so that the frilled edge peeps out.

TO CARE FOR PILLOWS

A pillow protector (see 'Bed accessories', p. 69) is vital for keeping pillows clean and prolonging their life. Barring accidents, a good feather or down pillow should last five to ten years; a synthetic one has a life of only two years.

Tip: To test whether a down or feather pillow needs replacing, lay it across your arm. If it flops sadly, its days are numbered. To test a

synthetic pillow, press it in the middle to see if it springs back. If it
does not, replace it.

Check the care label on pillows for washing instructions. Most pillows with natural fillings can be washed in the washing machine, but check first that the machine can take the weight. If the care label has become detached, wash on a lukewarm cycle, using a mild detergent. If the washing machine has a super-rinse facility, use it.

You can dry pillows in the tumble-dryer on a low setting (put a couple of dry towels in with it to absorb some of the moisture). Be aware that this can take a very long time. To economise on electricity, take the pillow out of the dryer when it is half-dry and finish off the drying outside (it is best, therefore, to wash pillows on a warm, sunny day). When drying outside, shake the pillow from time to time, to prevent the filling from clumping. When you think they are dry, give them another quick blast in the tumble dryer and then allow them to air before putting them back on the bed.

Make sure that the pillows are completely dry before using them again – this could take several days. If you leave them damp, they will smell and develop mildew.

Tip: Freshen up pillows by tumbling them in a hot tumble-dryer for
15 minutes or so once a month. The heat will also kill dust mites.

TO FOLD FLAT SHEETS AND PILLOWCASES

Folding bed linens of a regular shape, such as flat sheets and pillowcases, is a matter of common sense, though big things are folded more easily by two people. My mother used to dragoon me into helping her fold the sheets – we would fold sides to middle, then sides to middle again, pulling really tight until she gave the sheet a 'snap', nearly pulling me over if I was not paying attention. Then we walked towards each other to fold hem to hem a couple of times, making a neat parcel of cloth. When we got the rhythm going and I paid attention, it felt rather as if we were performing one of those stately old dances like the gavotte.

This is the way to fold all large rectangular linens, such as sheets and duvet covers, and also large tablecloths.

Pillowcases should be folded in half horizontally and then in half again. If you want the bed to look as they do in interiors magazines, iron the pillowcases to remove the creases before putting them on the pillows.

TO FOLD A FITTED SHEET

Hold the sheet the wrong side up – that is, with the fitted corners facing towards you. Fold it in half, hem to hem, tucking the top corners into the bottom ones. Fold in half again so that all the fitted corners are in a stack. Fold in half again to make a square, then again to make a rectangle. This is easier with two people, but if you are on your own, lay the sheet on a bed or large table.

TO STORE BED LINEN

Store bed linen (and indeed all household linen) in a cool, dry, well-ventilated cupboard. Slatted shelves are best, because they allow the air to circulate.

Do not store bed linen in a warm airing cupboard. Heat causes yellowing and premature ageing of linens. The yellow marks can be hard to remove.

Never put away linen unless it is completely dry. If it is damp, it can develop mildew, which means it will have to be washed all over again, or can develop a musty smell that permeates everything else.

If storing linens for any length of time, wrap anything old, delicate or precious in acid-free tissue paper, and place in boxes made from acid-free cardboard. Put moth-repellent sachets or lavender bags or sprigs of lavender in with them. Store linens unstarched, because other insects, such as silverfish, consider the starch a delicacy.

BLANKETS

A blanket's qualities are warmth, weight and durability. Absorbency is less of an issue because you do not normally sleep with a blanket next to your skin. Layered as they are between the sheet and the bedspread, blankets need laundering less frequently than sheets.

Blankets are generally made from wool, cotton or a synthetic fibre.

Wool blankets, which range from plain old lambswool to merino wool to cashmere, are warm and luxurious. They tend to be heavier than other blankets and suit those who like sleeping under a bit of weight. They are warm in cold weather. They can sometimes be machine-washed, but often have to be dry-cleaned. When buying, choose a blanket with a fuzzy, napped surface, which not only traps air, increasing the blanket's efficiency, but also means it is less likely to slide off the sheet in the night.

Synthetic blankets are made from polyester or acrylic. They are lightweight and extremely warm – sometimes even warmer than wool, and are generally machine-washable. Their drawbacks are that they are prone to pilling and in a dry atmosphere can develop static, leading to spectacular sparks and crackling when you get into bed.

Cotton blankets tend to be thin, often with a waffle or honeycomb construction. They are designed to be used in warm weather, and are fully machine-washable.

TO CARE FOR BLANKETS

Do not buy a wool blanket expecting to wash it frequently. Many wool blankets cannot be washed at all. Most have to be dry-cleaned. Heavy wool blankets that are to be put away for summer should be cleaned when they are taken off the beds and put into storage. (Obviously, if the blanket becomes dirty, clean it as needed.)

If the care label states that the blanket is washable, follow the instructions, but, frankly, unless it is machine-washable, I would not bother. Washing a blanket by hand is an exercise in masochism.

Synthetic and cotton blankets can be washed in the machine, according to instructions. They can usually be tumble-dried too, although domestic machines may be too small – in which case, take them to a launderette.

When a blanket is not in use, wash or dry-clean and air. Then store in a polyethylene bag in a cool place.

DUVETS

Both blankets and duvets have their passionate champions. I infinitely prefer the latter. A duvet is essentially a bag filled with down, feathers and down or artificial fibre. Although they have been used in northern Europe for centuries, they are relative newcomers to Britain. Today they are so commonplace that it is hard to remember that they used to be quaintly called 'Continental quilts', to show their exotic origins.

Now, ten duvets are sold for every one blanket. It is hardly surprising that we have taken them to our hearts in such a big way. They are blissfully warm, but do not weigh you down as blankets do. A good one settles round you in a cosy cocoon, with no tangled heaps of sheets and blankets. They are easy to look after and make bed-making the work of seconds.

All duvets work on the principle of trapping air within the filling, which is what keeps you warm. Choose a box construction, which means the duvet is sewn into a number of even-sized squares. These help to keep the filling evenly distributed and prevent it from slipping to the bottom.

In the US, the appropriate season or situation for a duvet is indicated on the package. In the UK, duvets are rated by togs – a tog being a unit of heat. The more togs, the warmer the duvet. In Britain, three tog values of duvet are commonly sold: 4.5 tog for summer use; 9 tog for spring or autumn use; and 13.5 tog for winter use. This does not mean that you have to buy three duvets. I feel the cold, so I have a 13.5 tog duvet for most of the year, with a 4.5 tog one for summer.

> *Tip: Look out for combi-duvets. These are two duvets (4.5 and 9 tog) that can be fastened together to create a 13.5 tog winter duvet.*

There are three main types of filling: down, feather and down, and synthetic.

Down is the fine undercoat of birds, located underneath the feathers. Goose down and duck down are available, and goose down is the best you can buy. It is very light and warm but also very expensive.

Feather and down is a mixture of down and cheaper whole feathers. Feather and down duvets are cheaper than all-down duvets, but the filling can be heavy – although some people prefer that. The feathers can sometimes bunch up.

The most superior synthetic duvet filling is Hollowfibre, a polyester fibre with a hole running up the middle. The hollow structure traps air more effectively and so makes the duvet warmer. Hollowfibre is the choice for anyone who might be allergic to feathers, and is also the best choice for children because it is machine-washable. These are the cheapest duvets and are very light, but because they do not settle around you in the comforting way that down does, many people do not find them as warm.

To put a duvet in its cover: There are all sorts of convoluted methods for getting a duvet into its cover. They involve folding the cover and duvet in four, or using clothespins and turning the duvet inside out, or even climbing inside the cover. Ignore them. The only way to put a duvet in its cover is to wrestle with it. Grasp one corner of the duvet and work it into the corner of the cover. Keeping hold of the first corner, do the same with the opposite corner. Pull the cover down as best you can, and then take hold of the duvet and shake it thoroughly. Finally, do up the fastenings.

TO CARE FOR DUVETS

Change the duvet cover weekly and wash it along with the sheets and pillowcases. Barring accidents, the duvet itself should not need to be washed more than once a year. Hollowfibre duvets can be washed in the machine and even tumble-dried, if your machine is big enough. Down and/or feather and down duvets cannot normally be washed at home, so either wash them at the launderette, where the machines will be big enough to accommodate them, or send them to the laundry.

Never dry-clean duvets. The fumes from the dry-cleaning fluid will become trapped in the filling, which is not just unpleasant but downright dangerous.

When a duvet is not in use, wash it or send it to the laundry. Store in a cool place – on a spare bed, under a bedspread, is ideal.

69

BED ACCESSORIES

Bedding departments of large stores have many tempting ways of getting us to part with our money. Of the following list, only the first two are absolute necessities. The rest are just pleasant extras. Absolutely vital are:

Mattress pad / protector: Not only is it uncomfortable to sleep directly on top of a mattress, but it is unhygienic. At night, we produce significant amounts of sweat (about half a pint a night) and shed quantities of dead skin cells (about 1 lb a year), so it makes sense to have something removable and washable between an expensive and difficult-to-clean mattress and us.

In addition, dust mites, which are a significant cause of allergies, live deep in mattresses and pillows, coming out at night to feast on all that dead skin, and a mattress protector will go some way to reducing their numbers (for more on dust mites, see 'Household pests', p. 322).

Bedding departments of large department stores will have a choice of protectors. I prefer a cotton quilted version that fits over the top of the mattress like a fitted sheet. People with allergies may prefer a special protector – sometimes called a 'mattress barrier', that completely encloses the mattress.

You will need one mattress pad/protector for each bed plus one spare one. Wash once a month.

> Tip: If you do not want to go to the expense of buying special mattress protectors, an old thick flannel sheet or washable blanket will do as well. The important thing is to have something between you and the mattress.

Pillow protector: Again, the idea is to protect the pillow (difficult to wash) with something that is easy to wash. Special zipped pillow protectors are available, but an old pillowcase, past its first flush of youth, will do just as well.

> Tip: When putting on the top pillowcase, make sure the openings of both pillowcases are at opposite ends to prevent slippage.

You will need one per pillow. Wash once a month, or as necessary.

The following are nice to have but not strictly necessary:

Mattress toppers: These are new to this country, but used a lot in the United States. They are feather- or down-filled pads that go on top of the mattress but under the sheet, and are extremely warm and luxurious. Lying on them, the effect is the nearest we will get these days to sleeping on the feather mattresses of our ancestors. They are an acquired taste, can be extremely hot and uncomfortable in summer and are not for those who like a firm bed.

Electric blankets: Electric mattress pads and blankets are both available. They are deliciously warm and toasty, but need to be used with care. Always follow the manufacturer's instructions. Clean and service every three years – the manufacturer or supplier will carry out servicing and may offer a cleaning service. Some blankets with detachable controls are washable, and a few are machine-washable. They should never be dry-cleaned.

Discard an electric blanket if it becomes frayed or if you can see scorch marks. Never use when damp. Inspect it regularly to check wiring inside (hold it up to the light and you will be able to see that none of the wires overlap). Also check the cord and controls.

Tip: If storage space is short and you want to take the electric blanket off a bed over the summer, lay it flat under the mattress (not plugged in), or lay it on a spare bed. If that is not possible, roll it up for storage. Do not fold it.

Bed skirts: These are frilled flat sheets that slide under the mattress and hang down the sides of the bed base. Their purpose is purely decorative – to cover up the sides of the divan base. They do not need laundering as frequently as once a week, but do not forget about them. They can easily become dust-traps.

Clothes

Not being a naturally tidy person – tidiness is a habit I have painfully acquired, rather than something I was born with – there are some areas where I fall sadly short of the standards I have set myself. And my Achilles heel is looking after clothes. I simply cannot bear to put them away. When I come home from work, I will dump my coat on a chair, step out of my shoes, leave them where they stand and then go and change. Naturally, my work clothes are left in a pile on the bed, from where they will later migrate to the floor. I then put on a pair of jeans, plucked from the pile I made when I went to bed the previous night.

I make this confession with no pride because I know that when I do make an effort to change, it makes all the difference in the world.

The first and most obvious benefit is that my clothes look better, stay cleaner and require fewer visits to the dry-cleaner. Second, the morning is not the usual rush of missing breakfast and leaving the house five times because I have forgotten something. Third, I seem to do less washing. When faced with piles of clothes on the bedroom floor, it is much easier to fling them all in the laundry basket than to sort through them and put away things that may have been worn only once and do not require washing.

I do not even have the excuse of saying I have no storage – the bane of living in a London flat. (A cunning ploy of property developers is to kit out show flats with stylish sofas, beautiful bed linen and dinky, must-have gadgets in the kitchen, such as an espresso machine. It is more convenient for their bottom line to 'forget' that people own things, and that those things need a home, too.)

TO STORE CLOTHES

Decide on a wardrobe system. You might decide to hang clothes according to colour, or – my preference – like with like: all the trousers together, all the skirts together and so on.

Try not to cram clothes into wardrobes. Give them enough space to allow creases to fall out and to let them air. For the same reason, do not pack things too tightly into drawers.

In drawers, put sets of underwear together. Organise sweaters, T-shirts and so forth according to colour, or by weight – heavy sweaters in one drawer, lighter-weight ones in another, T-shirts in another.

Put suits, jackets, coats and dresses in garment bags (which can be found in department stores and on specialist clothes storage websites) to keep out dust and moths. Garment bags should always be made of a breathable material, such as cotton, not plastic, and should be big enough that the clothes inside do not get crushed. For preference, clothes should always be stored in them. In practice, when one is busy, this is a Counsel of Perfection. A good compromise is to store your most precious garments in a bag, as well as anything that is not worn very often, such as evening dresses, winter coats out of season and fur coats. See also 'Seasonal storage', p. 76.

Never store clothes in plastic. It might seem like a good idea to leave dry-cleaned clothes in the dry-cleaner's plastic bags, but it is not.

For a start, if there is any hint of dampness in the clothes or the wardrobe, mildew may develop. More important, if clothes are stored in plastic for a long time, the polymers in the bags can migrate on to fabrics and cause yellowing, which is impossible to remove.

If you go in for hats, keep them in their hat boxes. Stuff the crowns lightly with acid-free tissue paper.

Store bags on shelves. If a bag was sold with a dust-bag, use it.

The best wardrobes – whether built-in, fitted or freestanding – have a hanging rail or rails and a set of drawers plus space at the bottom for shoes. The joy of fitted or built-in wardrobes is that they can be customised to fit your requirements. The advantage of a freestanding wardrobe is that you can take it with you when you move.

Wardrobes should be cool, dry and airy. Try not to site them near radiators (apart from anything else, this will damage the wood), and do not let hot pipes run through fitted wardrobes or built-in cupboards. Heat damages and prematurely ages fabrics.

Utilise the dead space at the very top of wardrobes to store items you do not use often, such as sleeping bags, suitcases, ski suits and hat boxes.

Line non-slatted shelves and drawers with paper to prevent them snagging fabrics. Old wrapping paper will do, but scented drawer liners can add a luxurious touch.

HANGING CLOTHES

Always hang dresses and jackets on a padded or broad wooden hanger. The thin plastic ones used by dry-cleaners are too thin and will not support the clothes properly. Wire ones are also too thin and can rust, leaving ineradicable marks on clothes. Proper hangers are not expensive – look for special offers of wooden hangers in newspapers and magazines, or try the internet for clothes storage sites.

> Tip: Get into the habit of buying a hanger every time you buy a new outfit.

Hang trousers on trouser hangers, either by the hems, or folded over the hanger. Buy double trouser hangers if you can – they allow you to hang two pairs on one hanger. Some of them have rubberised bars to prevent them slipping.

Hang skirts on skirt hangers by their waistband loops. Wrap the loops twice round the notch in the hanger. On plain hangers, twist rubber bands round the ends to prevent the skirts slipping off.

OTHER WAYS OF STORING CLOTHES

The main pieces of bedroom furniture are chests of drawers, which are useful for storing woollens, T-shirts, underwear and so forth in the absence of built-in drawers in cupboards. They can also double as a dressing-table, where space is short.

Trunks and ottomans are not really suitable for storing clothes for everyday

73

use, because it is difficult to find things easily. Use them for seasonal storage (see p. 76) and for large or bulky items such as bed linen, skisuits, sleeping bags and so on.

Many divan beds now come with drawers in the base, which also provide useful extra storage – they are surprisingly useful for shoes.

CARING FOR CLOTHES

Protect clothes by always wearing an apron when cooking or doing housework. Keep a set of old clothes for gardening, DIY and other dirty jobs.

Before putting clothes away, brush well. Clothes brushes are the best for removing dust. To get rid of fluff, use a lint-removing 'brush' which has little nylon barbs. Empty pockets, do up zips and at least some of the buttons, especially the top one. Fold sweaters and T-shirts before putting away. For more on folding clothes, see below.

Hang moth repellents in wardrobes and put moth-repellent sachets in drawers (or use lavender) to keep these hungry marauders at bay. For more on moths and other pests, see 'Household pests', p. 322.

To deal with very creased clothes: Rather than pressing very creased clothes or sending them to the dry-cleaner, try hanging them in a steamy bathroom for an hour or so. In shops, they use steamers to remove creases. These are available for domestic use, while steam cleaners can also be used to steam clothes (see 'Electrical equipment', p. 219). Note, however, that steam can bring out stains on clothes.

To fold shirts and blouses: For preference, these should always be hung. If folding a shirt or blouse, do up the top, middle and bottom buttons and lay it on its front. Fold in both sides, aligning the sleeves with the sides. Fold up the tail, if it has one, then fold into three horizontally. Fold sweaters and T-shirts the same way.

To fold skirts: These would normally be hung on a hanger. If folding for packing, fold the sides into the middle and fold in three horizontally. Always fold clothes horizontally. Once unfolded and hung up, their weight and the force of gravity will force the creases out. Vertical creases just stay put.

To fold trousers: For tailored trousers, align the inner and outer seams of the legs to ensure a crisp crease and hang by the hems. Do not align seams on legs of jeans – creases on jeans are very uncool. Fold them in half vertically and hang on a trouser hanger.

To fold dresses: These should always be hung on a hanger. If folding a dress for packing, do up buttons or zips and lay it on its front. Fold in the sides to the middle, folding the sleeves back on themselves. Fold in three horizontally.

To fold jackets: Use a hanger and store in a garment bag. If folding for packing, turn inside out and do up top, middle and bottom buttons. Lay flat on its back and fold in sleeves. Try to lay it flat in the suitcase, or if this is not possible, fold up the bottom third.

To fold socks: Lay one sock on top of the other. Fold in three, starting at the toe end, then pull over the outside of the top sock to make a neat roll.

To fold underwear: Fold underpants in three, sides to middle, then tuck in the crotch. Fold bras in half, one cup inside the other, tuck in the straps, then tuck matching knickers (folded) inside the cup as well to keep them all together. The same technique applies with men's underwear (although not bras, obviously).

Men's boxer shorts should be folded in half vertically, then in half horizontally.

TO CARE FOR FUR COATS

Fur has had its ups and downs and is a particular target of the animal rights lobby. This is not the place to discuss the whys and wherefores of wearing fur. Either you wear it or you do not.

If you do have a fur coat, here is how to look after it.

Fur is a paradoxical fabric – both strong and delicate. A well-made and well looked after fur can last for years, but moths can destroy it in one summer. Rather like feathers, fur is anti-static, which means it will not attract dirt. It does, however, get greasy, especially around the collar and on the sleeve cuffs, and this grease will attract dirt. A fur coat needs cleaning only every other year, and must be done by a specialist. Furriers and specialty dry cleaners are listed in the Yellow Pages.

A fur coat has two sides – the fur side and the leather side. The leather is four or five times thinner than a leather coat, so is far more susceptible to heat and moisture. If it gets wet, it will shrink, and if it gets too dry, it will harden. With average British temperatures – not too warm and not too cold – it will keep well in a dry, well-ventilated wardrobe. During the winter months, store it in a cotton garment bag when it is not being worn. If a fur coat gets wet, hang it on a hanger and let it dry naturally. Do not put in front of a radiator.

The fur part is susceptible to moth attack, and moths seem to have been multiplying in the longer, warmer summers we've had recently. During these months, when the coat is not being worn, do not just put it in the wardrobe and forget about it. Moths can destroy a coat in a single summer. Instead, put it into cold storage, which costs around $50 a year.

Seasonal storage

It used to be general practice at the end of the winter and the end of the summer to bring out the new season's clothes and put the old ones into storage. This is not always possible in modern houses and flats, with their lack of storage space, but if you can do it, it is a worthwhile habit to get into.

A regular turnover makes space in the wardrobe so that clothes are not crammed together. It prevents chaos. You can see exactly what clothes you have, and spot thrilling gaps in your wardrobe, to be filled next time you go shopping.

TO STORE THE OLD SEASON'S CLOTHES

Before putting away the old season's clothes, assess if they still deserve their place in your wardrobe. Generally, I put on probation anything that has not been worn for one season; anything not worn for two seasons goes into a bag for the charity shop. Or you could try selling them if they are good quality and/or designer clothes.

Mend, dry-clean or wash clothes as necessary before storing them. This is important for several reasons. First, it is depressing to pull out dirty clothes from storage. Second, dirt encourages mildew. Grubby clothes often smell musty too, and the mustiness will permeate them all. Finally, insects, especially moths, are attracted to dirt on clothes and linens. To insects, it is not dirt, it is dinner. They find clean clothes much less attractive (for more on moths, see 'Household pests', p. 322). Ensure clothes are completely dry before storing.

For storing clothes, a large trunk (the more traditional department stores stock these in their luggage departments) is ideal. If not, large suitcases will do, as will the drawers fitted in some divan beds and storage boxes designed to fit under beds, as long as they have well-fitting lids.

Fold the clothes carefully (see above), and put in the trunk/box, with layers of tissue paper. The tissue paper helps prevent clothes from creasing and should ideally be acid-free. This is widely available – try art suppliers.

Put heavy winter coats and suits in cotton garment bags, padding the sleeves with acid-free tissue paper, and putting a couple of lavender bags in the pockets. It is best to hang them somewhere if you have room. If not, lay them in a cool, dry place (in a little-used spare room on top of the bed is one possibility).

> Tip: Use tissue paper when packing for a holiday as well. Your clothes
> will emerge as uncreased as when they went into the suitcase.

To be double sure that the clothes are protected from moths, put moth-repellent sachets in with them. There are several brands available – herbal, cedar or chemical. Even nicer is to strew dried lavender stalks on top of each layer of tissue paper. Lavender is a traditional repellent and smells delicious. Another traditional remedy is to put several handfuls of horse chestnuts in with the clothes. Though they smell innocuous to us, moths apparently hate them. I have not tried this myself, but a friend swears by their moth-repelling efficacy.

To store woollen clothes: Store woollens in compression storage bags. These are a great way to save space. You put the clothes in a bag and then suck the air out with the vacuum cleaner, squashing them down to a fraction of their original bulk. Look out for brands with a double layer of plastic, which gives protection from puncturing. Because the bags are sealed, the clothes are protected from damp and moth attack. Interestingly, they do not seem to come out too creased.

> Tip: These bags are also recommended for packing clothes to go
> on holiday. The only problem is that unless you can guarantee that

77

there is going to be a vacuum cleaner at the other end, how will you get them all home again?

TO PREPARE THE NEW SEASON'S CLOTHES

Take the new season's clothes out of the trunk/box and hang them up to air. Meanwhile, clean out all wardrobes and drawers. Dust will have accumulated over the previous six months, and clothes moths may have laid their eggs there too. It is not the moths that you can see that do the damage; it is their larvae, which you cannot see, but which may be lurking in crevices and cracks.

Vacuum well, going into all the corners, then wipe the interior surfaces, using water with a little all-purpose cleaner and a well wrung-out cloth. Leave doors and drawers open until you are sure that everything is completely dry. Re-line drawers. Hang fresh moth deterrents in wardrobes and put moth-deterrent sachets in drawers before putting clothes away.

Shoes

'When there's a shine on your shoes, there's a melody in your heart,' as Fred Astaire so memorably put it in *The Band Wagon*. Life was obviously much simpler in 1953. Nowadays, having shiny shoes is a vital component of any job interview, and if you want to know the mark of a man, look at his shoes. It doesn't matter how smart his suit, how well ironed his shirt: if his shoes aren't clean, he will look like a scruff. (Actually, the same applies to women.)

As well as aesthetics, it makes practical sense to look after your shoes. On average, we spend four hours on our feet and take between 8,000 and 10,000 steps each day. Every time we take a step, we exert a force about 50 per cent greater than our body weight.

Tip: Buy shoes at the end of the day, because feet can swell by up to five per cent in hot weather. Always try both shoes on, because one of your feet may be larger than the other.

CARING FOR SHOES

Before wearing a new pair of leather shoes, clean them with shoe cream. Shoe creams contain lanolin, which will nourish the leather and give it a protective coating. Fabric, suede and nubuck shoes should be treated with a protective spray. Do not wear new shoes in wet weather.

I often rub the leather soles on new shoes with fine sandpaper just to remove the shiny surface – it stops them being so slippery.

Do not wear the same pair of shoes day in, day out. They need time for the leather to dry. Store on racks. Finding I had no room for shoe racks in my new flat, I put my shoes in one of the drawers in the base of the bed – they make surprisingly useful and accessible storage for shoes.

If you prefer to keep your shoes in boxes, a favourite trick of the fashion tribe is to take a Polaroid of the shoes and stick it on the end of the box, so you can see at a glance what it contains. However, it is far simpler to buy see-through boxes. Trawl the clothes-care department of large stores and internet sites for suitable options.

Always use shoetrees. Wooden ones are best because they absorb any moisture in the shoes, and cedar varieties are best of all because their scent permeates the leather. Wooden shoetrees will not work on flimsy sandals – for these, use the foam rubber variety that just fits into the toes of shoes.

When travelling, stuff shoes with socks to help them keep their shape (this also helps economise on space), and put into shoe bags before packing.

> *Tip: Some of the upmarket brands of shoes are sold with felt storage bags. Do not throw these away. They are very useful for packing shoes when going on holiday.*

TO CLEAN LEATHER SHOES

Clean shoes after every wearing and before putting them away. If they are wet and/or muddy, stuff with newspaper and allow them to dry naturally in a warm, dry place. Do not put them in front of a radiator, or the leather may crack or dry out and become stiff.

Brush the mud off when it is dry, using a stiff brush. If the shoes are still dirty, wipe all over with a barely damp cloth before polishing. For really dirty shoes, an old-fashioned remedy that works well is to clean them with saddle soap before polishing. This is readily available from saddlers and shops selling tack. To use, follow manufacturer's instructions. The important thing is not to let it lather too much. As well as cleaning, it will condition and preserve the leather.

Once any dirt is removed, polish the shoes. Apply a small amount of polish with a soft cloth. Start at the toe and rub the polish in, using a circular motion. Fold the cloth and lightly buff the shoe, then insert a shoetree and put the shoes away. Before wearing, buff the surface again with a soft, clean cloth.

To clean patent leather shoes: Clean with a soft damp cloth. Use a little vinegar to remove finger marks. Patent leather is covered with a fine plastic film. Do not leave it in contact with patterned or coloured polythene bags – they can leave a permanent imprint.

To clean suede and nubuck shoes: Brush gently with a suede brush. Go easy or you will remove the top layer. Use short, quick strokes to raise the nap. Or (for suede), wrap sticky parcel tape round your hand, sticky-side up and pat the shoe all over to remove dust and bring up the nap. This is useful for delicate suede that might be damaged by a wire brush. For oily spots, use a suede stick. One brand currently available is Janie, which you can find on internet sites.

> *Tip: To revive worn suede, put the kettle on and hold the shoes over the steam (being careful not to burn yourself). Allow them to dry and then brush well.*

TO CLEAN NON-LEATHER SHOES
Wipe with a damp cloth as necessary.

TO CLEAN ATHLETIC SHOES
If they are very wet and muddy, leave to dry naturally in a warm place (do not put on a radiator). Brush off the dried mud and clean with mark and stain eraser. Finish off with a sneaker whitener. To clean the laces, put them in with a load of washing.

Another method is to clean the fabric parts of the shoes with upholstery shampoo or carpet shampoo. Work the foam in with a cloth, then 'rinse' with a damp cloth and plain water. Finish off with a sneaker whitener.

Some trainers can be washed in the machine – and it will say so on the label. Washing ordinary athletic shoes in the machine will damage them, but while it is probably not a good idea to machine-wash the shoes you plan to run a marathon in, you might risk it with sneakers that are past their best. One mother I know always washes all her sons' sneakers, with no bad effects.

> Tip: Wash athletic shoes with some towels to stop them banging about in the washing machine.

Jewellery

As Anita Loos's exuberant and illiterate heroine, Lorelei Lee, said in *Gentlemen Prefer Blondes*, 'A kiss on the hand may make you feel very very good, but a diamond and safire [*sic*] bracelet lasts for ever.'

There is certainly something comforting about owning a good piece of jewellery, be it a present, an inherited piece or the fruit of one's own labours. Several years ago, I worked for a brief time on a tabloid newspaper. When I left, my pension contributions were returned, and I decided to buy my first 'good' jewellery with the money (a pair of Tiffany bow earrings – platinum, inset with minute diamond chips).

I tried to kid myself that the earrings would be 'an investment', portable wealth, as if at any moment I might be forced to flee an invading army with my jewellery sewn into my petticoats. Of course, they were nothing of the sort – I bought them because they were beautiful. It was an act of sheer frivolity, but I still get a thrill of pleasure every time I wear them.

Jewellery comes and goes out of style, but it is worth hanging on to until the wheel of fashion turns again. Silver, which has been in the ascendant for the past ten years or so, suits pale northern skins; gold, less so. Unless you are absolutely sure of what you are doing, do not buy jewellery, especially stones, abroad.

TO STORE JEWELLERY

Always store jewellery in padded boxes. The box a piece came in is probably the best because it was designed specifically for it. I do possess a large leather jewellery

81

case that my mother gave me for Christmas a few years ago. It is lovely, with special padded ring holders and earring mounts, but I do not use it for good jewellery because it always seems to me that it just makes a handy holdall for burglars.

Storing jewellery in boxes maintains humidity, keeps out dust and prevents breakages, quite apart from keeping it safe. If you do prefer to use a large jewellery box, keep items separate. Hard gemstones, particularly diamonds, can scratch softer metals, and some more fragile gemstones, such as topaz, can crack. Before putting away, fasten the clasps of necklaces and bracelets and put earrings on their special mounts. If you do not have enough boxes or compartments in a jewellery case, wrap each piece in acid-free tissue paper or use special jewellery rolls.

> *Tip: If you find that a chain has mysteriously formed into a Gordian knot, untangle it by dusting with talcum powder and using two needles to tease out the knots.*

TO KEEP JEWELLERY CLEAN

Always take rings off before washing up or doing housework. Chemicals such as alcohol and ammonia will damage some gemstones, while chlorine bleach can pit gold and tarnish silver. You could use a safety pin to attach rings to your lapel or apron while doing housework, but I never seem to have a safety pin to hand, so I have a small bowl on the kitchen window sill specifically for rings and other jewellery.

A glamorous friend tells me that jewellery should not be packed in checked-in luggage when flying. Apart from the danger of theft, the extreme temperature changes in the hold can crack gemstones. However, with ever-changing security regulations, it may not be possible to carry jewellery in hand-luggage, so it's probably best to leave it at home.

TO CLEAN JEWELLERY

All jewellery collects grease, soap scum, dirt, skin cells and so forth, which build up and eventually cause the metal or stones to look dull and dirty. There is another reason to keep jewellery clean: detergents and other chemicals accumulated on the backs of jewellery can cause allergies in susceptible people – particularly rings and earrings that are in close contact with the skin.

When embarking on cleaning a piece of jewellery, proceed with extreme care, and if in doubt or if a piece is very precious, delicate or an antique, take it to a jeweller to be cleaned professionally.

Do not be tempted to use an ultrasonic cleaner. They clean by vibration and can cause stones to crack or even shatter. They are not worth the expense or the risk.

TO CLEAN GOLD AND PLATINUM JEWELLERY

Gold and platinum jewellery, whether plain or set with diamonds, sapphires, rubies, garnets, amethysts and other transparent gemstones apart from emeralds and aquamarines (see below) can generally be washed. Do not wash if set with opaque stones, such as pearls.

Use a small plastic bowl, not the sink, in case something slips down the drain. Fill with lukewarm water (hot water can cause thermal shock to stones) and add the merest drop of unperfumed, colourless dish soap. Special jewellery cleaners are available, but detergent is fine. Some people recommend adding a drop of ammonia, but while diamonds and other stones might not be harmed by ammonia, the settings might be. It is not worth the risk.

Drop the pieces in the water, one at a time, give them a gentle stir and leave to soak for a few minutes to start dislodging the dirt. If the pieces are very dirty use a very soft brush, such as a baby's toothbrush, to clean them. This is especially useful on rings, where dirt can get lodged behind the stones. Do not use a cloth when cleaning rings because it could catch on the claws holding the stones and loosen them. Rinse in clean plain water and lay each piece on a clean, dry tea towel. Finish drying by gently polishing with a chamois leather or a spectacle cleaning cloth – again, use nothing that will catch on the settings of the stones.

> Tip: Before discarding the washing water, drain it through a sieve in case a stone, bead or earring back has been overlooked.

An old remedy for cleaning diamonds is to soak them briefly in gin – the idea being that the alcohol will cut through grease on the ring. This has a certain sluttish glamour about it, and will not harm the diamonds, but detergent and water do just as well.

Did you know that the commonest time to lose stones from a ring is after cleaning? This is not necessarily because of the cleaning but because the stones have been held in their settings only by the build-up of dirt and grease.

83

TO CLEAN SILVER JEWELLERY

Plain silver can be washed as above, or if it is tarnished it should be cleaned as normal using silver polish (for full instructions see 'Silver', p. 149). But silver set with enamel, or with opaque stones such as opals and turquoise, needs special care, not because of the silver but because of the stones, which will be damaged by water or chemicals.

Proceed with extreme caution. If the piece is only lightly tarnished, try rubbing the silver gently with a proprietary silver metal polishing cloth (not the kind that is impregnated with polish). If that does not work, graduate on to a soft pencil eraser (use an Artgum eraser, available from artists' suppliers).

If there is still a problem, pour a small amount of silver polish or dip into an eggcup. Dip a cotton swab into it and squeeze out excess. Rub the silver only with the cotton bud, making sure that no chemical comes into contact with enamel or gemstone. 'Rinse' by rubbing with another barely damp cotton swab, dipped this time in plain water, then immediately polish with a soft cloth. Wrap silver jewellery in special silver protecting cloths (found in many department and jewellery stores).

84

TO CLEAN EMERALDS AND AQUAMARINES

Emeralds and aquamarines are porous and extremely sensitive to extremes of temperature. Emeralds have often been treated with an oil to close up the fissures and cracks to which the stones are prone. The oils will be lost if the stones are immersed in water.

Some authorities say that these stones can be washed in soapy water as above, but I would not risk it. Instead, wipe them with a soft cloth, and if you think they need further cleaning, take them to a jeweller.

> *Tip: A reputable jeweller will know not to clean emeralds and aquamarines in an ultrasonic cleaner, but check first before handing over your precious baubles.*

TO CLEAN OPAQUE STONES

Opals, coral, jet, lapis lazuli and turquoise are porous and can absorb water and other chemicals. They should never be immersed in water, but polished with a soft cloth. Opals are a special case in that they are actually a solid gel, a hydrous silicon dioxide, and contain water. As such, they require humid conditions or they may dry out and crack. The best way to keep opals 'alive' is to wear them.

Amber is also porous and should not generally be washed. However, I have been told that it can be briefly dipped in milk and then immediately wiped dry. Apparently, the milk gives the amber a lovely shine.

TO CLEAN PEARLS

Pearls are very delicate. When not being worn, they should be kept separately from other jewellery in a soft pouch because they can easily get scratched. Like opals, they can be damaged by too dry an atmosphere (they begin to peel) and the best way to keep them lustrous is to wear them.

Pearls can be easily damaged by chemicals. Never immerse them in water or cleaning solutions, especially those containing ammonia. And be careful with perfume and hairsprays. The old-fashioned advice, which still holds good, is to put on your pearls after doing your hair and make-up.

After wear, wipe the pearls with a barely damp cloth before putting them away. Polish them gently with a chamois leather to bring up the shine. Check the string regularly and have them restrung before they break. There are two signs that they probably need restringing: discolouration of the string between the pearls, and uneven gaps appearing between them (which means the string has begun to stretch). If the string does break, a good tip is to put the pearls on a round tray, which makes it easier to see the gradations of size.

85

> *Tip: How do you tell a real pearl from a fake? Rub the pearl gently against your teeth. Real and cultured pearls will feel gritty; fakes, which are made of plastic, will feel smooth.*

Brushes and combs

It is easy to forget to wash hairbrushes, combs and make-up brushes. But even if you wash your hair every day, hairbrushes and combs will pick up dust, dirt and residue from hair gels and sprays. As for make-up brushes, there is no point in following a rigorous skin-cleansing routine, only to then brush dirt all over your face along with your foundation. As well as being unhygienic, clogged make-up brushes are also less efficient at applying make-up.

TO WASH HAIRBRUSHES

Wash brushes once a month. All brushes – bristle, plastic and rubber – should be washed in the same way. First remove any hair from the bristles by running a comb through them (go easy on natural bristles to avoid pulling them out).

Brushes should not be immersed in water. This rule applies not just to wood- or bone-backed brushes, which can crack. Even cheap rubber-cushioned brushes normally have a couple of air holes in them, which can fill up with water and rot the rubber from inside.

To clean, fill a small bowl with lukewarm water and add a little dish soap. Dip the bristles only in the water. Use your fingers to clean in between the bristles. Rinse by dipping the bristles in plain water. Give the brush a good shake to get rid of excess water, gently squeeze the bristles with a soft, dry cloth, then place the brush face down and allow to dry naturally.

TO WASH COMBS

Once a month, soak plastic or metal combs in warm water and dish soap for ten minutes to loosen dirt. Use a small scrubbing brush, such as a nailbrush, to clean between the teeth of the comb. Rinse in plain water and leave to dry.

TO WASH MAKE-UP BRUSHES

Always wash make-up brushes if you have had an eye or skin infection. Otherwise, wash at least once a month (once a fortnight is better). Use lukewarm water and a little dish soap. Dip the bristles only in the water – avoid getting the handles wet. Rub through the bristles with your hands to clean and rinse in plain water, again dipping just the bristles in the water. Wrap the bristles in paper towel to squeeze out excess water, then place the brushes on their side on a flat surface, with the bristles hanging over the edge, and allow to dry naturally.

Children's bedrooms

Children's bedrooms are not generally bastions of restrained good taste. As children get older, their bedrooms cease to be a nursery and become the part of the house that is their own, where they can rest, do schoolwork and expand their interests and personalities. And they should be allowed to have a say in how they are decorated.

When it comes to furnishing a child's bedroom, the priorities are comfort, obviously, a place to do homework (although you might prefer to keep an eye on them while they work at the dining-room table) and plenty of storage. Hamster, mouse, gerbil and guinea pig cages should be banned from children's bedrooms, because they are really nothing more than big litter boxes in which the animals defecate and urinate. And cats and dogs should not be allowed to sleep on children's beds. I also do not think that children should be allowed to have a television or computer in their bedroom. Firstly, children need their sleep and these are distractions. Second, parents can monitor their children's viewing and internet activity more easily if they are not tucked away on their own.

TO CLEAR UP AND CLEAN OUT

Children's rooms should routinely be cleaned along with the rest of the house – tidied daily, when the beds are made, and cleaned once a week.

The housework can be incorporated into play even with very young toddlers. You just have to reconcile yourself to the fact that it is going to take a lot longer and be patient. Every day, get children to help put their toys away by making it a game. Children love being helpful, so during the weekly clean, give them a duster and let them help 'dust' while you get on with the job in hand. Give them the waste-paper basket to empty too. Get them to help make the bed – they are just the right height to tuck sheets in – and when changing the sheets, let them hide underneath the duvet cover and sheets and play peek-a-boo.

When I was very little, an occasional treat was to be allowed to ride on the vacuum cleaner while my mother cleaned. It was probably wildly unsafe and did the vacuum cleaner no good, but it was fun.

Do not forget that children's hairbrushes and combs need cleaning frequently (see 'Brushes and combs', p. 85).

When it comes to getting rid of things, it is only right to consult children before throwing out things such as toys they have outgrown – how would you like it if someone came into your bedroom and decreed that you had got too many shoes and then arbitrarily decided which ones to get rid of? Explain that some things must go and let children be part of the process.

I strongly believe that the above lays the foundations for later years, when older children's bedrooms truly become their private space. They should know how to make the bed (even if they choose not to do it), that clothes not put in the laundry basket will not be washed, and that once a week you will do a trawl for dirty mugs and plates and anything else that does not belong in their bedroom, so if they do not want this invasion, they should take things downstairs.

Other than that, if they choose to live in a slum, so be it.

TO STORE TOYS

Try to confine toys to children's bedrooms. That is easier said than done. The Second Law of Thermodynamics states that entropy – disorder – of a closed system always increases. In other words, everything falls into chaos eventually. A perfect demonstration of this law can be seen in houses with young children. You feel as if you are being engulfed in a sea of plastic, and guess what – you are.

Store larger toys in clear plastic storage boxes so it is easy to see what they contain. Stackable boxes are useful, as are those with wheels.

The trouble with toys is that most of them are so small – as anyone who has experienced the exquisite pain of treading on a piece of Lego with bare feet can attest. Do not throw everything randomly into one large toy box. Sort Lego, small toy figures and animals, and all the other tiny inhabitants of Plastic Toy Hell into smaller plastic storage boxes. Or use shoeboxes, labelled if you have the energy.

Clear things out occasionally. Throw away anything that is broken or anything old or unwanted – but allow children to have a say.

A good half-way house between having everything out and getting rid of things is to rotate toys. Put half away in the loft or somewhere similar and bring them out six months later. That way, you halve the mess and the children renew their pleasure in a rediscovered toy.

CLEANING TOYS

It is neither possible nor desirable for children to live in a sterile environment, but toys need to be kept reasonably clean: they lie on the floor, they go in children's mouths, they are taken into the garden; the dog is allowed to play with them too. Make life easier for yourself by trying to buy toys that are washable.

To clean plastic toys: The simplest, most labour-saving way to wash plastic toys is to put them in the dishwasher on a low temperature. Either put them in the cutlery basket, or tie them to the top rack with a freezer tie. Larger items should be washed in a bowl of soapy water, rinsed and dried. Involve smaller children in this – it can become 'dolly's bath time'.

Pacifiers and other things that have been in children's mouths should be washed every day. You may also want to sanitise them by leaving them in boiling water for five minutes.

To clean stuffed toys and dressing-up clothes: Teddies and other cloth toys should be washable – most are these days. Launder them weekly in warm water. After washing, check that the seams are still securely stitched and that nothing has become detached.

Launder dressing-up clothes regularly as you would any other clothes. It is easy to forget them.

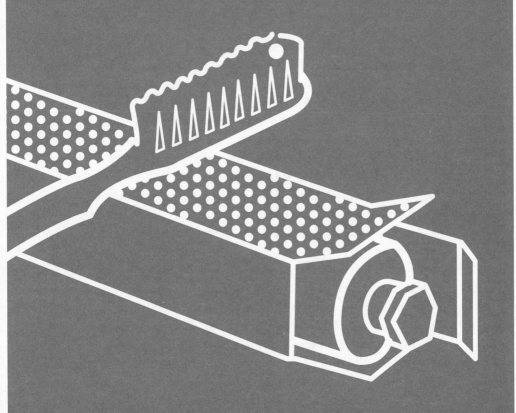

CHAPTER 3
The Bathroom

The only time the world beats a path to your door is if you're in the bath.

Anonymous

After kitchens, the room on which we spend the most money is the bathroom, and before you know it, you have parted with a small fortune – labour and installation often costing twice as much as the fixtures and fittings.

But it is only recently that the bathroom has achieved such elevated status. When I was growing up, one bathroom was the norm in most houses. Nowadays, a second or even a third bathroom is considered a necessity, one of which must be en-suite. In new houses, the only constraints are space and money. In older houses, rooms are often carved up in order to accommodate extra bathrooms – which is a neat mirroring of what happened in the 19th century when the first bathrooms were put in. A bathroom would be shoehorned into an existing room – often a dressing-room – so would be small and inconvenient, not to mention cold.

In these days of wet rooms, power showers, double basins, whirlpool baths and underfloor heating, it is hard to remember that British bathrooms were for a long time an international joke, giving rise to accusations that we are a nation of soap-dodgers. And it must be admitted they were pretty Spartan.

Well into the 1980s, I was invited to a party in a large country house, which had what must have been the original Victorian bathroom, 'modernised' in the 1930s. The water, heated by a geyser, ran at a trickle, and it took about 20 minutes to run a bath. The one tiny radiator proved entirely inadequate to heat the room, so as the hot water hit the icy surface of the cast-iron bath, it was transformed into vast, impenetrable clouds of steam, which condensed on the ceiling and rained down in cold droplets on to the occupant of the bath.

British showers were another joke. Poor water pressure was the main reason for the miserable dribbles that passed for a shower in many houses. And lack of a proper thermostat meant that if someone turned on a tap elsewhere in the house while you were in the shower, you were either scalded or doused in cold water. Even today, in some British hotels, the promised 'shower' turns out to be a rubber hose attached to the faucet.

Part of the problem was the gravity system of water supply that is common in most British homes. Cold water supply for every room in the house but the kitchen is stored in a tank at the top of the house. To get reasonable shower pressure, the tank must be at least three feet above the fitting. Power showers, with their pumping systems and controls independent of the rest of the hot water system, have changed all that, but with all the improvements in modern showers, shower usage in this country is still only a quarter of that of baths.

After the kitchen, the bathroom and lavatory are the areas of the house that require the most attention. The bathroom is shared; it is where human waste is disposed; it is where we are ill. There is no escaping the fact therefore that bathrooms need consistent, regular cleaning. The good news, though, is that their hard, shiny surfaces make this an extremely quick and easy job.

The essentials

Bathrooms are easy to keep clean as long as they are kept tidy. It is the work of seconds to run a damp cloth over a clear surface, but a complete nuisance if it is cluttered with bottles and jars of potions, lotions and make-up.

The ideal is to keep everything out of sight. For some reason, a cluttered bathroom looks grubby, even when it is not. A cabinet is better than open shelves, which can get very dusty, and drawers are even better. You can see exactly what is in the drawer at a glance and everything is easily accessible. In one house I lived in, there was a little alcove in the bathroom, about 12 inches wide and 15 inches deep, which we turned into a cupboard. We fitted narrow shelves from top to bottom, but kept them about 6 inches deep at the back of the alcove. On the inside of the cupboard door, we fitted wire baskets. This kept everything in reach and enabled us to make the most of the entire space.

LIMESCALE

Hard water is water with dissolved mineral salts in it – usually calcium or magnesium carbonate. Rainwater, which is naturally soft, does not contain any minerals, but as it seeps through rocks such as limestone or chalk, these minerals are dissolved in it. If it passes through hard rocks such as granite, or through peaty soils, it does not pick up minerals and remains soft.

Hard-water areas in Britain follow the rock formations, and tend to go from north to south, with the softest water in Scotland, northern England and the westerly parts of Wales and Cornwall, and the hardest in East Anglia and south-east England.

You will know if your water is hard because soap will not lather very well, soap scum will be left in sinks and baths and crusty deposits will form in showerheads, on pipes and taps, and around drainholes. This is limescale. It is formed when the dissolved salts in the water are precipitated out when the water is heated, or remain after cold water has evaporated. The former causes limescale to build up in your kettle; the latter causes it to build up around a dripping faucet.

The good news is that hard water is generally believed to be good for us. In the past, when lead was used for water pipes, hard-water deposits on the pipes protected people from lead poisoning (some lead pipes can still be found in old properties, but they are gradually being replaced). In more recent times, it has been noted that patterns of cardio-vascular disease tend to follow the same patterns as soft-water and hard-water areas: even after adjusting for socio-economic and other factors, there are higher rates of cardio-vascular disease (heart disease and strokes) in the soft-water areas of the north than in the hard-water areas of the south and east. People who live in hard-water areas also claim that their water tastes better, but as the same claim is made by people who live in soft-water areas, that is probably a matter of what we are used to.

If you are renovating the house, you may want to consider a permanent water-softening system. These are installed in the plumbing system and normally work by replacing the calcium and magnesium with sodium. You cannot drink the softened water, so you will still need a supply of drinking water. Magnetic and electrical devices can alter the calcium ions so they do not build up on pipes, but some of them are of limited effectiveness. They do not soften the water.

TO TREAT LIMESCALE

A steam cleaner is very effective at removing limescale deposits from bathroom fittings, but if you do not want to go to the expense of buying one, equally effective and much cheaper is white vinegar, used either as is or diluted with water (for specific instructions, see 'Vinegar', p. 232). Vinegar can be used safely on porcelain basins and on modern vitreous enamel and acrylic baths. On older baths, go carefully and allow the vinegar to stay in contact with the enamel for a minimum amount of time. Proprietary limescale removers are effective but expensive. They are worth using on vertical surfaces such as tiled walls in shower enclosures where vinegar would run off.

To avoid limescale building up in the first place, make sure that taps are fully turned off and fix dripping faucets.

Tip: If you are taking a tap apart to replace a washer, always plug the drain first. If you do not, some vital component is bound to disappear down the drainhole.

VENTILATION

Mould develops in damp, poorly ventilated areas, and bathrooms, which are prone to condensation, are particularly vulnerable. Mould is a fungus. It shows as black spots and usually appears on tiles but can sometimes develop on the walls and ceilings of bathrooms. It can also burrow below the surface of paint or wallpaper.

Prevention is better than cure, so keep bathrooms well ventilated and well heated: open the window after a shower or hot, steamy bath, and leave towels off heated towel rails until the room has dried off a bit.

If mould does develop, it can be killed and removed with a solution of chlorine bleach. Proprietary mould removers are also available, but their main ingredient is bleach, so why pay more?

Make a solution of bleach (equal parts of bleach and water) and scrub off mould with a soft brush (an old toothbrush is ideal). Rinse with plain water and dry well.

Tip: In a shower cubicle, run the hot shower first so that the steam starts loosening the mould.

When you come to redecorate, choose a special paint (probably called something like 'For kitchens and bathrooms') that has anti-mildew properties.

If mould appears on sealant, you can try using a toothbrush and straight bleach, but in my experience, once those black spots appear, nothing will remove them. Your only recourse is to cut away and replace the sealant.

95

Baths, basins and showers

If kept in good condition, bathroom fitments can last for years and will need replacing only if you get tired of them or they go out of fashion. And they do. For a while, acrylic baths were the rage because they were cheap and not too cold to sit in. But then people realised they looked cheap too, and also creaked and scratched easily. Free-standing baths, too, had their moment until everyone realised that for all their retro-glamour, there was nowhere to put the soap. For the past 20 years, the only colour for bathroom fittings has been white, but I wouldn't mind betting that coloured suites – yes, even avocado – will come into fashion again one day.

I wouldn't mind betting either that baths will have disappeared completely within the next 20 years for the simple reason that a shower uses so much less water. In these times of long-term drought (the past 100 years have been the driest century on record), water conservation is likely to become a hard and fast habit. And the fact is that a typical bath uses 18 gallons of water compared to 8 gallons for a five-minute shower – though power showers are deceptively large users, with some actually using more water than a bath.

With one or two exceptions, most materials used in bathrooms are extremely hard-wearing and can withstand a lot of wear and heavy-duty cleaning. The best choice for basins and toilets is porcelain (it is too heavy for baths), which is extremely easy to clean and only likely to get damaged if a heavy object is dropped on it.

The material used in all older baths and basins and in more expensive modern baths is cast iron or steel coated in vitreous enamel. It is important to use only products recommended for vitreous enamel (check on the back of the bottle), because some acid-based products can damage the enamel.

The exceptions to the hard-wearing rule are acrylic baths and shower trays, which are easily scratched, and glass or plastic shower screens, which are prone to smearing and getting covered with soap scum.

TO CLEAN BATHS AND BASINS

Wipe basins daily. Once a week, clean thoroughly using a soft cloth and household detergent, paying particular attention to the drainholes and the base of taps, where limescale can form. To prevent water spotting, wipe dry after cleaning.

Get into the habit of cleaning the bath immediately after it is used. Apart from anything else, it is then much easier to clean than it is after the tidemark has been allowed to harden into a dried-on ring.

While the bath is emptying, squirt a little household detergent into the water, quickly wipe the bath with a cloth and allow the water to drain away. Rinse quickly with a blast from the cold tap or a hand-held shower. This method is suitable for all types of bath. With acrylic baths in particular, do not use any abrasive product, which could scratch the surface.

If the bath is always cleaned after use, the weekly cleaning becomes so much easier – in fact, you may need only to clean the edges and faucet. Once a week, clean the drainholes. Remove any hair or other debris, and if the water seems to be running slowly, implying a blockage, see 'To unblock a drain', p. 50.

> *Tip: To make baths easier to clean, do not use bath oils, which can leave a sticky residue. Stick to bubble bath, which is itself a detergent. Bath oils can stain acrylic baths.*

To descale baths and basins: Limescale builds up around the base of faucets and the rim of drainholes, where water can pool. Soak a rag or white paper towel in vinegar and place it over the limescale deposit. Leave for a couple of hours or until the limescale has softened and can be wiped away with a cloth (to remove from the base of taps, use an old toothbrush). Stubborn spots of limescale might need the help of a slightly abrasive cream cleaner (one occasion you can use it).

> *Tip: Put cream cleaner on the end of an old cork and rub the spot – this enables you to rub harder.*

97

TO CLEAN FAUCETS

Things like toothpaste can damage the metal of faucets, so wipe it off as it appears. Once a week, clean faucets thoroughly with a damp microfibre cloth, then shine with a dry cloth.

Modern faucets generally do not need polishing. In fact, most have been lacquered or given a special coating, which will be damaged by metal polish. Old

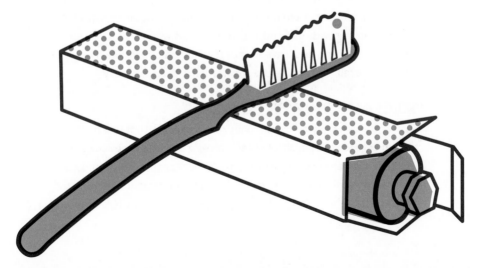

brass faucets can be polished (see 'Metal', p. 280), but it is a bit of a chore, so most people do not bother.

To descale faucets: Soak a cloth in vinegar and wrap it around the end of the faucet. Leave for an hour and then have a look to see if the limescale has softened. If so, wipe it off with the cloth. If not, leave for a further 30 minutes, then check again.
   Or:
   Stick half a lemon on the end of the faucet and leave for an hour or so. The lemon juice will have the same effect as the vinegar.
   Limescale deposits at the base of faucets can be removed by the same method. Use an old toothbrush to remove the softened deposits.

> *Note: Use vinegar on stainless steel and chrome taps only. It can corrode old, brass or plated taps.*

TO CLEAN A SHOWER

Shower trays are generally made of acrylic material – just like baths – and should be cleaned in the same way. Clean with a mild detergent once a week and be aware that oils and strong perfumes can stain the shower tray and that it can get scratched.

> *Counsel of perfection: Wipe it dry after every use.*

Every week, check that the plughole is not blocked with hair or other debris. Once a month use an enzyme drain cleaner/freshener.

To descale a showerhead: Do not bother dismantling the showerhead. Instead, half-fill a plastic bag with half and half vinegar and water. Fix it to the showerhead with a rubber band and leave it until the limescale has gone. Flush out any little bits of limescale by running the shower hard, then wipe dry.

TO CLEAN SHOWER CURTAINS

Shower curtains can quickly get scummy and mouldy. Try not to leave them so that the bottom edge sits in a puddle of water – hanging them over the shower rail helps.
   Wash shower curtains regularly to prevent soap build-up and staining. Wash in the washing machine on a hot wash, using biological detergent. If they are very dirty, washing them along with some towels seems to help remove dirty marks.

TO CLEAN A SHOWER SCREEN

With really powerful modern showers, a shower curtain will not keep the water in. You need an integral screen fixed on the side of the bath, or a separate cubicle. If you have the space, opt for the latter. The best shower enclosures are made using ¼-inch glass. Choose one with drip strips that channel water back into the tray, so it does not drip on the floor when the door is opened, and seals that can withstand the force of water generated by a power shower.

Shower screens can be difficult to keep clean. Often, their construction – especially if there is a sliding door – means there are parts that can never be cleaned. And in hard-water areas, limescale can be a problem. Water droplets evaporate on the surface, leaving behind a characteristic dappling of limescale spots. The good news is that many modern shower screens and enclosures are now treated to make them less prone to limescale.

There are several ways of dealing with limescale.

The green solution is a rubber squeegee, of the type that window cleaners use. The idea is to give the screen a quick once-over after a shower. It is a good habit to get into.

The speedy solution is to use one of the special shower sprays. You spray them on to a wet shower screen, and leave them. They are designed to be used after every shower and are extremely effective, but are pointless unless they are used every time and unless the screen is clean in the first place.

> Note: Some people report that shower sprays encourage mould. This seems to be a problem in damp bathrooms and shower rooms. If mould develops, stop using them, tackle the mould (see 'Ventilation', p. 95) and use a squeegee.

99

To clean a really filthy shower screen: First deal with any limescale. Although vinegar mixed with water is the best and cheapest way to remove limescale, it will run down vertical surfaces. On this occasion, use a proprietary gel cleaner, which will cling to the screen. Follow instructions and rinse well.

To clean, swab the entire screen with straight all-purpose cleaner and leave overnight. The next day, wash off using a cream cleaner (you need an abrasive, but it must be a gentle one, in case of scratching). Rinse well with plain water and – important – dry with soft cloth. Now, if you like, apply a shower spray (but see note above).

The toilet

In 1851, one of the unlikely hits of the Great Exhibition was the flushing lavatory – something that many people had not seen before. Around 827,000 people – 14 per cent of the visitors to the Exhibition – tried them out. The Parliamentary papers reported that the largest amount of money taken for use of the women's 'waiting-rooms', as they were called, was £32.16s. 3d (£2,355.55, or $4,500, in today's money) on one day, 8 October (the men's urinals, by the way, were free).

After this date, flushing lavatories began to be installed as a matter of course in British homes. That the modern lavatory was invented by Thomas Crapper has passed into modern legend. Sadly for lovers of toilet humour, this is not true. Thomas Crapper was a master plumber based in London and a tireless proponent of the new sanitary systems. His contribution was, as the history of his company, which is still going strong, puts it, to 'promote sanitary fittings to a somewhat dirty and sceptical world' by registering patents and championing the siphon system to remove the smells that made early lavatories so unpleasant.

A Victorian transported to the 21st century would recognise modern lavatories immediately (though he would think them sadly plain – Victorian lavatories were decorated with characteristic exuberance), for they are still largely based on Thomas Crapper's siphon system with its familiar S-bend.

TO REDUCE WATER USAGE IN A TOILET

The amount of water used every time a toilet is flushed is a major cause of concern. The average toilet uses around 5–8 gallons each time. Toilet flushing accounts for about a third of household water usage.

There are various things you can do to use less water. If you are installing a new tank, choose one with a low-flush or dual flush system, which use around a third less water. Otherwise, install a water displacement device in your tank to reduce the amount of water used for each flush – typically by up to a gallon. Some of the more strident green campaigners recommend flushing only 'when needed'. Well, I'm sorry, but that's every time if you don't want your lavatory smelling like a medieval privy.

TO CLEAN A TOILET

A daily brush and squirt of cleaner should keep the loo at an acceptable level.

Tip: If brushing alone will not remove obstinate deposits, wrap a cloth around the bristles. This seems to work much better than the brush alone.

Once a week, clean the entire toilet using an all-purpose cleaner. Clean all surfaces, inside and out, and do not forget the flush handle and the underside of the seat, which are major repositories of germs. For this reason, keep one pair of rubber gloves specifically for cleaning the toilet and, to avoid cross-contamination, do not use them for any other cleaning jobs around the house. Always lift the seat when cleaning the toilet bowl, because cleaning fluids can bleach wooden seats and discolour plastic ones.

Tip: To clean the parts of the toilet bowl that are usually under water, shut off water supply, then flush twice to empty the bowl and tank.

To clean a really filthy toilet: If no amount of cleaning has worked, try spirits of salt. This is a charming and old-fashioned name for hydrochloric acid, which is sold in builders' stores and hardware stores (if you cannot find it, or it is sold only in large containers, a proprietary patio, drive and paving cleaner, available from any DIY shop, will do the same job). Be careful when using spirits of salt: wear gloves and protect your eyes and clothing. Carefully dilute one part of spirits of salt with ten parts of cold water and pour into the toilet bowl. Leave overnight. If this does not shift stains, nothing will.

101

Note: After using spirits of salt, flush the toilet several times to clear out all traces of the chemical and ensure that there is nothing but clean water in the bowl before using it. Never mix it with any other chemicals or cleaners, or you risk producing deadly chlorine gas.

To tackle limescale in toilets: The water sitting in the toilet bowl means limescale builds up quickly. Daily use of a toilet cleaner that contains a limescale remover should prevent this. Remove heavy build-up using either ¼ pint straight vinegar or 2 denture cleaning tablets and leave overnight. A can of cola is also very effective – so effective, in fact, that one wonders what it does to our teeth. The next day, flush the toilet and remove any remaining deposits with a brush.

TO UNBLOCK A TOILET

First, try to poke out the blockage with an old wire coat hanger. If it seems to have shifted and the toilet is not full to overflowing, try pouring a bucket of water into the bowl and, at the same time, flushing the toilet. The combined force of the water is often enough to push the blockage through. If this does not work, bail out excess water and use a plunger. If this does not work (and it usually does), call a plumber.

To prevent blockages in the future, make it a rule that the only things to be flushed down the toilet are human waste and toilet paper – no tissues, no sanitary napkins or tampons, no nappies.

Bathroom surfaces

By its very nature, a bathroom has to be waterproof and washable, so the surfaces – mirror, tiles, floor – will be hard-wearing and easy to clean. The bathroom is one of the most satisfying rooms in the house to clean – it takes no time to make it sparkle.

TO CLEAN MIRRORS AND GLASS

Clean once a week, using water and a microfibre cloth. Spray the mirror with water and clean with a dry cloth.

> *Tip: To prevent mirrors steaming up, put a small amount of undiluted dish soap on a dry cloth and rub very well on to the surface of the mirror.*

TO CLEAN TILES

Clean bathroom tiles once a week, using household detergent. After washing, dry with a soft cloth to make them shine and to prevent limescale forming. Tiles in bathrooms are particularly susceptible to mould. To find out how to deal with it, see 'Ventilation', p. 95.

To clean really filthy tiles: Turn to the method described above for really filthy shower screens. You will probably not have to remove limescale, so start with the straight detergent. Swab the tiles with it and leave overnight. Next day, moisten the tiles with water and sprinkle with scouring powder (ceramic tiles are tougher than shower screens, so you can use a harsher abrasive). Clean the tiles, using a scrubbing brush to get at the grout. Rinse and dry with a soft cloth.

CHAPTER 4

The Sitting-Room and Hallways

Homily was proud of her sitting room:
the walls had been papered with scraps
of old letters out of waste-paper baskets,
and Homily had arranged the handwriting
sideways in vertical stripes which ran floor
from ceiling.

Mary Norton, The Borrowers

The sitting-room — or living-room, lounge, drawing-room, or whatever you choose to call it — is one of those rooms that has been superseded by the exigencies of modern living — the dining-room is the other. Who, these days, has a 'best' room that is used only when guests arrive? The lack of space in modern houses means this would be a criminal waste of space. But, more than that, the laissez-faire, 'take-us-as-you-find-us' spirit of 21st-century living means that we are not ashamed of being caught — as it were — with our pants down. We do not feel the need for a room that is used only for show, to impress others. In fact, even when that was the ideal, the stuffy parlour, with its oppressive 'Sunday best' feel, was often used as a metaphor for the hidebound insularity of middle-class life. No one would advocate a return to that.

You may not want a room for 'best', but you may want a room that is for grown-ups. It's not a bad idea to keep the sitting-room as the one room in the house that is kept apart from the children, the one room in the house that is not engulfed by a tide of primary-coloured plastic. Some parents I know do not allow their children into the sitting-room, unless it is to be quiet: they have been taught that this is their parents' special place and it becomes a treat to be allowed in to watch television with them or to listen to music, or to have a grown-up conversation.

The sitting-room is where you are likely to spend the most money — on carpets, curtains, furniture and probably a television, all of which are expensive. It is also where you are most likely to display pictures, ornaments and other precious objects (of course, these things are not only found in this one room, but it felt right to group them together in this chapter) but first and foremost it is a room in which to sit and be relaxed.

Is this terribly out-of-step in this child-centred 21st century? Maybe it is; although I like to think it is a small step in reclaiming a part of the house for peace, quiet and contemplation.

Along with the bedrooms, the sitting-room is unlikely to need much heavy-duty cleaning. A daily tidy-up and a weekly clean (see 'Schedules', p. 289) should suffice. Spring cleaning is the time to tackle more specific tasks, such as cleaning ornaments, light fittings and so forth. All the instructions for these are given in this chapter.

Upholstery

Upholstered sofas and armchairs are likely to be some of the most expensive items we have in the home, and on that account we expect them to last a long time. They are subject to an amazing amount of wear and tear and, from a housekeeping point of view, are difficult to keep clean because the upholstery (with the obvious exception of loose covers) is generally fixed: if you spill a cup of tea on an armchair, you can't put it in the washing machine.

105

TO CARE FOR UPHOLSTERY

Turn cushions on sofas and armchairs regularly to ensure even wear. Upholstery fabrics, though tough, are subject to fading by sunlight, as is any other fabric.

Try to avoid placing chairs and sofas in such a way that shafts of sunlight will hit one particular spot. Certain colours, such as yellow, are more vulnerable to fading than others – something to bear in mind, perhaps, when choosing the furniture or upholstery fabrics.

Consider having slipcovers made for any chairs and sofas that are subject to particularly heavy wear. In sunlight, the covers will fade instead of the furniture. It is cheaper to replace the covers than to have the sofa reupholstered. In fact, slipcovers are almost compulsory if you have lots of children and animals in the house, or if you favour very pale fabrics.

Counsel of perfection: Have two complete sets made and change covers on all the furniture at the same time, to ensure even wear.

The disadvantage of slipcovers is that they can look cheap unless properly made by an upholsterer – in which case, they can cost as much as a new sofa – but that is made up for by the convenience of just being able to whip them off and wash them or have them cleaned.

Tip: If full sets of slipcovers are prohibitively expensive, just have sets of removable arm covers made (the arms are the where the furniture gets most wear).

In general, try to keep pets off chairs and sofas. If you cannot, one way to remove pet hairs on furniture is to wrap parcel tape round your hand, sticky side out, and run it over the cushions. Another way is put on a rubber glove, dip it in water and run your hand over the chairs or sofa. Do not let it get too wet.

To vacuum upholstery: **Vacuum sofas and armchairs thoroughly once a week. Remove cushions and vacuum in all the cracks and crevices, using the crevice tool. Then vacuum all surfaces, using the upholstery tool. Do not press too hard, but run the cleaner head lightly over the surface.**

TO CLEAN UPHOLSTERY

Because of its size and construction, cleaning upholstery is awkward, so it is better to prevent it getting dirty in the first place. When buying new upholstery fabrics, look for fabrics that have been pre-treated with dirt-repellent coatings, such as Scotchgard. You will still have to mop up spills quickly, but there is less chance of permanent staining.

It is also possible to have existing upholstery treated. Doing it yourself is a tedious business and results can be patchy, so it is better to spend the money and get it done professionally.

However careful you are, general grime builds up on upholstery over time. Have upholstered furniture cleaned once a year. It is possible to hire machines for cleaning upholstery, but as with carpets, the professionals do a better job. Their machines are stronger and they have specialist cleaning materials.

In between cleaning, tackle spills as soon as they happen. For a full explanation of how to treat stains on upholstery and an A–Z of the most common stains, see 'Stains', p. 305.

TO CARE FOR LEATHER FURNITURE

Leather furniture is extremely hard-wearing and easy to care for, and should last for a lifetime. Over time, it acquires a pleasing patina of age. Position leather furniture away from direct sources of heat, such as radiators, which can cause the leather to crack, and keep it out of direct sunlight. The sun can fade leather and cause it to deteriorate. Do not allow leather to get wet.

New leather furniture should be supplied with care instructions. In general, all that is required is a good dusting once a week. With caution, you can wipe off grime with a damp cloth, wrung out until nearly dry, but do not allow the leather to get wet and do not sit on leather furniture when it is damp.

Occasionally apply specialist hide food or leather conditioner, available from department stores, to keep the leather supple. Do not use furniture polish, which contains solvents that can damage leather.

107

Curtains

Curtains come and go in fashion – remember the elaborate swags and 'window treatments' of the 1980s? – but are still the best way to make a room feel cosy and welcoming, in a way that blinds, with their cool elegance, never can.

It used to be a normal thing to have two sets of curtains for some rooms – one set for summer and one for winter. I vaguely remember my mother doing this. In our sitting-room, we had a heavy pair of velvet curtains, which were put up as autumn approached, and taken down and replaced with a lightweight pair of cotton curtains for summer.

If you have the money or the inclination, this is not a bad habit to get into. Apart from anything else, replacing the curtains gives the room an instant makeover, without any extra expense, apart from the initial cost of the curtains. Simply by swapping over the curtains, you can have a look that is light and airy in summer, and warm and cosy in winter.

Curtains can be hung from tracks or rods. Curtain tracks are fitted to the wall or ceiling and are designed not to be seen. Corded tracks mean that the curtains can be drawn or closed without your having to touch fabric, which helps to keep them clean. Curtain rods are a design statement in themselves and are made to be seen. They come in wood or metal and are usually supplied with rings.

TO CARE FOR CURTAINS

Curtains become so much a part of a room that it is easy to neglect them and ignore the fact that they have soaked up dust and grime. Smoke, dust and other pollutants in the air become embedded in the fibres of the curtains, making them smell and spoiling their appearance. They are also the first line of attack from sunlight, which beats down on them, fading their colour and weakening the fabric. Although this can happen very quickly – over the course of a month for some very fugitive colours, such as yellow – because one is looking at the curtains every day, one sometimes does not notice the fading until the curtains are taken down for cleaning.

Vacuum curtains once a week, using the upholstery brush and a gentle suction. Close the curtains so you can vacuum as much of the curtain as possible. Pay attention to the tops and vacuum both sides. Apart from making it easier to vacuum them, curtains that are kept tied back a lot of the time benefit from being untied and shaken out once a week to discourage moth attack and to stop permanent creasing.

If the curtain treatment is not too elaborate or the curtains are not too heavy, take them down once a quarter and hang them outside on a dry, breezy day to air and remove musty smells.

If it is difficult to take the curtains down, there are also sprays designed to remove smells from fabrics. Before using, however, test on an unobtrusive piece of the curtain first in case of staining. In general, though, fresh air is a better remover of smells and these sprays should be used only as a last resort, and never instead of cleaning.

TO WASH CURTAINS

Curtains in sitting-rooms or bedrooms can be washed or cleaned once a year. Generally, the best time to do this is as part of the spring cleaning, especially if you are planning to wash them – it is easier to dry them on a breezy day.

Kitchen and bathroom curtains, which get dirtier, will need to be cleaned more frequently.

> *Note: If you have fabric valances, swags or tiebacks, wash or clean them at the same time as the curtains so that one component does not look cleaner or more faded than another.*

Always choose a washable fabric for kitchens or bathrooms. When buying curtain fabric, check that it is pre-shrunk. Otherwise, allow ten per cent extra for shrinkage (ready-made curtains usually allow five per cent extra for shrinkage). Check with the shop assistant when buying, or consult the care label on ready-made curtains before washing.

Before washing curtains, measure them so that you can stretch them back to the correct size. If you are worried about shrinkage, let down the hems. Now take down the curtains and remove the curtain hooks. Loosen the header tape.

Shake the curtains well and then vacuum on both sides, using the upholstery brush. Soak them in a bath of cold water, to loosen the dirt. Then wash either by hand or in the machine (see below – in general, wash by hand if the curtains are old or delicate or if you are worried about shrinkage).

Dry outside, hanging over the line – or two parallel lines if they are very heavy. Iron, if necessary, while still damp. Iron on the wrong side, working along the vertical length. As you do so, stretch the seams gently. Pull the curtains into shape, then reinsert hooks and pull the tapes to the correct length before rehanging.

To wash curtains by hand: Remove the curtains from their cold soak. Fill the bath with lukewarm water and add a mild liquid detergent. Wash the curtains by squeezing them, not rubbing (you could also get in the bath and tread on them in the manner of a grape-treader). Rinse thoroughly, at least three times, to remove all the detergent, then wring or spin dry.

To machine-wash curtains: Only use a washing machine if you are sure your curtains are machine-washable. Check the weight of the curtains and the maximum load your machine can take. You may have to wash them one at a time. If the curtains are very large, make sure that they fit inside the drum.

109

Give the curtains a cold-water soak as above before washing on a very gentle wash. Remove from the machine as soon as possible to prevent creasing, and dry outside as above. Do not put in the tumble-dryer.

TO HAVE CURTAINS PROFESSIONALLY CLEANED

Many curtains are not washable, whether because they are made of a non-washable fabric, such as silk, or because they are trimmed with something that is not washable, or because they are lined with a fabric that will shrink at a different rate from the main body of the curtain.

Sometimes, even dry-cleaning will cause shrinkage, and although it is a terrible chore, it is sometimes better to remove the linings and dry-clean the linings and curtains separately. If shrinkage does occur, it is cheaper to reline curtains.

> Note: If curtains return from the dry-cleaner smelling strongly of cleaning solvents, take them out of their plastic wrapping and hang outside to air until the smell has gone. Do not use the tumble-dryer, because the heat of the dryer could cause the inflammable solvents to catch fire.

110

Even easier, though not cheaper, is to have the curtains professionally cleaned in situ. The best way to find a reputable cleaner is by word of mouth. Your dry-cleaner may do it, or may be able to recommend a cleaner specializing in curtains. Otherwise, look for a member of the Drycleaning and Laundry Institute International (www.ifi.org).

TO CARE FOR NET CURTAINS

Wash nets and sheers regularly, before they become grubby. Wash either by hand in lukewarm water or, if possible, machine-wash on a very gentle wash (follow the care label). If in doubt, wash by hand.

Dry outside and hang while still just damp. They do not generally need ironing.

If nets have become yellow, a biological detergent should sort out the problem. Otherwise, net whitening products are readily available.

TO CARE FOR CURTAIN ACCESSORIES

While the curtains are being washed or cleaned, clean the tracks or rods. Vacuum tracks, using the crevice tool, then run a damp cloth over the track. Take off the gliders and soak them, along with the curtain hooks, in a bowl of warm, soapy water. Rinse in clean water. Dry the gliders. Dry curtain hooks by putting them in a clean tea towel, gather up the ends to make a bag and rub them vigorously. Spray the channel in the tracks lightly with a lubricant such as WD40, to ensure smooth running of the hooks – but make sure all lubricant is wiped off the surface of the track before rehanging curtains.

Curtain rods just need dusting. Metal rods are usually lacquered so will not need polishing. Wooden rods may need a light application of furniture polish, but make sure all polish is removed before rehanging curtains.

Tiebacks and fabric valances cannot normally be washed. Use a foam upholstery shampoo, following instructions. Be careful not to get them too wet. Use an old towel to get them as dry as possible. Wooden cornices just need dusting.

Blinds

Blinds fit in perfectly with the modern taste for the sleek and streamlined. They can be as plain or as decorative as curtains and are immensely practical – keeping heat in and light out. My last flat had Victorian sash windows in deep recesses, making curtains impracticable. There was also rather a large number of them. The huge expanses of glass made the flat very cold in winter as the heat escaped through it, and very bright in summer, with the result that a lot of my furnishings were faded by the sun.

My remedy was to fit Roman blinds which were lined with a fabric to block out the light and interlined with an insulating layer to keep the heat in.

Blinds are practical, durable and cost-effective. They are the first choice for kitchens, bathrooms and small rooms that would be swamped by curtains. If made to measure, they are not necessarily cheaper than curtains, particularly if you have specific requirements, but the vast range of ready-made blinds should suit all but the most design-conscious.

Cleaning fabric blinds poses the same problems as cleaning and/or washing curtains (see above) because the fabrics from which they are made will shrink if washed, or even if dry-cleaned. Venetian blinds, being made of plastic, wood or metal, are easier to clean – if fiddly.

111

FABRIC BLINDS

Fabric blinds are usually made into Roman blinds They are attached to a batten at the top of the window with Velcro and have a series of rods sewn at regular intervals along the length of the blind, which, when it is pulled up, cause it to fall into flat, broad folds. They give an elegant, sophisticated effect, but generally have to be made to measure, which can be expensive.

You still occasionally see Austrian blinds, where tapes attached to the back of the blind are pulled up to give a characteristic 'frilly-knicker' effect.

Conservatory blinds are essential for cutting heat and glare, and are made from special, hard-wearing fabrics that reflect sunlight and/or have insulating properties.

TO CARE FOR FABRIC BLINDS

Vacuum every now and again using the upholstery brush on a low setting. Austrian blinds in particular attract vast amounts of dust.

As long as you are conscientious about vacuuming, fabric blinds should not need washing or dry-cleaning for years. But if they do need it...

Austrian blinds may be washed or dry-cleaned, depending on their fabric. Take them down and loosen the vertical tapes. Wash or dry-clean as appropriate.

Roman blinds must be dry-cleaned, because exact right angles are crucial to their look. Some dry-cleaners will take Roman blinds intact. Others will ask you to remove the rods from the lining, which you will then have to sew back in when the blinds have been cleaned.

After cleaning, rehang. Pull the blinds up and smooth in the folds with your hands. Leave the blind pulled up for a few days to set the folds in place.

> Note: If Roman blinds have blackout linings or insulating interlinings, you may have a problem with shrinkage when they are dry-cleaned. In which case, you may have to disassemble the whole thing before dry-cleaning. In general, try to avoid having to clean blinds at all. Regular vacuuming should see to that.

TO CLEAN CONSERVATORY BLINDS

Many conservatory blinds are designed to be dirt-resistant. Dust with a cloth or lambswool duster, and occasionally wipe with a damp cloth.

Tip: Blind cords inevitably get grubby from people's hands. Replacing the cords is the work of about five minutes and instantly makes blinds look as if they have just been cleaned, even if they have not. Always replace blind cords after cleaning blinds.

An alternative is to have a professional cleaner come in to clean blinds in situ. This is worth considering if the blinds were very expensive.

ROLLER BLINDS

These are made from fabric that has been specially treated and stiffened. They traditionally use a spring mechanism, which can be fantastically irritating to operate. Better is a beaded cord system. Roller blinds can look a bit Spartan in living areas, but often work well in conjunction with curtains, especially if you want them to block the light or to give privacy. Ready-made blinds can be cut down to fit.

TO CARE FOR ROLLER BLINDS

Vacuum using the upholstery brush and a low setting, paying attention to the roller mechanism where dust can accumulate. Take the blind down occasionally, lay it flat and vacuum the reverse side.

If the blind is washable (to test, sprinkle a little water on an out-of-the-way corner: if it does not sink in, the blind is washable), take it down and open fully. Weigh down the end so it does not spring back suddenly. Using upholstery shampoo, sponge the blind, then sponge again with plain water to rinse. Dry with a soft cloth. Turn the blind over and clean the other side. Do not let the blind get too wet, and rehang while it is still damp.

VENETIAN BLINDS

These are made of horizontal slats of wood or aluminium, and come in a variety of widths. Wooden blinds used to be very expensive, but can now be bought ready-made at a reasonable price and cut to fit. Venetian blinds are particularly suitable for bathrooms, kitchens and minimalist interiors, and can be easily adjusted to give light, shade or privacy, but can be tricky to clean. Their main drawback is that they accumulate dust and grease and can be extremely fiddly and tricky to clean, particularly in kitchens. Aluminium blinds can mark paintwork if they bang against window frames.

TO CARE FOR VENETIAN BLINDS

Dust and grease can make cleaning Venetian blinds a bit of a nightmare (it once took me three hours to clean one blind).

Close the slats so they lie flat and then vacuum using the upholstery brush on a low setting. Hold the blind steady so it does not bang against the window frame. Start at the top and vacuum first the centre section of the blind, then the sections on either side of the tapes. Reverse the slats and do the other side. Do this at least once a month. If more is needed, wipe the slats occasionally with a barely damp cloth. Wooden blinds should never be immersed in water. For this reason, it is not a good idea to put wooden blinds in a kitchen – the combination of grease and dust in the atmosphere can stain the wood irrevocably.

For metal blinds, a second option is to use a blind cleaner. This consists of two furry prongs that fit tightly over each slat and which you then slide along the blind to remove dust. You could also use a put on a pair of cotton gloves (or use cotton socks as mitts) and run your fingers along each slat.

114

> Tip: Go easy on metal blinds. It is surprisingly easy to bend the slats and, once bent, they cannot be unbent, but will have an irreversible kink. If a slat is bent, the only solution is to restring the whole blind and add a new slat.

TO WASH A VENETIAN BLIND

Once metal blinds get very greasy, you will have to wash them.

Pad the window sill with an old towel to catch drips and to prevent the blind banging against the woodwork. Fill a bowl with water and dish soap. Open the blind fully, with the slats horizontal.

> Note: Do not use ammonia-based detergents – ammonia reacts with aluminium.

Wearing heavy-duty cotton gloves (or using cotton socks as mitts), dip your hands in the water and run your fingers along each slat. Work from top to bottom, being careful not to bend the slats. Take care also to avoid getting the cords wet. Blinds can get very dirty, so replace the water frequently.

Rinse the blind in the same way, using plain water to which you have added a generous splash of vinegar. Finally, wipe dry with a soft cloth. The vinegar will give a good shine. Do not pull the blind up until the slats are completely dry.

> *Tip: To prevent aluminium blinds getting dusty, after cleaning, spray with an anti-static spray or the type designed for computer screens.*

VERTICAL BLINDS

These consist of vertical slats that run on a chain control unit. They are a bit office-like, but useful for very large windows.

To clean them, use one of the furry blind cleaners for the slats. Work from top to bottom to avoid unhooking the slats. Alternatively, have them professionally cleaned.

Sun damage

115

Several years ago, after the break-up of a long relationship, I was looking for a change: I wanted to move house and to move from the area we had been living in for ten years. I wanted to change everything – swap suburban for urban, a house for a flat, a garden for a balcony (I dislike gardening). Eventually, I found a flat located in the top two floors of a corner house, with windows on all sides, which meant it was bathed with light on even the gloomiest winter's day.

What I had not bargained for was the damage that all that light slowly and insidiously wrought on some of my most prized possessions. A year or so after I moved in, I noticed that a 1920s walnut desk, which had lived on a dark landing in the old house, had a bleached strip down one side where the sun hit it in the afternoons. A pair of Roman blinds in the bedroom originally had bright yellow linings. By the time I left the flat, they were bleached white. A dark blue curtain over a door ended up with sun-bleached stripes at the top of each fold of fabric. And one afternoon a pair of silk cushion covers featuring rather charming elephants, which I had bought in the Jim Thompson shop in Singapore, literally fell to ribbons in my hands.

And all this was caused by sunlight.

THE ESSENTIALS

Ultraviolet light destroys paper and natural fabrics such as cotton, linen, wool and silk and will also cause them to fade. Sunlight bleaches and breaks down finishes on wood, and can literally turn dark wood white. I once saw a Georgian mahogany chest of drawers in an antiques shop, which had been so exposed to sunlight that it had turned from its original dark brown to a pale blond colour.

Sunlight attacks watercolours (and, to a lesser extent, oil paintings), causing them to fade. It bleaches photographs and coloured textiles, but prolonged exposure to sunlight turns white cottons and wool yellow (conversely, laying white cottons outside in the sun is a cheap and good way of bleaching them – see 'The Laundry', p. 155).

Sunlight does not attack metals, stone, ceramics, glass (including stained glass), enamels and non-organic pigments.

It is worth remembering that it is all levels of ultraviolet light we are discussing here, not just bright sunlight. Even at low levels, light can damage objects, something that conservators and people who work in museums and historic collections know very well.

116   Sun damage is cumulative and irreversible.

TO REDUCE SUN DAMAGE

There are no clever tricks to restore sun-damaged materials. It is intimations of mortality writ large upon your curtains.

The only way to reduce sun damage is to reduce light levels. In this, our Victorian forebears had the right idea. We may think of them as mad piano-leg coverers (not true, by the way – if this was ever done, which is unlikely, it was to preserve the piano's legs, not the modesty of female piano players), but the plethora of cloths, rugs and doilies with which their houses were festooned was there for good, practical reasons. Partly, it was a matter of taste – a reaction against the plainness of Georgian furnishings – and partly it was a necessity. The dyes that were available then were unstable, and the only way to preserve their brightness was to keep furniture covered and sunlight out.

I am not advocating a return to Victorian fussiness, merely the following simple procedures:

DRAW THE CURTAINS

This is the simplest and most effective remedy. When a room is not in use, or is used infrequently, keep the curtains closed or the blinds drawn. This has the added advantage in summer of keeping a room cool, and if you are out at work all day, it makes no difference if the curtains are drawn or not.

> *Tip: If you are lucky enough to live in an old house that still has its original shutters, use them. They are not purely decorative, but were designed with the idea of protecting the house. They are both an extremely effective blackout during the day, and also provide extra security and thermal insulation.*

FIT BLINDS

If all the rooms in the house are in use throughout the day, it may not be practicable to draw curtains and plunge them in darkness. In which case, fit semi-transparent roller blinds in addition to curtains at all your windows. Blinds should be pulled half-way down at most times, fully raised when it is really dark and pulled right down when the sun is at its height. The furnishing department of any good store should be able to advise on suitable fabrics.

117

MOVE THINGS OUT OF THE SUN

Check if any light-sensitive objects are sitting in direct sunlight and, if you can, move them into new positions. Watercolours and other works of art painted in chalks and pastels, are particularly vulnerable, but furniture is easily damaged too, especially if the sun moves round and hits one spot at a certain time of day. If you have lots of objects at risk and limited space, rotate things so that they are not all in the light at the same time. If a room is very light, consider not having pictures in it, or only one picture at a time.

> *Tip: A very good place to hang pictures is in hallways and stairwells, turning them into a mini gallery. These areas are often darker than the rest of the house, with few sources of direct sunlight. And as the walls tend to be larger, there is ample space to display paintings well.*

MAKE SLIPCOVERS FOR UPHOLSTERED FURNITURE

That way, the covers will fade, not the furniture. It is cheaper to replace the covers than to have the sofa reupholstered.

UV film: A high-tech solution to reduce light is to apply special transparent film with UV filters to the inside of windows. This is available from specialist suppliersbut can be expensive and fiddly to apply, so is not always appropriate. It is worth considering if you have a great many precious objects, and does have the added advantage of making the glass virtually unbreakable.

Lighting

These days our homes seem to be flooded with light. Interestingly, this phenomenon is less than a century old.

I once attended a conference on the technology of the country house. Its premise was that, after the Industrial Revolution, the newly rich magnates realised that the technology they had developed in their mills and factories could be used to make their homes more comfortable. Thus, for example, the great boilers that heated and pumped water in the mills were scaled down to produce the first rudimentary central heating.

In the afternoon came the most fascinating lecture of the day – a demonstration of lighting down the centuries.

All the lights in the lecture theatre in the Royal Institution were turned off and we were plunged into darkness. For the next hour, we experienced the illumination – or lack of it – in our ancestors' lives. It is astonishing to think that lighting technology did not move on significantly from the Greeks and Romans until the end of the 18th century. For the majority of people the source of light was a fire, a rush light, an oil lamp or candles.

Light was a privilege of the few and an indicator of wealth and status, for only the rich could afford to illuminate their homes beyond the basic.

Now, the thought that we cannot turn on a light is intolerable. And yet lighting is a major source of energy consumption. As a result, the EU has decreed that the traditional incandescent filament bulbs, which date back to the late 19th century, are to be replaced with low-energy fluorescent bulbs. Could it be that lighting will once again become the preserve of the rich?

TYPES OF BULB

At the time of writing, the main types of light bulb are incandescent, halogen and fluorescent. It is likely that traditional incandescent bulbs that we all grew up with will be used less and less as they are gradually phased out. While it is true that traditional bulbs are not energy efficient (90 per cent of the energy they produce is heat), I cannot help regretting their passing. They give a warm, clear light, work well with dimmers and, because they come in a range of wattages, are very versatile.

Like incandescent light bulbs, the popular halogen bulbs work by heating a filament, but in this case, the filament is enclosed in a glass tube filled with halogen gas. They give a crisp, bright white light and are extremely long-lasting, which makes them a favourite for areas where good lighting is important, such as kitchens and bathrooms. In fact, low-voltage halogen spotlights are so popular that they have become a modern design cliché. Their main drawback is that they get extremely hot (and are thus not energy-efficient), which means they must be installed only in places where they do not come into contact with anything inflammable. A halogen spotlight igniting cleaning fluid caused the fire that swept through Windsor Castle in 1992. When replacing halogen bulbs, be very careful not to touch the bulb with your bare hands. The oils in your skin can cause the bulb to deteriorate and crack or even explode. Hold them with tissues.

Fluorescent bulbs are phosphor-coated glass tubes filled with argon gas and mercury. They are extremely long-lasting and energy-efficient, but they cannot be fitted to dimmers and their reputation has suffered because of the rather sickly light and flickering and noise they used to produce. Modern versions are much better.

The energy-efficient bulbs we are all supposed to be using are sometimes called compact fluorescent bulbs. They work in the same way as normal fluorescent bulbs, but the tube has been made smaller and folded over so that they fit into spaces designed for an incandescent bulb. They are extremely efficient and long-lasting – they last ten times longer than a standard incandescent bulb – but they generally cannot be used with dimmers, many still give a dim, flickering light and they are relatively expensive. They are beginning to improve in looks, though many are still extremely ugly.

APPROPRIATE LIGHTING FOR DIFFERENT ROOMS

Whatever the ins and outs of energy-efficient lighting, it is still important to get the right lighting for each room. A lighting designer or the lighting studios in some large department stores can help you see how different combinations of lighting can work in different settings, the effect of different beam widths and bulbs, and how lights recessed into the ceiling compare with those on tracks. Bear in mind the following:

Sitting-rooms need a variety of different lights, including reading lamps, to accommodate the different activities – reading, watching television – that take place there.

Halls, stairs and landings should be very well lit, with no sudden differences in light levels. A light that switches on as anyone approaches the front door is a useful security measure.

Kitchens require good light for working, but if the family also eats in there, dimmers are a good idea to give a more relaxing light. Lights should be angled in such a way that they do not cast a shadow over the worktop where anyone is working. Halogen is particularly suitable for kitchens.

Bathrooms should be well lit, with good, direct light on mirrors to aid putting on make-up, shaving, etc. Because of the possibility of electrocution, light fittings must be designed for use in bathrooms.

Dining-rooms need flattering, soft light. If using pendant shades, ensure they are positioned in such a way that the light does not shine in everyone's eyes.

Bedrooms need soft, relaxing light – halogen is not suitable. Bedside lamps are a must – to ensure domestic harmony, there must be one for each partner in a double bedroom.

LAMPSHADES

Lampshades are a matter of taste and can be made in virtually any material – fabric, paper, parchment, plastic. The heat from light bulbs attracts dust, which could have a bearing on which shade to choose: fabric, for example, can get grimy very quickly and is very difficult to clean.

When choosing a new lampshade for a table lamp, a rule of thumb is that the width of the shade should be roughly the same as the length of the base. Fit a round base with a round shade and a square base with a square shade. A plain base can take an ornate shade and vice versa.

TO CLEAN A LAMPSHADE

Once a month, give light fitting, shade and bulb a good dust.

Shades made from fabric or paper are almost impossible to wash or dry-clean (in fact, real parchment shades will dissolve if they come into contact with water). Vacuuming is preferable to dusting with a cloth. Do it frequently, using the upholstery brush and a low suction. If there are fringes or tassels, cover the attachment with an old stocking to protect them. Hold the light steady but be careful not to get dirty finger marks on the shade.

> Tip: For best results with bulbs use a microfibre cloth (see 'Basic cleaning equipment', p. 213).

Plastic shades are normally washable. Wipe with a damp cloth.

121

Fabric shades present more of a problem. If a little more than vacuuming is needed, try a chemically treated dry sponge. These have names like 'magic sponge' and are made of a specially treated rubber that feels slightly sticky and picks up dirt on non-washable materials.

To clean a really filthy fabric shade: Fill a sink with enough lukewarm water to take the whole shade (if the sink is not big enough, use the bath) and add a small amount of dish soap. Immerse the entire shade in water (this is important to avoid water marks).

Using a soft brush, gently scrub the shade, starting at a side seam. Clean the outside, then the lining, then rinse in clean lukewarm water, again immersing the shade. Dry immediately with a towel, then put the shade on another towel and dry completely using a hairdryer.

To be honest, it might be less trouble just to go out and buy a new shade.

> *Note: Kitchen and bathroom light fittings get very dirty and greasy. Recessed halogen fittings do not present too much of a problem, but other types will need regular cleaning. Turn off the electricity, dismantle the fitting and wash the shade in hot, soapy water.*

CHANDELIERS

Fashionable and beautiful, chandeliers give instant glamour to a room. The drops are normally of glass or crystal and sparkle beguilingly in the light. New chandeliers can cost a fortune, as can valuable antique ones, but it is possible to pick them up at auctions for very reasonable prices. If doing this, it is imperative to get the chandelier checked by an electrician before installing it. It is generally safer to get it rewired.

TO CLEAN A CHANDELIER

Huge antique chandeliers need specialist cleaning. Consult the Yellow Pages to find a cleaner in your area. Or ask in a local antiques shop. If you do have to take one down, lay thick material under the lamp and get someone to help you. It can be a tricky, difficult job. Who has not seen the classic episode of *Only Fools and Horses* with Del, Rodney and the chandelier?

Smaller chandeliers can be cleaned in situ. Turn off the electricity. Spread newspaper underneath the chandelier to protect the floor below it. Spray the chandelier with a specialist cleaner (available from lighting shops and hardware stores), following instructions. Allow it to dry naturally or help it along a bit with the hairdryer (go easy, though).

The television

To dust a TV screen – or anything that attracts static – use a barely damp cloth to pick up the dust. If you have a tumble-dryer and use fabric conditioner sheets, dust screens with a used one. The residue will reduce static. Clean TV remotes with a soft brush, such as an old blusher brush. If they are very sticky, clean between the buttons with a damp cotton swab.

123

Pictures

The pictures I remember best from my childhood were an old map of Norfolk (a copy, I think, of a 17th-century one) and two etchings of Norwich – the cathedral and Norwich School. They hung in my grandmother's house and, after she died, in the hall of the house I grew up in. They are now rather faded and – as the saying goes – 'foxed', but I am extremely fond of them because they remind me of my childhood and – more than that – because they seem to give substance to the stories my mother and uncles told me of their childhood in the 1930s. The first time I visited Norwich, I instantly recognised the cathedral from those pictures.

Anyway, I digress. When I bought my own home, I started to collect pictures for it. For vague reasons of family history, I find myself drawn to Cornish artists. My favourite painter is a young Cornish artist called Kurt Jackson, who specialises in landscapes, the best of which are painted en plein air in Cornwall and the Isles of Scilly. He is the only artist I know who can precisely capture the silvery gunmetal glitter of the sun shining on the sea off Cornwall's north coast.

TO HANDLE PICTURES

Hold and carry pictures at the shortest sides, supporting them underneath the bottom of the frame to support the weight. Keep them upright. Do not try to lift a heavy picture by the top of the frame because it is very likely to break. Heavy paintings should be lifted by more than one person, and if you are carrying a large picture from one room to another, check the height of door frames beforehand. With unglazed pictures, take care not to touch the painted surface.

TO HANG PICTURES

When hanging pictures for the first time, check the condition of the wall. If the plaster is crumbling, soft or flaking, it may not be able to support the weight of the picture (and the combination of painting, frame and glass can be surprisingly heavy).

For heavy pictures, nylon picture cord, which is extremely strong, is preferable to picture wire, which can snap suddenly. Wire is fine for smaller pictures. If using wire, make sure that the ends do not protrude into the back of a canvas.

When attaching the cord/wire, do not make it too tight. It needs to be slack enough to allow the picture to hang slightly away from the wall. This looks better, allows air to circulate (poor ventilation can cause mould to develop) and gives a sloping surface to allow dust to fall off.

Older houses often have a picture rail running about three-quarters of the way up the wall. Before hanging a picture from a rail, make sure it is sound. Pictures are hung from the rail using a picture-rail hook (normally brass) and wire or a chain, which is designed to be seen. Decorative hooks and wires are available, which look very attractive.

In the absence of a picture rail, pictures will be hung directly on the wall. Traditional brass picture hooks can take a surprising amount of weight. They normally come in single or double sizes, complete with strong metal pins. Check how much weight they can support (on the packet) and do not exceed the stated weight. If in doubt, weigh the picture first on the bathroom scales.

> Note: You cannot support a very heavy picture by using more than one picture hook. Simple physics dictates that two picture hooks do not support double the weight. Each supports the same weight and is therefore under equal strain.

124

For really heavy pictures, a hook will not suffice. Instead, drill two holes into the wall and fix screws. Put a washer on each screw to prevent the wire from slipping off. Two screws are safer than one.

The nails that come with traditional brass picture hooks can often not be knocked into solid concrete walls. In this case, look for plastic solid wall hooks, which contain three integral pins.

A common mistake is to hang pictures too high on a wall. A third of the way down is about right, whatever the height of the wall.

TO CLEAN PICTURES

Pictures will generally not need anything more than dusting – once every few months is all that is necessary. Instead of a duster, use a brush to whisk dust off. A brush is less likely than a duster to catch on splinters on the frame or loose flakes of paint on canvases. An alternative is to use an artist's puffer brush to blow any dust off. Even easier is to blow the dust off yourself as you are brushing.

The glass should also only need dusting. If you feel you must clean it, never spray any liquid on to the glass. It is very likely to run down in the crack between the frame and the picture and cause staining of the picture or allow mildew to develop on the picture or the inside of the frame. Most little spots on the glass can be removed by the simple method of licking a finger and gently rubbing the mark until it disappears. Shine with a dry duster afterwards.

If the glass is so dirty that you consider an all-over clean is required, take the picture down from the wall. Use a dry microfibre glass cleaning cloth. As the very last resort, you could spray a tiny amount of water, to which you have added the merest splash of vinegar, very lightly on to a cloth so that it is barely moist, and carefully go over the glass with that. Generally, though, dusting is all that is needed.

125

> *Tip: Never polish the glass of a pastel or chalk drawing. The static electricity created can attract loose particles of pigment on to the inside of the glass.*

TO CLEAN PICTURE FRAMES

If frames need cleaning, follow the same procedure. Take the picture down from the wall. To avoid any cleaning product running down between the frame and the painting, spray a very little plain water on to a cloth, again until it is barely damp, and then clean the frame. Make sure the frame is completely dry before rehanging.

Gilt frames should never come in contact with any liquid because gilt is extremely fragile. Dust every few months with a soft brush – or simply blow the dust off.

With wooden frames, dusting is all that is needed. Little spots of dirt can be removed by licking the end of your finger and gently rubbing the mark off.

If you really think frames need polishing (and I have to say I have never polished a picture frame – a job I put in the 'life is too short' category), use the merest smidgen of polish and clean the frame, making sure that no polish gets between the frame and the painting (the same applies to metal polish and metal frames, particularly silver photograph frames).

When spring cleaning, or if the paintings have been taken down for redecorating, deep-clean before rehanging. Dust all over with a brush, then, using the vacuum cleaner on the lowest setting, clean the backboard, the stretcher bars at the back of the canvas and right into the corners of the frame. Check the condition of the wires and hooks before rehanging.

Never attempt to clean unglazed oil paintings yourself. If they are very dirty (the likely result of a smoky or sooty atmosphere), consult the Yellow Pages to find a conservator to give them a professional clean.

TO STORE PICTURES

If taking pictures down for spring cleaning or redecorating, stack them upright against a wall. Stack them facing inwards to protect the painted surface, in descending order of size (i.e. larger ones first), no more than three deep, so the weight does not damage them. Cover with tissue paper to protect them from dust.

Wrap in bubble wrap if they are going to be stored for any length of time. If you do not want to use a lot of bubble wrap, just put it on the corners of the frames to protect them.

Do not store pictures in damp rooms, nor in rooms that have been newly replastered, until they have completely dried out, nor newly painted rooms, until the smell of paint has gone, nor on cold stone floors, which are prone to damp.

Note: Unless properly insulated, attics are not suitable for long-term storage of pictures. Fluctuations of temperature and humidity are

126

particularly acute in this part of the house, especially in modern houses, with their excessive emphasis on draught proofing. Store in a spare room, if possible. If you really hate the picture so much that you do not want to hang it, sell it or give it away.

TO CARE FOR PAINTINGS

Paintings can be adversely affected by sunlight, heat and air pollution. With one or two obvious exceptions, such as not siting pictures above an open coal or log fire, there is not much that can be done about the last of these. But care can be taken with the first two.

To protect against sunlight: When hanging pictures, make sure they are not going to be hit by direct sunlight. Watercolours and pastels are particularly vulnerable to fading; oils, to a lesser extent. Once faded, the colour cannot be restored. A good place to hang pictures is on a wall between two windows, as long as shafts of sunlight cannot hit the painting through gaps at the sides of curtains or blinds.

127

If a room is very sunny, hang only one picture in it and move pictures either round a room or from room to room so that they get equal exposure.

Draw the curtains when you go out or when you are not using the room, to minimise exposure to sunlight. Somebody once said that this makes a room 'gloomy', but what does it matter if you are not there?

If you have several paintings of actual or sentimental value, you might put them all in the darkest part of the house, which is usually the stairwell, and turn it into a mini gallery.

Delicate, light-sensitive pictures are better glazed. Choose a low-reflecting glass with a UV filter (sometimes called museum glass). This is more expensive than ordinary glass but will protect the painting from sunlight very effectively. Some of it is virtually unbreakable, too.

To protect against heat: Central heating can cause damage to paintings – not just because of the heat but because of the dry atmosphere it creates. Problems arise when the heating is turned on once or twice a day – as most of us tend to do – because it causes fluctuations in temperature. When a room is warm, the humidity falls; as the temperature drops, the humidity rises. Pictures are particularly prone to damage from these fluctuations in heat and humidity because their constituent parts are affected by heat and moisture at different rates. This applies even to the canvas itself and the paints upon it. Too many changes in temperature can cause the paint to crack and even flake off the canvas. In some cases, wooden frames can expand and contract and break the glass in a picture.

Avoid this by having the central heating on all the time at a constant low temperature (you can always boost it if it turns cold). In any case, turning the heating down saves energy and is probably better for our health.

Do not place pictures directly above a radiator or any other source of heat. And do not hang them on walls carrying internal hot pipes.

Do not site picture lights too close to the top of a painting. The danger comes not so much from the light as from the heat of the light, which can scorch the painting.

Conversely, cold and damp do not do pictures much good either. In these conditions, pictures are likely to develop mould (the light brown spots known as 'foxing').

If you want to use a picture light, make sure it is placed far enough away so as not to cause damage, but near enough to give a reasonable light pool. Make sure, too, that the covers on the lights are long enough to ensure the painting does not get too hot.

To protect against air pollution: Fewer of us have open fires these days, but if you do, have pictures glazed (see above) to stop soot damaging the surface. The same applies if there are heavy smokers in the house. It is far easier to clean the glass than to clean the surface of a painting. Do not hang pictures directly above a fireplace that is used frequently.

TO ORGANISE PHOTOGRAPHS

Most of us have piles of old photos sitting around unseen and unloved. If no one ever looks at them, what is the point of keeping them? Go through each packet of photos and select the best ones. Throw out the obvious candidates, such as pictures of someone's foot. Also take the opportunity for a ruthless, Soviet-style excision of pictures of former boyfriends, ex-wives, old enemies and any snap that shows you in an unflattering light.

Buy photograph albums made from acid-free paper, with pockets for

128

photographs, or plastic film that you lay over them. Ensure that the plastic is made from clear polyester film, not PVC, which gives off vapours that can damage photographs. Forget adhesive photo mounts, which are too fiddly.

Do not glue photographs into albums or use sticky adhesive tape because they can damage them, and you will not be able to remove them from the album.

Write captions in the album, not on the photographs. If you must write on a photograph for any reason, write on the back in soft pencil, not ink.

TO CARE FOR PHOTOGRAPH ALBUMS

Store albums upright unless they are very large. To clean, treat them as books. Occasionally dust gently along the top, from the spine outwards, with a soft brush. Hold the album tightly closed so that dust does not slip down between the pages. Alternatively, vacuum along the top, using the upholstery brush attachment on low power.

Some of the more expensive albums are supplied with a storage box (which should preferably be made from acid-free card). If your album has a box, use it to prevent dust getting into it.

If the inside of the album is dusty, remove dust from the paper surrounding the photographs with cotton wool, working from the centre outwards and away from the photographs. Remove dust from the surface of the prints themselves by brushing very gently with a soft brush (an artist's brush or an old, well-washed, soft make-up brush).

129

To deal with water spillages: Water damage can be minimised by acting quickly. The National Trust recommends soaking up the spill by holding a piece of paper towel vertically at the edge of the spill. The water will be soaked upwards, so there will be less danger of it spreading. Once the water has gone, lay the photographs face up (do not touch the surface of the print) on paper towel and allow to dry naturally.

Old photographs need special care and attention. Consult a specialist photographic shop for advice.

SCRAPBOOKS

It may sound madly Jane Austen, but a scrapbook is the perfect solution to the question of what to do with all those bits of paper that usually lie neglected in drawers and shoeboxes – stuff that is intrinsically worthless but means a lot to its owner.

Buy a large, old-fashioned photo album, without plastic film or pockets and preferably made from acid-free paper. Using paper glue or a product designed for artists, such as Spray Mount, stick the bits and pieces in. If you are feeling wildly creative, you can theme your pages, but it is easier to stick stuff in any old how.

Ornaments

We British love our bric-à-brac. Partly this is a result of our history. Unlike the rest of Europe we have not been invaded for 900 years and, give or take the odd civil war, we have been remarkably peaceful. As a result, things survive.

There cannot be a household in the country that does not have at least one little piece – a painting, or piece of china or furniture – that has been handed down, and which is treasured because of the family connections. A couple of years ago my mother gave me a pair of Dresden figures that had been passed down through the family. They are a slightly vacuous-looking boy and girl – both dressed in what must have been Le Petit Trianon notions of shepherdess chic and carrying a basket of flowers. I have to admit they are not really to my taste, but I love them because of the childhood memories they revive. I remember them sitting on the mantelpiece in my grandmother's house, and just looking at them gives me a sense of warmth and continuity. This section is really devoted to old and precious pieces like them.

TO DUST ORNAMENTS

Generally, ornaments need little more than dusting. And some materials, specifically unbaked clay, unglazed earthenware, or ceramics where the glaze is flaking, should not get wet at all. Dust in itself will not harm glazed objects, although it will detract from the sparkle that makes them so attractive. But it will damage unglazed objects, working its way into the fabric of the pot and making it impossible to clean.

Tip: When cleaning ornaments, be careful that dangling necklaces do not bang against them.

A very effective way to dust ornaments is to use a brush. Starting at the top and using a soft brush (see 'Basic cleaning equipment', p. 213), flick the dust into a duster or, even better, the nozzle of the vacuum cleaner on low power. A brush helps to dislodge dust from nooks and crannies that a duster cannot reach and will not rub it into the surface of the object. The vacuum technique is a bit awkward at first, but once you get used to it, you can thoroughly clean a lot of objects quickly. Avoid dusting gilding, which might wear away.

On flat items such as plates, use a duster, folded into a pad so no loose ends are trailing. Press it softly on to the object and try to lift the dust off rather than rubbing it in. Microfibre dusters are very good at lifting off dust. Never use a feather duster – broken quills can scratch ornaments.

Tip: If you notice the odd dirty mark, the simplest way to get rid of it is to spot clean it with saliva. It is quick and easy, and saves having to wash the entire object. The enzymes in saliva help break down dirt quickly. Lick the end of your finger or, if you prefer, a cotton swab, and rub the mark out. Polish off with a soft dry cloth.

131

TO WASH AN ORNAMENT

With regular dusting, you can go for literally years without washing ornaments. Eventually, however, you may decide that they are beginning to look grimy and in need of a wash. Before going ahead, have a good look at it. What is it made of? That will dictate how it can be cleaned. Plain, undecorated glass, bone china and other glazed porcelains and stoneware can all be washed.

To wash a china ornament: Use a plastic washing-up bowl. Line it with a thick towel. Fill the bowl with warm (not hot) water and add a few drops (literally) of a neutral, unperfumed, uncoloured dish soap.

Wash objects one at a time, using a soft cloth. A soft hogshair brush (available from artists' suppliers) will lift dirt from crevices on more elaborate objects.

Remove the object from the bowl before emptying it, then refill it with plain warm water and rinse. Dry with paper towels, mopping rather than rubbing, and then put on a clean tea towel and leave to finish drying for 24 hours.

If the object is too big for a washing-up bowl, you can use the sink, again lining it with a towel. Push swivel faucets well out of the way. Or wrap faucets in a soft cloth – a clean dish cloth will do. Proceed as above.

> *Tip: It is best not to wear gloves, rubber or otherwise, when handling ceramic objects. China, as I have learnt to my cost, is very slippery when wet.*

To wash an ornament that cannot be washed: Some materials such as unglazed earthenware or damaged or cracked porcelain should not be immersed in water, because water can enter tiny cracks in the glaze and carry dirt into the clay underneath. Gilt-decorated objects should also not be washed because the gilt will be washed off. Metal mounts can rust or corrode if they get wet.

The following method is recommended by ceramics experts as the best way to clean such problem pieces. You need:

1 small plastic bowl filled with lukewarm water to which you have added one drop of mild, unperfumed dish soap
1 small plastic bowl filled with plain lukewarm water
2 hogshair paintbrushes
Cotton wool

Work at a table with a towel covering it. First brush the dust off the object, avoiding any gilding.

Dip a small piece of cotton wool into the detergent mixture and squeeze out the water. Holding the ornament steady, swab the cotton wool over a small patch, until it is clean. Use the paintbrushes (one for washing, one for rinsing) to get into any nooks and crannies.

When one patch is clean, 'rinse' the area with the plain water, using a cotton swab (or brush), before going on to the next patch. Work methodically from top to bottom, replacing the cotton wool as it gets dirty, avoiding any gilding or metal mounts.

Pat all over gently with paper towels and then leave to finish drying in a warm place for 24 hours.

I have used this method myself and I cannot pretend it is not time-consuming. It once took me nearly a whole afternoon to clean two china figures. But the job does not have to be done more than every two or three years as long as things are kept dusted. And fragile old objects are worth treating with care if we want another generation to enjoy them.

Flowers

Flowers are very much a part of modern living. No self-respecting makeover show would be complete without those five minutes at the end when the makeover genius puts a few vases of flowers here and there and magically 'dresses' the room. And you don't even need to make an elaborate arrangement: one of the virtues of flowers is that you can just plonk them in an old coffee jar and they will look beautiful.

For years I worked in women's magazines. Though they were all quite different from each other, the one thing they had in common was the fashion departments, and the blasé sophistication of the girls who worked there (people in fashion departments are always 'girls', even the men). The paradoxical result of inhabiting a world whose raison d'être is innovation is that they quickly ceased to be surprised by anything. This attitude was at its most marked when they received the enormous, mouth-watering bunches of flowers that regiments of couriers daily — no, hourly — delivered to the office as tokens of esteem from adoring PRs and designers.

Those of us toiling away in the sub-editors' department would have given a month's salary for the cachet of having a

133

bouquet from the boyfriend delivered to the office, but the fashion girls were unimpressed.

'Oh God, not orchids again,' I remember one ungrateful minx saying. Then, catching sight of me scurrying in apologetically with a proof, she said, 'Here you, do you want these?' For the record, I said no. I've got my standards.

The more conventional response on receiving a bunch of flowers is to be completely thrilled and to want it to last as long as possible.

TO PREPARE FLOWERS

If cutting flowers from your own garden, cut them in the morning, before the dew has dried, or in the early evening. Use sharp stem-cutting or pruning shears and cut above a node or dormant bud to encourage new growth. Take a bucket of lukewarm water with you and put the cut flowers into it as you work. Leave them for several hours before putting in a vase so they can have a really good drink.

With a commercial bouquet, remove the flowers from the wrapping and using a sharp knife or very sharp scissors cut at least 1 in off the stems on the slant. Blunt scissors will crush the stem. (Don't bash hard or woody stems for the same reason.)

Strip off any leaves that will be below the water line, otherwise they will rot.

Place the flowers in a bucket of deep, lukewarm water – up to their heads if possible – and leave in a cool place out of direct sunlight for several hours or overnight. In florist's parlance, this 'conditions' the flowers.

An exception to this softly-softly approach is with sunflowers and zinnias, whose sap tends to ooze. To avoid this, scald the stem ends in boiling water for 20 seconds. You could also use a candle flame.

To prepare hand-tied bunches: These came into vogue about 15 years ago and look like old-fashioned posies, tied tightly with string. They are normally delivered with their stems sitting in a cellophane reservoir of water.

Lift them out of the packaging (do this over the sink, for obvious reasons), being careful not to knock the flower heads. Gently lay the bouquet on its side and then cut the stems at an angle as above. Give them a good soaking in a bucket of lukewarm water, still tied, then put them in a vase (with cut flower food) that is wide enough to take the whole bunch in one go. Florists say that the string should be left intact, but I find that if you cut the string, holding the bunch firmly to keep the arrangement in place, the shape is retained, while the flowers sit more naturally in the vase.

TO CARE FOR FLOWERS

Ensure all vases are sparkling clean. Dirty vases may contain bacteria from the last lot of flowers, which will rapidly multiply and shorten the life of the flowers. Place flowers in lukewarm water, not cold. Lukewarm water has fewer bubbles, which could get into the stem and prevent them taking up water. Add cut flower food if it has been supplied with the bouquet, made up according to instructions – usually one sachet to 1 quart warm water. Traditional 'flower foods' such as aspirin, copper coins and bleach make little or no difference to the life of the flowers, and in some cases they will wilt more quickly (but see 'To make your own cut flower food', below).

TO CLEAN A VASE

Flowers breed masses of bacteria – hence that revolting old-flower stench. Always wash vases thoroughly after use. Use hot water and detergent and then rinse in hot water to which you have added a dash of bleach.

135

Some people have reported that cut flower food stains glass vases, leaving a rainbow bloom that is difficult to remove. This seems to be more common in areas where the water is very hard.

To remove the marks, first wash the vase thoroughly as above, then fill with half and half water and white vinegar. Leave overnight, empty out the vinegar, wash, rinse and dry. If this does not work, put in more vinegar and water and leave the vase for up to a fortnight if necessary. Empty out nearly all the water, then add some dry rice and swill it around inside to remove any residue.

Finally, wash again. Rice is gentler than metal decanter beads, which are used in the same way, but these are very efficient. They are the commercial equivalent of the lead shot that old household manuals recommended as the best way to clean decanters. If you have access to lead shot, try it. Otherwise, decanter beads are widely available (see 'To clean decanters', page 29).

Once the vase is clean, try to use cut flower food specially designed for glass vases: look for names like 'crystal clear'.

TO MAKE CUT FLOWERS LAST LONGER

Some flowers simply last longer than others, for instance alstroemeria, aster, celosia, cosmos, gypsophila, lilies, lavatera, rudbeckia, scabiosa, snapdragon, statice, sunflower, yarrow and zinnia. Flowers with hollow stems, on the other hand, have the shortest vase life. But there are still ways to make them last longer.

Keep flowers out of direct sunlight, which can scorch petals and causes bacteria to breed, and away from heat and draughts, which chill them. Do not sit the vase too near the television. Apart from the obvious fact that water and electricity are a lethal combination, the heat from the television will cause the flowers to wilt.

Keep flowers away from pets and small children.

Do not put the vase near bowls of fruit. Fruit gives off ethylene gas, which ripens fruit but ages flowers. Dead flowers give off the same gas, so remove dead or dying blooms daily.

Top up the water level daily too or, even better, if the arrangement is not too elaborate, replace the water completely. This seems to make all the difference with roses. Flowers like a damp atmosphere, so mist the arrangement daily.

> *Tip: The easiest way to remove the dead bunch of flowers from the vase is, leaving the vase in situ, to invert a large plastic rubbish bag right over the whole bunch. Hold the vase in one hand, gather the plastic in the other and grasp the bouquet by its stem, lifting it out inside the bag. This saves trailing dead leaves, petals and seed heads through the house.*

To make your own cut-flower food: The ingredients in commercial cut flower food are a fiercely guarded commercial secret (I know – I tried to find out). But the principle is a sugar to feed the flower (usually fructose or dextrose), a biocide anti-bacterial agent to kill the bacteria present in the water, and an acidifier to lower the ph value of the water (flowers take up water better in an acid environment).

Commercial cut flower food is widely available from florists, garden centres and DIY stores – and this is what I use.

But at a pinch, try the following:

Mix ½ pint each lemonade (not diet lemonade) and water with ½ tsp bleach. The lemonade is acidic and contains sugar, and the bleach kills bacteria. Put the flowers in this mixture. If your vase is very large and you need more liquid, just increase the amounts proportionately.

PROBLEM FLOWERS

Some flowers pose particular problems, shortening the life of the whole bouquet. If a bouquet contains some of the following flowers, it is best to dismantle and put the flowers in separate vases.

Daffodils: Do not mix daffodils with other flowers because they exude a slimy sap that contaminates the rest. If you feel your arrangement will be incomplete without a few heads of narcissi nodding tremulously in the vase, cut the flower stems and soak in water for 12 hours, then add to the vase without cutting again. Special bulb cut flower food is also available.

Lilies: The main problem with lilies is their pollen, which stains fabrics and carpets irrevocably and will eat into wood if it drops on furniture (see below). Removing the stamens will prevent this, as well as prolonging the life of the lilies. Pull the stamens off; do not cut them. I drop them straight into an old envelope, screw it up and then throw it away.

If pollen falls on to a wooden surface, remove it immediately with a soft duster. If it falls on to carpet or upholstery, do not wipe because you will rub it into the fabric and leave an indelible stain.

First, vacuum up as much as possible, hovering the nozzle over the pollen (do not touch the fabric). Any residue can simply be lifted off using sticky tape.

Roses: Roses are so often a scentless, drooping disappointment, but try the following. Remove all leaves except the last set nearest the flower head. After cutting the flower stem, stand the bottom 2 in of stem in boiling water for 20 seconds. Soak for 12 hours in cool, deep water before cutting again and arranging in the vase in fresh water. Use flower food. Keep as cool as possible.

Tulips: Tulips have a tendency to droop languidly over the edge of the vase in a dispiriting way. To avoid this, after cutting the stems and removing most of the leaves, wrap the bunch of tulips very tightly in kitchen foil, leaving an inch or two of bare stem at the bottom. Soak in deep water for 12 hours. Wrapping the tulips allows the stems to take up water while remaining straight. Next day, unwrap them and put in a vase of fresh water.

137

The hall

The first part of the house that visitors see is the hallway. In modern houses, this is often little more than a narrow corridor leading from the front door, but in older houses hallways are much more impressive, in some cases almost constituting another room. When I was moving house a couple of years ago, I was thrilled to find a flat with a large, square hall, which was roomy enough to have bookshelves on one wall and fitted cupboards on the other. The latter is the equivalent, in the absence of a staircase, of the 'cupboard under the stairs' – an essential part of any house.

Ideally, the hall should have plenty of storage for coats, boots and so forth, and it must be well lit. First and foremost, though, it is the part of the house that is subject to the heaviest traffic and therefore the most wear and tear. Bear this in mind when choosing floor coverings and when redecorating. Tiled, stone or vinyl flooring is preferable to carpet, possibly with a rug to make it more comfortable. Walls and paintwork are bound to get a lot of buffeting, so keep decorating schemes simple. Paint is preferable to wallpaper in hallways because it can be cleaned more easily, and if it gets too grubby, can easily be given a fresh coat. Finally, to prevent dirt being tracked into the rest of the house, always use a doormat (see below) and encourage the family to remove their shoes when they come in from outside.

TO CLEAN THE HALL

Daily: hang up coats and other outdoor clothes. Sweep or vacuum the floor as necessary.

Weekly: Clean all paintwork and vacuum or mop the floor. If the weather has been wet, you may have to mop or vacuum more frequently.

THE DOORMAT

Why, I wonder, has the word 'doormat' come to mean a downtrodden, miserable sort of person? In terms of housework, a doormat is a hero, a first line of defence against grit, dust and dirt entering the house. Without a mat, grit is ground into the pile of carpets and scratches the surface of hard flooring. Place a doormat at the entrance to every outside door and make it as large as possible. Ideally, it should be long enough for anyone entering the house to be able to take a stride and still have both feet on the mat. Large doormats can be difficult to manoeuvre, so place two smaller ones side by side.

Traditionally, mats are made from coir (coconut matting). Coir's tough bristles can easily remove dirt from the bottom of shoes, and its loose-weave construction enables it to trap dust and grit efficiently. If you also want to have a mat outside the door, make sure it is weatherproof (a rubber backing is best).

TO CLEAN DOORMATS

Coconut matting is extremely effective, so much so that if it is not kept clean, it can get clogged with dust and then start recycling dirt round the house. Once a week, take mats outside, turn upside down and shake vigorously to get the dust out. Vacuum, using the strongest suction.

> Tip: Roll the mat right side out, tie it and beat it. The rolling forces the fibres apart and lets the dust and grit out.

Old-fashioned household books give instructions for cleaning coir mats with salt water. But, frankly, this comes into the 'life's too short' category. If a mat is so dirty that it needs washing, go and buy a new one.

Before replacing the mat, sweep or vacuum the floor where it has lain.

> Note: Mats backed with rubber or latex can stain some floors, particularly vinyl and resin floors (for example, Amtico).

THE CUPBOARD UNDER THE STAIRS

If it is large enough, the cupboard under the stairs is the perfect place to keep virtually anything that does not otherwise have a natural home. If there is no room in the kitchen, this will be the home of the vacuum cleaner. If you do not have a utility room, it will house the ironing board and the iron. And it is the natural home for spare light bulbs, fuses, picture hooks, batteries – the stuff you do not need every day, but when you do, it has to be immediately to hand.

TO ORGANISE THE CUPBOARD UNDER THE STAIRS

Think of this as an enormous filing cabinet for bulky things, so keep everything to hand and labelled. Put small items in old jam jars and label them, so you know

139

at a glance which are, say, 13 amp fuses and which are the 5 amp ones. Use clear plastic storage boxes for bigger items such as light bulbs.

Group like with like, so you are not running round the house looking for things. Thus the cupboard may contain not only the ironing board, but also the iron and the clothes-drying rack; near the vacuum cleaner should be the spare bags and the filters. Along with spare fuses and light bulbs, keep candles in case of power outages, along with a flashlight and some matches.

> Note: If you keep dry dog or cat food in the cupboard under the stairs, make sure they are in closed containers. Otherwise, they may attract mice. Do not store chemicals in the cupboard under the stairs, especially if there are children in the house. If there is no alternative, keep the cupboard locked.

To prevent the cupboard turning into a disaster, turn it out once a year. Throw out everything you have kept for more than three years without ever needing or looking at it. Vacuum it thoroughly and wash down paintwork and shelves. Reline shelves if necessary and make sure everything is dry before replacing the contents.

CHAPTER 5

The
Dining-Room

Poor Mr Woodhouse's feelings were in sad warfare. He loved to have the cloth laid, because it had been the fashion of his youth, but his conviction of suppers being very unwholesome made him rather sorry to see any thing put on it ...

Jane Austen, Emma

When space is short in the modern home, the dining-room is the first room to be sacrificed. It is seen as a quaint anachronism from the days when people had dinner parties and a set of 'best china' and a bit of a luxury, a sad waste of space that is used only for celebrations and holidays. In the 1980s, of course, everyone wanted one. They were often decorated in a style that was elaborately baroque even for that over-the-top decade. I remember longing to have a dining-room painted dark green, which was to be lit only by candlelight, and was desperately envious when a friend did something along those lines, painting her dining-room dark blue.

This was very much in keeping with that other Eighties phenomenon – the 'dinner party', which was less a social occasion with friends than an exercise in one-upmanship. I remember spending an entire day cooking for a dinner party. The object was always to impress, though one never admitted this. There were never fewer than three courses and always a choice of two, sometimes three, puddings.

While formal dining was possible in the days when people had servants, it makes no sense nowadays. In fact, it made no sense 20 years ago either: what normally happened was that the poor cook spent the whole evening in the kitchen while her guests sat in the other room, having a hilarious time and getting sloshed.

Now that very few families regularly sit down together for meals, formal dining is completely out of fashion. And one wonders if it will ever be revived.

Changing social and demographic patterns would seem to say not. Growing numbers of people live alone these days – it is projected that by 2010 one in three households will be single-person – which makes the former demarcations of cook in the kitchen and guests in the sitting-room completely impossible if the host or hostess actually wants to see the guests.

Second, and more important, the kitchen has increased in importance, becoming not just the place where food is cooked, but very often the social centre of the home. The fashion now when entertaining is for people to congregate in the kitchen with the cook, often while the food is being cooked. Instead of trying to impress, the idea is to create an atmosphere of artless informality – as if the cook has just thrown everything together with effortless stylishness. I have to say that from the point of view of the cook, rushing home from work and trying to throw a relaxed 'kitchen supper' – as dinner parties are now called – can be every bit as taxing as the old three-course affair.

Another change in fashion has been the rise in home computing – up to three-quarters of homes now have a computer. This trend might not seem to have any connection with the demise of the dining-room, but it does. Computers are unlovely objects and, with their wires and associated paraphernalia such as hard-drives, printers and scanners, take up a lot of room. What people want is a study or home office, and increasingly, the dining-room has been co-opted into this role, making a home not just for the computer but for all the paperwork with which the modern home seems to be inundated. For more on how to run the home office, turn to 'The Study', Chapter 7.

143

The dining-room in its traditional form may be dead, but many people still like to push the boat out once or twice a year, get out the silver, put candles on the table and – like Mr Woodhouse – lay the cloth.

If most family meals are eaten in the kitchen, and the dining-room – if it exists – is kept 'for best', it is likely to be one of the least used rooms in the house. This has several advantages. First, the dining-room is going to need little more than a cursory clean once in a while. Second, you can use the dining-room to store precious things such as good china, silver and linen. With little general traffic or children rampaging through, it will all keep safe. This chapter looks at the care and cleaning of all those special things.

The dining table

In a formal dining-room, the table may well be one of the most expensive pieces of furniture you own – probably wooden, possibly even antique.

To keep it in good condition, never put hot plates directly on to it: they can scorch or mark the surface. Use mats, or a cork or cloth table protector. Even these may not be enough with very hot dishes – such as a casserole taken straight from the oven. Remember that when mats are described as 'heatproof' – even up to 500°F – it means that the mats are safe from the effects of heat, not the surface on which they are resting. Even with heatproof mats, heat can be transferred and will leave a mark on the furniture. A cloth will protect it from food spills, but if you prefer not to use one, wipe up any spills immediately with a barely damp cloth. In general, wood and water are not a happy marriage. For more about how to care for a wooden table, see 'Wooden furniture', p. 272.

Table linen

Formal, starched linens have gone the way of formal dining, but many people still like to use a tablecloth, especially when there are guests, or it is a special occasion, such as Christmas. For normal family meals, if you adhere to this quaint tradition, many people use plastic cloths, especially on the kitchen table.

Note: If the table underneath is of good quality, the plastic cloth should not be left on permanently. Plasticisers in the cloth can migrate to the wood and permanently mark it.

TABLECLOTHS

When calculating which size of tablecloth to buy, allow an overhang of up to 1 ft all round. Buy larger than you need, rather than smaller, to allow for shrinkage.

Laundering table linen can make a lot more work, so be kind to yourself. For everyday use, look for easy-care cloths – the best choices are non-iron linen or cotton/synthetic blends.

For 'best', heavy linen or cotton table linen is still the first choice, but it will need ironing and possibly starching.

> Tip: It may sound contradictory, but white table linen is easier to launder than coloured, because it can withstand higher washing temperatures and you don't have to worry about loss of colour. It can even be bleached if necessary.

If you like the look of a formal white tablecloth occasionally, or have inherited an old damask cloth, use it. Many old linens are perfectly acceptable. And some really are old. Their extraordinary high quality means that 19th-century linens have survived right down to the present day.

People often do not want to use them because they think they require a great deal of looking after. That may have been true in the days when the tablecloth was made. But modern washing machines and detergents have made this a thing of the past.

NAPKINS
Napkins are always a good idea, because they protect clothes. Use cloth rather than paper napkins because they are better at soaking up spills. There are no standard sizes for napkins, and they seem to be getting smaller. I have some damask napkins inherited from my great-grandmother, which are nearly two foot square – a testament to Victorian good sense in the days before washing machines

Unless you want to launder napkins after each meal, supply every member of the family with a napkin ring and wash napkins as necessary. A silver napkin ring used to be a standard christening present – I use my grandmother's – and quite often these are inherited and then never used. If you have them, get them out and use them. Otherwise, napkin rings can be bought in any department store.

Again, when buying, look for easy-care or non-iron napkins, to reduce the amount of ironing. If buying synthetic-mix fabrics, make sure that there is a high proportion of natural fibre because it is more absorbent than synthetics.

TO CLEAN TABLE LINEN
First attend to any stains. The main problems are likely to be grease and other food stains, candle wax, wine and coffee. Most stains will respond to a soak and a hot wash (140°F), using oxygen bleach if necessary. If this does not work, turn to

145

the detailed instructions on removing specific stains in 'An A–Z of fabric stains', p. 307.

If the table linen is going to be used straight away, iron it if necessary. If it is tumble-dried, removed promptly from the drier and then folded, ironing is rarely necessary, even for cotton. In any case, just give it a quick once-over with the iron and fold. Do not iron in creases. Tablecloths and napkins that are used only occasionally can be left until needed.

Heavy cotton and linen cloths, including damasks, will probably need starching (see 'Starch', p. 163).

TO FOLD A TABLECLOTH

Fold in half, then lengthways in half again and if necessary in half again. Then fold crossways once or twice to make a square. Or fold lengthways loosely and roll up.

Fold a round tablecloth in half, wrong sides together, making a semicircle. Fold the curved edge up to the straight edge to make a rectangle with two curved edges. (If the cloth is very large, fold in half again.) Fold the two curved ends into the middle, then fold in half again and, if it's large, again, to make a square.

TO FOLD NAPKINS

Fold small napkins in quarters to form a square and, if you like, fold the square into a triangle.

Fold large napkins in half, then in half lengthways. Finally fold crossways.

TO STORE TABLE LINEN

The rules for storing bed linen apply equally to table linen (see 'To store bed linen', p. 66). Store somewhere cool, dark and dry, avoiding hot places such as airing cupboards or near radiators. The heat will cause yellowing and may even make the fabric crack. If storing long-term, you may like to wrap linen in acid-free tissue paper to protect it. Keep an eye out for moth infestation and if you suspect the little blighters may be present, take the necessary steps (see 'Household pests', p. 322).

Fine china and glass

The demise of the dining-room is reflected in other changes of habit. For example, that set of 'best' china – probably given as a wedding present – may see the light of day only a couple of times a year. We are more likely to have one set which is used every day and replace things as they get broken (some companies even make a virtue of this, manufacturing different variations on a colour theme, so you can mix and match). And though china at the top end of the market is still as fantastically expensive as it was when Josiah Wedgwood was making cream ware for the aspirant middle classes of the 18th century, in general china and glass are cheap enough for us to do this.

However, if you own or want to buy a set of really good china or glasses, you will realise that replacing broken pieces is going to be a very expensive business, so it pays to know how to look after it.

TO CARE FOR FINE CHINA AND GLASS

Ceramics are surprisingly durable. They can withstand heat and they will not fade in sunlight. They are not susceptible to pest damage. What they cannot withstand is rough handling. Washing them in very hot water can cause thermal shock and crack them. Even putting something down sharply can cause hairline cracks that can 'travel' down a piece at an alarming rate. And when there are children or pets around you are asking for trouble. A friend of mine had a Burmese cat whose party trick was walking along the mantelpiece and batting things off it with its paw. Of course, everyone thought this was hilarious, which only encouraged it.

Always lift large pieces of china and glass with both hands. Hold glasses by their stems. Do not lift anything up by its spout.

If you need to move an object any distance – when, say, a room is being emptied before redecorating – carry it in a box that you have padded with a towel. This enables you to carry more than one piece at a time, but do not cram them in. To carry several plates at a time, slip paper plates between them to cushion them.

> *Tip: For testing to see if your dishes are suitable for the microwave oven, I pass on this tip from a friend. Fill a Pyrex jug with some water and put it on the microwave turntable with the dish that you are testing (if there is no room for both, put the jug inside the dish). Heat them both on High for a minute. If the dish is microwaveable, it will feel cool to the touch, but the water inside the jug will have started to feel warm.*

TO WASH FINE CHINA AND GLASS

If you want fine china to last, it should never be washed in the dishwasher, even if it is marked 'dishwasher-proof'. The chemicals in dishwasher detergent are very harsh. They take off the glaze, and over time the decoration will wear away. Nothing is 100 per cent dishwasher-proof. Always wash fine china by hand.

Lead crystal glasses washed in the dishwasher will quickly develop a bloom that is impossible to remove. Wash glasses in warm water with a dash of dish soap. Do not hold the glass too tight, especially round the rim.

Rinse in plain water to which you have added a splash of vinegar, and put to drain on a clean tea towel. Finally, polish off the last few water spots with a soft, dry tea towel. Microfibre cloths are particularly good at polishing glasses. Polish gently, and avoid holding the stem and twisting the glass to dry the bowl – this is when breakages occur. For more on washing china and glass, see 'To wash up by hand', p. 26.

> *Tip: Always remove rings when washing glasses, especially diamond rings. The diamond can scratch the glass and it does not do the jewellery much good either (see 'Jewellery', p. 81).*

TO STORE FINE CHINA AND GLASS

Stack plates and saucers according to size (not too many at once), interleaving them with a white paper towel or paper plates to prevent the pattern or glaze getting scratched. Bowls of the same size can be stacked, again interleaved with paper towel, but do not stack bowls of different sizes because the accumulated weight may make them stick together. Do not stack cups at all, for the same reason. If the shelves are deep, store smaller items at the front.

Fine china cups should not be hung on hooks (only suitable for everyday mugs and things that you do not mind getting broken), but should be placed on shelves right side up. People often store cups and glasses upside down because it keeps the dust out, but the rims of glasses can easily get chipped and gilt decoration on teacups can get worn away. If you do not use them very often, store them in the boxes they came in where possible. If they are to be kept on a shelf, lay a sheet of acid-free tissue paper over the top to keep the dust out. Of course, that isn't desirable in a glass-fronted display cupboard.

When storing china and glass that is not in daily use, wrap each piece individually in acid-free tissue paper. You can also get specially designed cotton storage bags in different sizes for teacups, coffee cups, plates and so on.

Silver

To say that silver is a soft, white element with the atomic number 47 and the highest conductivity of any metal does not begin to capture its romance. In 1985, when Lord Stockton attacked the then Conservative government for 'selling off the family silver', people knew exactly what he meant, because a fine collection of silver has always been a mark of wealth in this country.

Silver has been widely used since 3,000 BC. It is mentioned in the Old Testament, when Abraham is described as being 'very rich in cattle, in silver and in gold'. For some, it ranked above gold in desirability. The Vikings had a passion for silver, and to this day some of the world's best silverware and jewellery is made in Denmark. The British share this love – and I wonder if the reason silver is so highly prized among northern peoples is because its soft, deep sheen is particularly suited to our cold, grey light. Certainly, our long, dark nights gave us ample opportunity to see how well silver is enhanced by candlelight.

It will be obvious by now that I love silver, too. It is the most tactile of metals – when I see it, I immediately want to stroke it. But silverware – cutlery, candlesticks, teapots and so forth – is out of fashion. For one thing, it does not suit the modern taste for minimalism. For another, it does not easily fit into a world where everything must be 'easy-care'. All of which is good news for us fans of silver. While it remains in the fashion doldrums, there are bargains to be had. The reason that Lord Stockton's criticism seemed so stinging is that silver has always been prized as something to hang on to and to pass on to future generations. So though we may not be buying silver in great numbers, many of us will have inherited silver, family pieces that are brought out for special occasions and repay looking after.

TO CARE FOR SILVER

Is the piece to be cleaned solid silver or silver plate? In fact, 'solid' silver is something of a misnomer because all silver is an alloy – usually of copper.

Silver plate, sometimes called electroplate, is made by fusing a thin layer of silver electrolytically on to a base metal. The most commonly seen version is labelled EPNS, which means electro-plated nickel silver (the base, nickel silver, does not contain any silver at all, but is a mixture of nickel, zinc and copper).

The basics of cleaning and care of solid silver and silver plate are the same. Silver looks at its best when it is used regularly. The patina that develops on it is caused by light catching on minute scratches on the surface. But the very quality that gives silver its lustre also shows that it can be dented and scratched. The silver coating on silver plate is very thin and can wear through with over-zealous rubbing.

Silver tarnishes very easily. Tarnish is caused by the silver reacting with sulphur in the air or with other compounds to form a yellow film. If it is not removed, it turns brown and eventually goes purplish black.

All sorts of things can tarnish silver, including eggs, onions, spinach, mayonnaise, wool, newspaper, brown paper and rubber. If you have worn rubber gloves to polish silver and have noticed that it actually seems to become more tarnished, you would be right. The sulphur in the rubber creates tarnish even as you are trying to clean it off. Wear cotton gloves.

As well as tarnishing, silver can be corroded by salt, chlorine bleach and acids. Always clean it after use and before putting it away. Silver salt cellars have a glass lining to protect the metal. Even so, empty them and wash them after use. The same applies to mustard pots.

Silver that is on display should be dusted regularly. Dust particles attract moisture and pollutants in the atmosphere, which encourage tarnishing. Use a soft duster and rub gently to bring up the shine. A soft brush, such as an old, well-washed blusher brush, is useful for getting dust out of crevices and elaborate decoration.

> *Note: The best way to keep silver in good condition is to use it. Frequent use and washing up will keep it bright and shiny without polishing (which can wear both silver and silver plate). Worn modern silver plate can be re-silvered, but it can be expensive and is probably not worth it unless the piece is of great sentimental value.*

TO WASH SILVER

If an object has got dirty, wash to remove surface grime. If the piece of silver is solid – in other words, it does not have hollow handles or feet, or handles made from wood or bone, or a resin base, an applied rim, or anywhere else that water or cleaners could get in – it can be immersed in water. Use warm water and a little dish soap. Wash with a soft cloth, rinse and polish with a silver polishing cloth. These cloths will bring up the shine and are also impregnated with tarnish inhibitors. Do not rub too hard, or you may scratch the surface. Use long, even strokes – do not rub crosswise or in circular movements.

151

Pieces of silver that are not solid should not be immersed in water. Instead, take two bowls. Fill one with warm water and a little dish soap and the second with plain water. Dip a cloth into the first bowl, wring it out well and gently swab the object all over, being careful not to let water get into any crevices. As you wash each area, dip a second cloth in plain water, repeat the process with that, then gently buff dry with a silver polishing cloth, as above.

Light tarnish can often be removed just with a silver polishing cloth. On small objects, you can also use a plastic (not rubber) art eraser. Rub gently all over with the eraser, then wash, rinse and polish with a dry cloth. This is a particularly useful trick to know for anything that is elaborately decorated, because the eraser can reach into small crevices. Cut it to fit, if necessary.

Heavier tarnish can be removed only with silver polish. Cream cleaners are very good. Silver dip is gentler but not as effective and has to be completely removed from a piece of silver or it can cause corrosion. Never use silver wadding, which is too abrasive.

Note: Do not use products designed to clean other metals on silver – and vice versa.

To use silver polish: Apply the polish with a soft cloth, working in long strokes, rather than in small circles. This is particularly important on flat pieces, such as salvers. On chased or engraved pieces, use a hogshair brush.

I always then rinse the piece before polishing. To polish, use a soft cloth on flat pieces, again working in long strokes. On chased or engraved pieces, polish with a brush – bristle, not nylon, to remove polish from all nooks and crannies.

TO WASH SILVER CUTLERY

Wash all silver cutlery immediately after use. Certain foods such as vinegar, mustard, Brussels sprouts, egg and salt tarnish and/or corrode silver, causing pitting to the surface.

Wash by hand in hot water with a little dish soap.

Do not wash silver and stainless steel cutlery together. A reaction between the two metals will damage the silver.

Do not immerse bone- or wooden-handled cutlery in water. Water can loosen the glue or rust the metal shaft inside the handle, eventually causing the handles to split (metal expands as it rusts). Wash each piece individually.

Rinse in hot water and dry immediately with a soft cloth. Silver should not be left to dry naturally because water droplets can corrode the metal (see also 'Stainless steel', p. 285).

Do not put silver or silver plate in the dishwasher (see 'Washing up', p. 26, for an explanation).

Old or valuable silver or silver-plate cutlery, and wooden- or bone-handled cutlery, should be cleaned as above. For less valuable cutlery, try the following:

Put crumpled aluminium foil in the bottom of a saucepan large enough to immerse the cutlery. Put the cutlery on top, fill with water and boil for about 10 minutes. The tarnish will transfer from the silver to the foil, turning it black but leaving the cutlery shiny. Remove from the saucepan, wash in hot, soapy water, rinse and dry.

Note: Strictly speaking, only knives are referred to as 'cutlery'. Forks and spoons are known as 'flatware'.

TO STORE SILVER

After cleaning, leave the object in a warm, dry place to ensure it is completely dry. Wrap in a special silver cloth or bag impregnated with a tarnish retardant. These are available from the home care departments of large stores. Anti-tarnish strips – paper strips that absorb sulphur in the atmosphere – are also available. Put them in bags or drawers where silver is stored. Store in a dark drawer or cupboard – in any case, out of direct sunlight.

Or use acid-free tissue paper. Do not use newspaper or brown paper, which will tarnish the silver.

Do not use chamois leather or felt to wrap silver because both contain sulphur and will cause tarnishing.

Do not use plastic bags – moisture can get trapped in them, and the plasticisers they contain also cause tarnishing.

Do not fasten bundles of silver with rubber bands; they contain sulphur, which will tarnish the silver.

TO REMOVE WAX FROM SILVER CANDLESTICKS

Wax dripping decoratively down a candlestick looks rather romantic when everyone is having a lovely time and, in any case, it is not very hospitable to start twittering about spills in the middle of dinner. But removing it is a tedious job. Avoid it in future by burning non-drip candles.

Do not freeze silver candlesticks to remove wax, as some people suggest. Many are made of more than one metal. Different metals contract at different rates, and the shock of freezing could cause the metal to split, or damage to enamel or paint.

Before you clean a silver candlestick, turn it upside down. How it is made has a bearing on how it is to be cleaned. It will either be hollow or have a filled resin base. Each has an advantage: hollow candlesticks are easier to clean; resin-filled bases are more stable. To clean, proceed as follows.

Hollow candlesticks: Run the candlestick under the hot tap and then prise out the wax, using an orange stick (the wooden stick used by manicurists) or a wooden cocktail stick. Once the obvious bits of

153

wax have been removed, rinse again under the hot tap to remove the rest. Dry very well with a soft duster, then polish with a silver cleaning cloth.

Candlesticks with a resin base: It is important not to allow water to get into the candlestick, because it can corrode the metal from inside. Never immerse in water.

To clean, start by taking the candlestick apart, removing the nozzles and so forth. Nearly all candlesticks unscrew: just be careful to support the candleholders from below with your hand and not to press too hard.

The removable parts can be rinsed under the hot tap, as above, then dried. The parts that cannot be immersed in water should be wiped with a cloth dipped in very hot water and wrung out. This is tedious, but eventually, the wax residue will disappear.

Or use a hairdryer to soften the wax. Use a low heat and do not direct the heat on one spot for too long. As the wax softens, prise it off with an orange stick or blunt cocktail stick – cut off the point.

Whichever method you use, once you have removed all the wax, dry the candlestick and buff gently with a silver polishing cloth.

> *Tips: To make a candle last longer, put it in the freezer for a couple of hours before using. To fit a difficult candle into a candlestick, dip the end in boiling water for a second or two. The end will soften enough to fit in easily, and it will sit tight.*

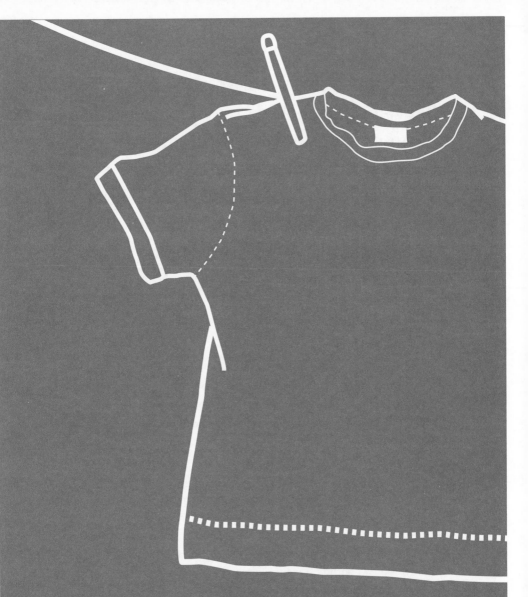

CHAPTER 6
The Laundry

Woollen socks, woollen socks!
Infuriating paradox!
Hosiery wonderful and terrible,
Heaven to wear, and yet unwearable.
The man enmeshed in such a quandary
Can only hie him to the laundry,
And while his socks are hung to dry,
Wear them once as they're shrinking by.

Ogden Nash, 'The Shrinking Song'

156

It is difficult now to comprehend quite how back-breaking housework was for generations of women until the 20th century, when the first mechanical household appliances began to come into general use. Nowhere was this more apparent than in the laundry.

For the rich, laundry was not a problem. Big houses would have had their own laundry rooms and employed their own laundry maids. The operation was industrial in scale. The middle classes hired the services of a washerwoman, who would either come to the house to do the washing and ironing, or take the laundry away with her and bring it back washed and ironed. Washerwomen, of whom there were 170,598 in England in 1871, were not very well thought of, but their absolute necessity to the fabric of life was borne out when a group of them went on strike in Hastings one Friday in 1860. Their employers, Hastings Town Council, settled on the Monday.

Laundry was back-breaking work. Mrs Beeton, the Victorian housework authority, devotes five pages to the duties of the laundry maid. After sorting the laundry, she attended to stains, using a variety of strong and toxic chemicals, including oxalic acid, salts of sorrel, sal ammonia and spirits of wine.

Ordinarily dirty whites were then soaked overnight in lukewarm water and soda, but greasy or very dirty cloths were left to soak in lye (water and unslaked lime). The next day, enormous copper tubs of water were heated up. Each item of clothing was removed from the lye, rinsed, rubbed and wrung; then put in more water and washed with soap; rinsed and wrung; washed again 'in water as hot as the hand can bear'; rinsed and wrung.

To remove soap, the laundry was then boiled in the copper for an hour and a half and skimmed to remove the suds. Two final rinses followed, one in plain water, one in water to which laundry blue had been added.

Once the laundry was clean, it was wrung out either by hand or with a mangle and dried. In warm weather, it was relatively easy to dry laundry outside, but wet weather proved a problem unless the house had a drying room. In cold weather, the washing froze on the line. For her work, the laundry maid got paid between £9 and £14 a year.

Something to think about while waiting impatiently for the washing machine to get through its cycle.

The essentials

My friend the builder tells me that one of the things that people most want in their houses is a laundry room. Years ago, at the height of the 1980s property boom, I remember being wildly impressed when some friends had their builders turn a redundant chimney flue into a laundry chute. Clothes went in through a hatch on the top floor and landed in a laundry basket in a laundry room in the basement.

If you haven't got a dedicated utility room in the house and are considering doing a bit of remodelling, try to find space for one: it is one of the most practical and useful rooms in the house.

For a start, all the paraphernalia connected with washing clothes is in one place. Second, locating the washing machine away from the kitchen saves valuable space and may make room for something equally useful, such as a dishwasher. (What is more, it will be out of sight and out of earshot.) Third, washing can dry at its own pace in a warm, dry room – especially useful in wet weather.

> Tip: If you do not have space for a dedicated utility room, consider a utility cupboard. In a flat I once lived in, the tumble-dryer was stacked on top of the washing machine in a small cupboard, with

*space at the side to slot packets of detergent, bottles of bleach and
the ironing board.*

In addition to the washing machine and tumble-dryer, the ideal utility room would contain a sink for washing articles by hand; storage cupboards; at least one drying rack (wooden or plastic-covered wire); the laundry basket(s); the ironing board and the iron; a large table for folding items. The cupboards would be used for storing detergent, fabric conditioner and stain removal products; starch and mesh nets for washing delicates; a small box in which to put buttons or belts that have been removed before washing; needles, thread, scissors (for quick repairs, such as tightening or removing buttons); clothes brushes; a noticeboard on which to pin care labels and washing symbol charts. If there is room for it, fit a cupboard with wooden slatted shelves for storing folded laundry, either permanently or before it is taken to its normal home.

A Dutch airer, i.e. a drying rack that is attached to the ceiling and lowered by means of a rope and pulley, would also be very useful – more useful than a single drying line because you can lay articles that need to be dried flat, such as woollens, across the top.

DETERGENTS

The number of different types of laundry detergent is truly astonishing: powder, liquids, tablets, plastic things that dissolve in the wash, detergent to be put in the machine, detergent to put in the dispenser with special cups to measure it, regular detergent and 'ultra' detergent which is a stronger formulation, so you can use less.

In addition to the formulation, consider the type of clothes you will be washing and how dirty they are. For protein stains, such as egg, blood and vomit, a biological detergent, which contains enzymes, is particularly effective. Detergents that have been specially formulated for whites usually contain oxygen bleaches and/or optical brightening agents. While they will brighten whites, they can cause fading or spotting if used on coloured fabrics.

Detergents formulated for cleaning coloured clothes contain no optical brighteners or bleaches. Some even milder formulations are designed for very dark colours. These are gentler than other detergents and could be used for washing delicates, but it is far better to use a 'mild' detergent specially formulated for washing wools and other delicate fabrics such as washable silk. They generally contain no brighteners or bleaches and are often unperfumed.

We are all becoming much more aware of how many chemicals we use in the home, and it is certainly worth considering an 'eco' product if you worry about your effect on the environment. Eco detergents are usually manufactured using plant-based formulations and do not contain petrochemical ingredients, chlorine bleach or phosphates. Some do not contain enzymes or optical brighteners. There used to be issues about their effectiveness – your conscience may have been clean, but your clothes were not – but these days they are very effective. Their main claim to fame is that they have a much lesser impact on the environment than ordinary detergents, whose residues are poorly biodegradable and have a significant effect on the natural environment and on wildlife.

All the above come in powder or liquid form (sometimes as tablets or capsules respectively). Powder is generally put into the powder dispenser of the machine; liquid is put into a dispenser or directly into the machine (but follow the manufacturer's instructions).

Follow the manufacturer's guidelines on how much to use, depending on whether your water is hard or soft (see also 'Water softeners', p. 163). Whether you choose powder or liquid, it is important to use enough detergent. It is tempting to think that manufacturers deliberately tell us to use too much detergent, but this is not the case. An inadequate quantity of detergent means clothes will not wash as well. In hard-water areas, there is also a danger that minerals will build up on fabrics, causing colours to fade, whites to look dingy and fabrics to feel stiff and harsh to the touch (see 'Troubleshooting', p. 173).

If you switch between ultra and regular brands, make sure you do not inadvertently use too little or too much detergent. When buying a new brand, follow the manufacturer's instructions until you get a feel for the right amount.

159

Powder detergents: For large families and people who do a lot of washing, powder is the most economical option because it is cheap, efficient and goes a long way. It is particularly effective at dealing with ground-in dirt, but it can cause fading and, if not dissolved properly, spots on coloured fabrics (this is more likely at low-temperature washes). Low-temperature washes in hard-water areas can also cause a built-up of powder which can clog washing machines and drains, and in the worst cases causes a thick white sludge that sets like concrete. If you are fairly scrupulous about maintenance washes (see 'To maintain a washing machine', p. 168), this should not be a problem.

Liquid detergents: These are in effect ready-dissolved detergent in water. They work out more expensive than powder detergents because you are paying for that water, but they are easier to use in cold-water washes because they will not spot coloured fabrics. They are particularly effective on grease stains and food marks, and can be used straight on these stains before washing.

Tablets: These are concentrated powder in tablet form and are designed to be used either in the machine's powder dispenser or placed in a net or some other proprietary dispenser directly on top of clothes. They come ready-measured, so you will not use too much detergent and are useful in small flats or houses with limited storage, but they are not versatile: they cannot be used for pre-wash soaking, treating stains or washing by hand. And they are expensive.

Liquid capsules: These are made from concentrated liquid detergent in soluble plastic capsules. Like tablets, they come ready-measured and are useful when storage space is short. But they are expensive and cannot be used for pre-wash soaking or washing by hand. The detergent in them is concentrated and can irritate the skin if the capsules split.

160

My advice is to use powder detergent for most washes (one for whites, one for coloureds, ultra or regular, according to your preference) and a mild liquid detergent for woollens and/or delicate items that need to be washed by hand.

> *Tip: Old-fashioned soap flakes are also very good for washing woollens by hand (they cannot be used in a washing machine). See 'Washing laundry by hand', p. 178.*

Fabric softeners: Liquid fabric softeners, which are added to the wash, contain substances that coat the fabric, making it feel softer and plumping up the fibres. As well as softening, they are designed to reduce static and make ironing easier. They are useful in areas where the water is very hard and are particularly effective when washing woollens and man-made fibres that are prone to static. But they can cause skin problems in certain sensitive people, and according to some schools of thought it is not washing powder that clogs up washing machines but fabric softener, especially in hard-water areas. Used too often, the coating they leave on fabrics will build up, making the garment feel greasy and reducing absorbency.

Use fabric softener when it is really needed. If you live in a soft-water area, you will not need it. Even you live in a hard-water area, you may find that you do not need to use a fabric softener for every wash. Do not use on items that are designed to be absorbent, such as tea towels, towels (but see 'Troubleshooting', p. 173) and cotton T-shirts. Used with discretion, fabric softeners are a useful weapon in the household armoury.

If you have a tumble-dryer, you could forgo liquid fabric softener and use fabric softener sheets instead, which go in with the load as it is drying. They are especially useful for reducing static on clothes made from synthetic fabrics or when something needs extra softness. Do not use them all the time – use every three four washes to prevent build-up of the product on clothes.

A green alternative is tumble-dryer balls. These are spiky rubber balls, which go into the tumble-dryer with the clothes and soften fabrics by friction.

BLEACH

To bleach something means to whiten it. The chemical in bleach (usually sodium hypochlorite or hydrogen peroxide) oxidises organic compounds within dyes, thus rendering them soluble so that they can be washed away. If not used correctly, bleach can seriously fade and weaken cloth or make it go into holes. Should we be using bleach? In short, no – at least not in every wash as a matter of course.

Modern automatic washing machines wash so well that heavy bleaching should really be a thing of the past. This can only be a good thing. Bleach is extremely toxic, so should be used only when really necessary.

Where bleach does come in handy is for heavily stained garments, or if you need to sanitise something – e.g. kitchen cloths, or clothes or linens that have been used by someone who has been ill. Do not get into the habit of using bleach all the time.

> *Tip: One of the most powerful bleaches is sunlight. The same action that causes your curtains, pictures and soft furnishings to fade can be put to good effect when laundering. Sunlight has the same drawbacks of yellowing of whites (in the long term) and fading of colours, but has the huge bonus of being completely free. For full instructions, see 'Line-drying', p. 180.*

Chlorine bleach (main bleaching agent: sodium hypochlorite): This cheap product is the strongest household bleach. It whitens whites (though too much will cause them to go yellow), brightens colourfast colours, removes stains and mildew, and sanitises and deodorises. But it also fades coloured fabrics; it is highly toxic, poisonous if swallowed, and can give off choking fatal fumes if mixed with other substances. Chlorine bleach should never be used on silk, wool, leather, nylon, many of the synthetic fabrics used to make sportswear (e.g. triacetate, polyamide, Lycra) and fabrics with special finishes, and is not recommended on any other sheer or delicate fabric.

> Note: Chlorine bleach will deteriorate over time. If a bottle is more than 12 months old, discard it.

Before bleaching, check for colourfastness. Make a solution (1 tsp of bleach to 1 teacup of cold water) and soak a small, inconspicuous corner of the garment to be bleached in it. Wait 10 minutes to see if the colour fades or changes in any way, and then press between two pieces of paper towel to check for colour run. Allow to dry, then check again.

To use chlorine bleach: Do not use more bleach than is recommended by the manufacturers (normally 3/4 cup for a standard load). Add bleach to water and mix thoroughly before adding items to be bleached. Do not pour straight bleach on to them. When prewashing, soak for the recommended time (usually 30 minutes). If it is more convenient to soak overnight, use half as much bleach. After soaking, rinse thoroughly in clear water before washing.

Oxygen bleach (main bleaching agents: hydrogen peroxide, sodium percarbonate): This is a more recent addition to the cleaning repertoire. It is sometimes called 'all-purpose' or 'all-fabric' bleach. It is gentler than chlorine bleach, thus it can be used on a wider range of fabrics; and it is safe on non-colourfast fabrics. But it cannot restore whiteness once it has been lost.

Oxygen bleach is normally added to the wash at the beginning. Put a scoop of bleach either directly on top of the wash or in the special plastic dispenser that comes with some makes.

ENZYME STAIN REMOVERS

Pre-wash detergents called 'biological' contain enzymes. They are invaluable for removing protein-based and other organic stains, such as blood, eggs, milk, urine, vomit, sweat, chocolate, fats and oils, starch and grass stains.

They are effective at temperatures between 104 and 140°F (warm and hot temperatures), which means they can be safely used on most fabrics, apart from wools, silks and some other delicate fabrics. Check the manufacturer's instructions for suitability before proceeding. The most readily available in the UK are Bio-Tex and Vanish, but new ones are always coming on the market.

Soak garments for half an hour so before rinsing and then washing as normal. The great thing about these products is that you can remove most stains without resorting to more complicated or harsher stain removal products. If stains persist, turn to 'An A–Z of fabric stains', p. 307.

> Note: Chlorine bleach deactivates enzymes, so if you are planning to bleach items, do so after soaking. It is generally safe to mix chlorine bleach with enzyme products and washing detergents, but check the label on the box/bottle first.

WATER SOFTENERS

If you live in a hard-water area, it is a good idea to add a proprietary water softener, which comes in either powder, liquid or tablet form. The best-known make is Calgon. Water softeners reduce limescale in the washing machine and mean you can use less detergent and can often do without fabric conditioner, thereby saving money. I like it for this and the effect of soft water on my clothes.

STARCH

Nothing beats the feel of crisp, starched cottons and linens. For a while only cold-water and spray-on starches were available, but traditional hot-water starch is now being made again and there are several brands available.

To use, the usual method is to mix starch with a little cold water, then add enough hot water, depending on whether you want a light, medium or heavy stiffness. Immerse the items to be starched in the mixture, then spin or wring out. Either iron while still damp, using a hot iron, or allow to dry and iron later. Before ironing, sprinkle the linens with water.

LAUNDRY SCHEDULES

Until about 50 years ago, housework was run on a cast-iron routine, and Monday was always wash-day. This was partly because it was back-breaking work and it made sense to do it at the beginning of the week after the day of rest on Sunday.

For single people or couples, doing all the laundry on one day a week can still make sense (for further discussion on housework routines, see 'Schedules', p. 289).

It is far more economical and efficient to do it all on one day than to do little bits throughout the week. Apart from anything else, a constantly running machine is an unwelcome reminder that dirty clothes – like the poor – are always with us.

For large families, a weekly wash-day causes unnecessary strain, but try not to do washing every day of the week.

If this is impossible, a busy mother of two suggests the following:

Buy four large laundry baskets – one for hot-wash cottons, one for warm-wash coloured cottons, one for delicates/wool and one for items that need to be washed by hand.
Every morning wash the contents of the basket that is the fullest.
Every evening collect all the dirty things and fill the baskets for the next day.
Every Monday do the hand-wash.

Total time spent sorting the laundry is about five minutes a day and there is always a full load for the washing machine.

164

TO REDUCE LAUNDRY

Dust and dirt cause fabrics to wear out. Substances such as sweat or spilt food also attack fabrics. Washable clothes and household linens should therefore be washed when they look, feel or smell dirty. Underwear, socks and very sweaty sportswear should be washed after each wearing.

However, washing can itself cause fabrics to wear out. I have seen a silk shirt literally worn into holes by over-zealous washing. All too often, laziness makes us wash more than we need. It is far easier to fling a piece of clothing into the dirty linen basket than it is to brush it and hang it up to air before folding it and putting it away. If you have worn a garment for only a few hours, always consider this before automatically putting it in the wash. Others ways to reduce laundry:

Hang towels to dry after use. If they sit in a damp pile on the floor, they will start to smell musty.
Always wear an apron when cooking and put on overalls when doing any dirty job.
Always make the bed so that bedding stays clean throughout the day.
Use napkins when eating.

Ban non-washable paints, pens and ink from the house.

Use a tray to carry food and drinks from one room to another (this also
  protects carpets).

Sorting laundry

Before doing a wash, sort laundry into different piles. Generally, this divides along lines of different fabrics, different wash temperatures and different colours. Study the care labels that must by law be sewn into garments, which will tell you if a garment can be washed – or whether it should only be dry-cleaned – and, if so, at what temperature, and whether it can be bleached or tumble-dried, along with any other instructions, such as whether it should washed inside out, or whether it is better not to wash it with biological detergent.

Begin by setting aside any very dirty items, to be washed separately, as well as any items to be washed separately by hand.

With the remainder, sort first according to colour – whites, light coloured and darks. Very light colours that you are sure are colourfast can go in with the whites if you are not planning to use bleach. Less light colours can go in with a darker load. If you have a really huge amount, sort by colour – so you have a blue/lilac pile, a pink/red pile, a grey/black pile and so forth. If you are scrupulous at this stage, you are less likely to have colour-run incidents.

Then sort the piles according to wash temperature. Try to sort into items of the same weight and type of fabric, so that heavy fabric will not snag or tear more delicate ones. Put delicate items in a mesh wash bag to protect them.

There used to be umpteen wash cycles on machines, but manufacturers have now cottoned on to the fact that most people use only one or two of them, so they have reduced the number of general cycles, but have introduced others, such as a hand-wash cycle. These days, most people use variations on a warm wash for most fabrics. Modern detergents are designed to wash efficiently at low temperatures and this is the most eco-friendly thing to do (although sometimes, whites can seem a little dingy after repeated low-temperature washes – see p. 174). It also suits delicate fabrics, such as woollens. In addition, people will

165

sometimes use a hot wash for very dirty sturdy white and colourfast cottons and a warm wash for synthetics. Washing machines use a lot of energy, so always wash a full load, or use a half-load or economy programme if your machine has one. Always wash at the lowest temperature you can – it is much more ecologically sound. A warm wash uses about half as much as energy as a hot wash.

> *Tip: Remember that you can always wash garments at a lower temperature than the one recommended. If, for example, you have a couple of only slightly soiled cotton shirts that can be washed warm, alongside a large pile to be washed cold, wash them all together at the lower temperature.*

To test for colourfastness: Until you have washed a garment, do not assume that it is colourfast. If you are not sure, add 1 tsp of detergent to a teacup of warm water and saturate an inconspicuous corner with it. Press between two pieces of white paper towel, and if the colour comes off, wash separately or with like colours. Some dyes cease to bleed after a few washes; others, such as the indigo dye on jeans, never seem to become colourfast.

166

The washing machine

In the 1930s, when my grandmother was bringing up her family, household linens, such as sheets, were sent out to the laundry and the washerwoman came once a week to help with the rest of the washing. It was only on reading a book called *The Complete Household Adviser*, which was published around that time, that I realised how extremely unusual she was in that she had a washing machine, bought for her by my grandfather, who was constantly fascinated by anything new or innovative. The machine was American or Canadian and pretty rudimentary by today's standards, but a rarity in between-the-wars Norwich.

Even in the 1960s twin-tub machines similar to the one my grandmother used were still pretty much the norm: there was a tub which was filled via a hose from the tap. The water was heated up, detergent was added and the dirty clothes were put in, and the washing was done by an agitator. When the washing was done, the clothes were lifted out with large wooden tongs and put into a second tub, containing clean water, for rinsing. Some older models included a mangle for squeezing water out of the wet washing.

Automatic washing machines of the type with which we are now familiar only really became commonplace in British households in the 1970s. According to the latest statistics, 99 per cent of households with two adults and two children have a washing machine, and even in one-person households, the figure is 78 per cent.

Our great-grandmothers would have been astonished to think that we can just fling dirty laundry into a machine, switch it on and come back an hour later to find the clothes washed and spun nearly dry, and that another machine could then dry it for you.

When you consider the ease with which we can now get clothes clean, the time, effort and labour saved, how there is no need for anyone ever to have dirty clothes, and how much sweeter-smelling and is when there is a plentiful supply of clean clothes, a washing machine seems little short of a modern miracle.

CHOOSING A WASHING MACHINE

167

When buying, check energy efficiency, energy consumption, water consumption and noise levels. Ask the sales assistant for advice, and note that this information will be on the label. Most large electrical appliances in the US must carry an EnergyGuide label, which shows how efficient the appliance is relative to others. Noise levels are usually indicated somewhere in the product documentation. Only the most rigorous eco-warrior would consider not having a washing machine (few eco-warriors, I find, are women with a large family to wash for), but we can all do our bit by choosing the most energy-efficient model we can and by using the machine sensibly.

Front-loaders: The majority of washing machines sold in the UK are front-loading automatic machines. The clothes are put into a drum, which rotates. As the clothes are turned and tumbled in the drum, soapy water is forced through the fibres, and it is this action, together with the fibres rubbing against each other, that cleans the laundry.

Front-loading machines clean well but gently, making for less wear and tear on clothes, and rinse well, which is good for clothes and for people with sensitive skins. They also dry clothes well because of their fast spinning, saving energy, money and time. Some have a limited size, which could be a problem in large families, but larger machines are becoming more and more commonly available.

Top-loaders: Top-loading machines, which are normally found in launderettes in Britain, but which are the norm in American households, clean clothes by means of a central winged post in the tub, which agitates the clothes back and forwards. They have a large capacity, making them good for larger families, and you can retrieve or add items of laundry throughout the wash cycle, but they clean less than front-loaders (hence the American addiction to bleach) and cause more wear and tear on clothes, owing to the agitation of the central post.

Washer-dryers: These combined washing machines and tumble-dryers are worth considering only in households that are very short of space. Although they have improved in recent years, washer-dryers still tend not to wash as well as standard machines because wash times are shorter. Their main drawbacks are that you have to wait to dry clothes and you cannot dry a full wash load: you have to take the damp washing out and divide it in half for drying so as not to overload the machine, leaving piles of wet washing lying about.

TO MAINTAIN A WASHING MACHINE

Always leave the washing machine door open when it is not in use. This allows any water inside to evaporate, so it cannot stagnate and breed bacteria.

Sometimes washing machines can get extremely smelly. The problem seems to be waste water getting trapped and going stagnant. Bacteria multiply in the water, and these are what cause the foul smell. Unfortunately, the smell is extremely pungent and long-lasting and will permeate every load of washing.

There is some evidence that things are made worse by the modern habit of washing everything at low temperatures, so you could start by running the machine empty on a hot wash with a little detergent to see if this sorts it out.

If the smell remains, check your connections. Where the washing machine is plumbed into the same outlet as the sink, waste water from the sink can run into the machine's sump or pump. It then sits in the machine and begins to smell. If the washer has its own waste pipe, check that there is a trap in it.

168

Without one, foul odours from the drain come up the pipe into the machine.

If you are a plumbing novice like me, or are in doubt about what to do, call a plumber or washing machine technician to make the necessary adjustments to your pipework. If the plumbing all seems OK, a little regular maintenance should sort out any problems.

Once a week: Check the rubber door seal, in case water is lurking inside it. Water in the seal is one of the main reasons that washing machines can smell musty. Wipe it clean, and if it does smell musty or mould has developed, wipe with a weak solution of bleach.

Check the powder dispenser. Pull it right out to make sure there is no build-up of detergent and/or fabric conditioner in the cavity. It is amazing how quickly you can get a thick build-up inside it. If you do, there is nothing for it but to scrape it out – use a kitchen spatula. Then clean the dispenser drawer.

> *Tip: I often put the dispenser drawer in the dishwasher on a short, low-temperature programme, to no ill effect.*

If your washing machine has a filter, remove and clean it. This is normally located behind a door at the bottom of the machine. Put a bowl under the filter – filters can discharge a surprising amount of water. You will find that it will be full of bits of fluff and limescale. Rinse it out and put it back, remembering to close tightly.

It is extremely important to do this. Otherwise, the washing machine will not be able to drain and you will find yourself faced with a service fee for an technician, who just empties the filter and charges you for it. I speak from experience.

Once a month: Do a maintenance wash, if you can run your washer empty. Set the machine on a hot wash with a little detergent. Alternatively, put a little straight bleach or white vinegar (not both) in the powder dispenser, or a cup of washing soda crystals in the drum, and run the machine on a warm cycle.

In either case, do not put any clothes in the drum at the same time.

If the machine is neglected, you may need to use a proprietary washing machine cleaner. But try the above methods first.

To descale a washing machine: Put a cup of vinegar in the detergent dispenser and run the machine empty through a full hot cycle.

Doing the laundry

Before putting clothes in the machine, empty out all pockets, fasten buttons, zips and buckles. Do up bras. Tie loose sashes, and button sleeves to the front of blouses and shirts to prevent them tangling up. Remove any belts and large buckles, and check that buttons are not loose; if they are, fix them before washing. Sometimes it is better to remove delicate buttons and sew them on again after laundering. Mend any small tears, which are likely to become bigger in the wash.

Check for staining, especially for grease spots or protein stains such as blood, which will set if exposed to heat, and deal with them before washing (see 'An A–Z of fabric stains', p. 307). For grimy collars and cuffs, rub in a little straight dish soap, or use a stick stain remover (dish soap is cheaper and just as effective).

> Tip: Dish soap also works well on greasy marks, which is unsurprising when you consider that removing grease is what it is designed to do.

Turn jeans inside out to reduce colour run. Other items such as fleeces also benefit from being washed inside out because they are prone to pilling, known in the UK as bobbles.

Wash sets of things together – e.g. sets of underwear, coloured sets of bedding, pairs of socks. This way, they will all wear at the same rate.

Do not overload the machine, because the water will be unable to circulate round the drum, leaving the clothes soapy and dingy. You can usually gauge by eye how much your machine can take – no more than three-quarters full is a good guide.

> Counsel of perfection: With a new washing machine, consult the instruction manual for optimum washing loads and weigh your first few loads on bathroom scales to get an idea of how much the machine can take.

Add detergent, fabric conditioner and/or bleach, if using.

TO WASH WOOLLENS

With gentle handling and a bit of common sense, woollens can be washed and worn for years. The most common problem with them is that they shrink or felt in the wash. This is caused by washing at too high temperatures, rough handling when washing by hand, and drying in a tumble-dryer or with direct heat. Unfortunately there is nothing to be done about this once it has happened; shrinking is irreversible. You can prevent it, though, by remembering the following:

Never machine-wash woollens unless the label specifically states that it is safe to do so. If in doubt, wash by hand and wash gently (see 'To wash delicates', p. 178).

Do not tumble-dry wool unless the care label says you can; dry flat, out of direct sunlight and away from direct sources of heat.

TO WASH SYNTHETICS

By this I mean, of course, all the polyesters, acrylics, Lycra, triacetate and so on and so on. They do require a bit of care (viscose in particular shrinks like nobody's business), so always use a special synthetics programme on the washing machine.

Synthetics can crease if you use the wrong wash programme (polyesters and other synthetics should normally be washed on a programme that includes either an anti-crease cycle or rinse-hold), or if you overload the machine, so clothes cannot move about. Washing at too high a temperature, leaving wet washing in the machine for long periods, over-drying, and leaving dried clothes in the tumble-dryer for long periods can also cause creasing. If this happens, you can either grin and bear it, or wash again at a lower temperature in a smaller load and using the right synthetics programme. ·

To prevent creasing, always check the care label for the correct wash programme and temperature; remove washing from the machine as soon as it is feasible to do so; do not tumble-dry at high temperature; remove clothes from the dryer promptly and fold or hang up.

TO WASH SPORTSWEAR

Considering that sportswear is designed for rugged use, it is surprisingly demanding. Look at the care labels. Much sportswear should not be laundered with fabric conditioner; or should not be tumble-dried; or should be washed inside out, which means that the outside does not always get clean.

Many modern fabrics are designed to 'wick' away moisture. This means that, while you are exercising, sweat is drawn out of the fabric, keeping your body dry. But while the moisture is drawn out, the bacteria that cause clothes to smell sweaty remain and seem to set indelibly into the fabric. To compound the problem, the synthetic fibres from which sportswear is made (for example, triacetate, polyamide and Lycra) should be washed only at low temperatures (usually a warm synthetics cycle), which can make it more difficult to get clean.

Wash sportswear as soon as possible after wearing. Do not let it sit in a sports bag, allowing mud and sweat to dry in and grass stains to set.

Soak in a lukewarm solution of enzyme pre-wash detergent, if available, for an hour or so. Wash according to the instructions on the care label. Dry naturally, not in a tumble-dryer, and iron, if necessary, using a cool iron on the reverse of the fabric.

Some washing machines now have a sportswear programme that includes long pre-wash soak and super-rinse cycles. If you are replacing your machine and have a lot of sporty types in your family, look for this feature.

172

Apart from sweat (and occasionally blood), the three stains on sportswear are mud, grass and (on cricket whites) red polish from the ball. For advice on removing all of these, see 'An A–Z of fabric stains', p. 307.

To revive dingy whites, soak for up to an hour in a solution of Calgon water softener, diluted according to instructions, rinse thoroughly, then wash as usual.

TO WASH COTTONS

Cotton is the most versatile of fabrics – light, yet strong and durable, and with the ability to take deep dyes and to be woven into different weights and textures, from the lightest muslin to heavy towelling. Cotton is also very forgiving, washes like a dream and can withstand quite hard handling.

Although cottons can be washed at very high temperatures, all except very hardy cottons will eventually fade or even shrink with repeated hot washes. A warm wash will be adequate for most cleaning purposes.

For best results use detergents specifically designed for whites or coloureds. Turn coloured cotton clothes inside out and in most cases wash warm. Cotton creases easily, so iron while still damp.

TROUBLESHOOTING

Even if you wash carefully, problems can arise in the laundry. Most, however, are easily remedied. The checklist below details some of the commonest problems and how to solve them.

Bobbles on clothes: Bobbles (pilling) can appear on any fabric, but are particularly noticeable on wool. They are a consequence of normal wear and tear and as such are virtually unavoidable.

What to do: Pick off bobbles from woollens by hand, or with sticky tape (as with lint, see below), or using a special lint-removing device (widely available). Pilling is virtually impossible to remove from poly-cotton bed linen.

How to prevent it: Because pilling is a result of normal wear and tear, it is difficult to prevent. Wash clothes inside out and use a fabric softener, so that at least most of the pilling is on the inside. Or wash in a mesh washing bag to prevent items rubbing against other fabrics during the wash. Once poly-cotton bed linen has started pilling, it is often very uncomfortable to sleep on, so replace.

Blue or pink spots or streaks: These streaks are caused by undissolved particles of powder detergent or fabric softener left on clothes.

What to do: Soak in a solution of white vinegar (I cup to I quart water), then rinse and wash again, at the correct temperature using the correct amount of detergent.

How to prevent it: Never put undiluted fabric softener on clothes, and use the correct amount of detergent so that it all dissolves. If you suspect powder detergent is not dissolving in low-temperature washes, use a liquid detergent instead.

Colour run: Colours run because of inadequate sorting of laundry. Non-colourfast fabrics will shed dye on to the rest of the washing load during the wash (who has not sat by helplessly as one fugitive red sock dyes all the white sheets pink?). This is the most obvious cause, but colours can also run if you let wet washing sit in the machine, or even if you tumble-dry mixed loads of colourfast and non-colourfast clothes.

What to do: Wash the clothes again, immediately before they have dried and the dye has set. You may have to use bleach (oxygen bleach for coloureds, chlorine bleach for whites). You may have to rewash more than once.

173

If this does not work, soak overnight in a solution of biological detergent, then wash again – or try a specialist colour run remover. For whites, the best of these is Rit Color Remover, which can be used to soak whites and then added to the machine when washing. Runs with coloureds can be problematic, and extra care should be taken beforehand to avoid the need to solve this problem.

How to prevent it: It is easy to avoid colour runs. Be scrupulous when sorting the laundry before washing.

If you are not sure of a new garment's colourfastness, do a colour test first (see 'To test for colourfastness', p. 166).

Do not leave wet washing in the machine for any length of time, because dye can transfer. Similarly do not put wet loads of white and non-colourfast fabrics together, e.g. in the laundry basket before drying or ironing.

Do not tumble-dry white and non-colourfast loads together.

Use a colour-catcher. This is like a sheet of thick, furry paper. One sheet (or several if the load is heavily dyed) is put into the washing machine along with the wash and it 'catches' the colour run. Use common sense: you cannot expect one of these sheets to catch all the colour if you were to put, say, a new pair of jeans in with a load of white towels. The best-known make in the US is Shout Color Catcher.

Wash clothes that run separately or with articles of like colour.

Dingy whites: White fabrics go grey if you don't use enough detergent. The dirt lifted out during the wash falls out of suspension in the water and instead of being carried away, gets deposited back on the clothes. Greying also happens if you regularly wash at low temperatures, use a detergent not designed for whites, or overload the machine so that dirt cannot be lifted away. Dyes from non-colourfast clothes can get transferred in mixed loads, turning white fabrics grey.

What to do: Soak white cotton in biological washing powder for an hour or so before washing. You may want to make this one of the rare occasions you use chlorine bleach (if appropriate for the fabric) – see 'Bleach', p. 161. After soaking/bleaching, wash at the highest temperature the fabric can take and run an extra rinse cycle (or use the super-rinse facility if your machine has one). Dry outside if possible, in full sunlight.

How to prevent it: Follow the care label instructions as to the correct wash temperature, using the correct amount of detergent, and not overloading the washing machine.

Fading: With repeated washings, all dyes will eventually fade, but the natural fading will be increased by over-use of too harsh detergents and over-washing or washing at too high temperatures. Bleach will fade colours, as will exposure to sunlight. Another possible cause is inadequate rinsing, which leaves a powdery detergent residue on the fabric.

What to do: It is not possible to restore colour that has gone. If something is very precious, you might try dyeing it, but the results are generally disappointing, and if the fading is patchy, the new colour will be, too. If you suspect that the fading is due to powder residue, try the following:

Soak clothes in a solution of white vinegar and water (½ pint of vinegar to 4 pints of water). Use hot water, at a temperature appropriate to the fabric, and soak clothes for an hour. Then rinse and wash as usual, using the correct amount of detergent.

How to prevent: Wash clothes less frequently. Always use a special detergent designed for coloured clothes and do not use bleach. Turn clothes inside out for washing and drying, and if drying outdoors, dry inside out, out of direct sunlig

Hard towels: Towels (and washcloths) become hard if you don't use enough washing powder, resulting in a build-up of minerals in the cloth, or if you don't rinse them adequately, or if they are dried at too high a temperature.

What to do: Soak towels in a solution of water softener, such as Calgon (2 tbsp to a gallon of water) for an hour or so.

Alternatively, soak the towels in a plastic bucket or bowl in a solution of 1 pint white vinegar to 1 gallon of hot water (from the tap) for 20 minutes. Rinse, then wash as usual on a hot wash. This should remove mineral particles trapped in the fibres.

After soaking, wash towels on a hot wash using the correct amount of detergent and run the rinse cycle a couple of times (or use a super-rinse cycle if your machine has it), to ensure all the detergent is removed. Add a cup of white vinegar to the dispenser drawer of the machine during rinsing.

175

Fabric softener is not usually recommended for towels because it can reduce their absorbency. But if used occasionally, it will make towels feel soft and fluffy again.

> Note: Wash new towels without fabric softener until they have lost their glassy shininess, then use as and when needed.

The motion of a tumble-dryer seems to soften towels. If you have not used fabric softener in the wash, tumble-dry occasionally with a fabric softener sheet.

How to prevent it: Always use the correct amount of detergent. If tumble-drying, take towels out of the dryer before they are bone-dry to prevent drying out the fibres. If drying on a radiator, remove them while they are still slightly damp.

Lint: Lint is an inevitable part of the washing process: bits of fuzz and fibre wear off fabrics during washing. Some fabrics such as new towels produce more lint than others, and some fabrics, particularly polyester and fleeces, seem to attract it. Other causes are tissues left in pockets and not using enough detergent. When washing, detergent lifts dirt and bits of lint from the fabric and holds it in suspension in the water, to be rinsed and drained away. If not enough detergent is used, the lint will be deposited back on the clothes, along with the dirt. Over-drying in the tumble-dryer will cause a build-up of static that attracts lint.

What to do: Remove lint from affected clothes using a clothes brush or lint-removing brush, whose surface is covered with tiny barbs that catch the lint. Or wrap sticky tape, sticky side up, round your hand and pat garment all over.

How to prevent it: Always empty pockets before washing clothes. Wash new towels separately until they have shed most of their lint. Always wash and dry lint-shedding fabrics separately from lint-attracting ones. Wash lint-attracting fabrics, such as fleeces, inside out, so at least the lint sticks to the inside. Do not over-dry in a tumble-dryer, and empty the lint filter in the tumble-dryer more frequently. A new product is lint-grabbers. These are balls made from microfibre which are put in the washing machine or tumble-dryer and attract bits of fluff, hair and tissue.

Wrinkled collars and shirt fronts: Incorrect washing temperature causes stiffening facings to shrink at different rates from the collars and button bands, puckering the top fabric.

What to do: Difficult to treat. Try steam-ironing the garment when damp and pulling it gently back into shape.

How to prevent it: Wash at a lower temperature to prevent shrinking.

Yellowing of whites: Whites go yellow from sweat and anti-perspirant stains under arms. As fabrics age, they will yellow from lack of use (one reason why it is a false economy to buy too much bed linen and then never use it), but the process will be increased if they are dried at too high temperatures or if clothes and linens have been stored in hot places such as in airing cupboards or near radiators, or if they have been stored in dry-cleaners' plastic bags. Although sunlight bleaches clothes, over-exposure to sunlight can turn whites yellow, as can drying bleached clothes without rinsing out chlorine bleach.

What to do: For sweat/anti-perspirant stains, soak, using an enzyme pre-wash detergent, then wash using a biological detergent. On less hardy fabrics, rub the stain with a stain stick, such as Shout (check suitability of fabric beforehand) before washing. For more ideas, see 'An A–Z of fabric stains', p. 307. On some synthetic fabrics, however, staining is impossible to remove.

For sun yellowing, over-drying, ageing and storage marks, soak in an enzyme pre-wash detergent, and wash at the highest temperature possible (hardy cottons can be boiled). If this does not help, bleach and wash again.

Paradoxically, bleach will not work for over-bleaching. Wash with biological washing powder at the correct temperature for the fabric.

It is impossible to remove yellowing from polymers in plastic bags.

How to prevent: Wash delicate items that are vulnerable to sweat-staining as soon as possible. Do not let clothes dry for too long in direct sunlight. Store clothes and linens in cool, dry, ventilated places, away from direct heat, such as hot pipes or radiators, and use a rotation method when storing bed linen to ensure that it is all used equally (see 'Bed Linen', p. 61). Take clothes out of plastic bags as soon as you get them back from the dry-cleaner.

177

Washing laundry by hand

If in doubt, wash the following by hand: woollens, including cashmere; washable silk; lace; delicate items of underwear; tights and stockings; anything labelled 'hand wash only' (although I have been known to disregard this and take the risk of washing in the machine when a garment is past its best, or is so dirty that only machine-washing will get it clean); garments with fancy trimmings that might get broken or spoilt in the washing machine.

> *Tip: If the main body of a garment is machine-washable, but the trimmings are not, and if you are confident of your skill with a needle, remove the trimmings, wash them by hand if necessary, wash the garment in the machine and then sew the trimmings back on.*

TO WASH DELICATES

The following technique works for all the items mentioned above.

Use a mild detergent specially formulated for washing wool and/or delicates. A liquid detergent is preferable, because powders may not dissolve effectively in the cool temperatures required.

Mild dish soap designed for sensitive skins can also be used for washing delicate items. It contains no optical brighteners or bleach. Use a small amount, just enough to make a few suds.

My preference, however, is for old-fashioned soap flakes. The leading brand in the UK used to be Lux flakes, but these are no longer made. The only supplier left in Britain is Dri-Pak, which used to make Lux flakes. Soap flakes are worth hunting down because they are cheap, they contain no chemicals such as bleach or enzymes which might harm delicate fabrics, and are unperfumed, which suits people with sensitive skin, and those who dislike the strong smell of some detergents.

To use, run a small amount of very hot water into the sink, add the soap flakes and allow to dissolve before filling up the sink with barely lukewarm water.

Whatever detergent you use, the water should be no more than lukewarm.

Before washing, attend to any grime, for example around the neck, or grease marks. Put a tiny amount of mild dish soap on the mark and gently squeeze it into the mark. Do not rub or you will break the fibres. Put the item into the sink of soapy water and leave to soak briefly (no more than ten minutes) to loosen the dirt.

After its brief soak, wash by squeezing it over and over with your hands. The point about washing any delicate item is to be as gentle as possible. Do not rub too vigorously and do not wring or you will damage the fibres and pull the garment out of shape. Pay attention to the cuffs and neckline if they were grimy, or to any other marks, but avoid rubbing.

When you are satisfied that it is clean, take it out of the water and squeeze out the excess, but avoid wringing.

At least three rinses are necessary to remove all the soap. Again, use only lukewarm water and squeeze rather than rub the garment. In the final rinse, add a small amount (about half a capful) of fabric softener, swirl the garment around briefly in the rinse water, remove from the water and squeeze out excess water.

Lay the garment on a flat, clean, white towel and pull gently into shape. Roll up the towel and leave in a warm (not hot) place for half an hour to start the drying process. Finish drying by laying flat on a drying rack out of direct sunlight.

Press, if necessary, on the reverse using a cool iron (follow care label).

179

An even gentler method: This is the way to deal with very delicate silks. It is also a last resort if you have taken something to the dry-cleaner but he has not been able to lift a stain. Try it – the garment is unwearable, so you have nothing to lose.

Fill a bowl with barely lukewarm water and, once it is full, add a drop of uncoloured, unperfumed, mild dish soap (you do not want bubbles).

Put the item in the water, stir it gently and leave for 15 minutes. Then stir again, moving it gently through the water, and leave for another 15 minutes.

Rinse in barely lukewarm water, again gently moving the item about to remove the detergent residue. Add half a cup of vinegar to the final rinse – it brings out the colours.

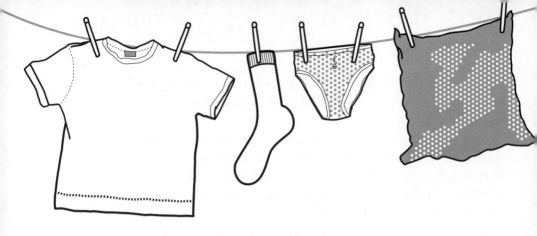

Drying laundry

For preference, washing should always be dried outside in the open air. But electric tumble-dryers have their uses, especially in a wet country like Britain. In flats, which often have no outside access, they may be the only option; some leases may preclude your drying washing outside. Used intelligently, tumble-dryers can help reduce ironing to a bare minimum (See 'Further non-ironing tips', p. 191).

LINE-DRYING

Is there anything more cheering than seeing freshly washed clothes billowing in the breeze as they dry on the line? No detergent manufacturer has yet been able to produce a product that replicates the unique, delightful smell of washing that has been dried in the open air. Other benefits include the bleaching and sanitising effect of sunlight and, best of all, the fact that it is totally free.

On the other hand, you are totally dependent on the weather, and there are a few other drawbacks. Clothes can feel stiff after drying, and sunlight can fade susceptible coloured fabrics. Stretchy fabrics and down-filled items cannot be dried flat, except on a rotary dryer.

For choice, the best weather for drying laundry is a warm, dry and sunny day with a good breeze. On warm, humid, windless days the washing never seems to dry, and on very cold days the washing will freeze.

Always wipe the washing line or rotary dryer with a damp cloth before pegging washing to it. Check that clothespins are clean too. Wash occasionally in a bowl of warm water and dish soap. Wooden clothes pegs look pleasingly retro; plastic ones with a spring are more readily available.

As you hang each garment on the line, give it a good shake; pull T-shirts and so forth into shape, smoothing seams, collars and pockets flat.

Peg out clothes so that the wind can billow into them to reduce drying time, making sure there is an ample overhang so that clothes do not slip off the line. With particularly heavy items, such as blankets, you will probably have to hang them over two lines so that they do not drag on the ground.

Dry coloured items in the shade to prevent fading, or turn them inside out to dry. They will still fade on the inside, but it will be less noticeable. If pegging the ends of two garments together to save space and clothes pegs, ensure that both garments are colourfast; otherwise you might leave dye marks.

Take down anything that is to be ironed while it is still damp and, if not ironing straight away, roll up in a clean towel to keep it damp.

As you unpeg each garment, give it a sharp snap, like a whip crack, and fold it before putting it in the laundry basket. Do not put everything in higgledy-piggledy, or it will get creased and wrinkled. By folding each item methodically, you may be able to reduce ironing, or avoid it altogether. Take down towels while they are still damp and, if possible, give them a short tumble in the dryer to fluff them up.

181

To line-dry blouses and shirts: Hang them upside down, opening both sides out and pinning at the tails.

Delicate blouses should be dried flat, but the more robust can be line-dried. If you do not want the pegs to mark the fabric of a delicate blouse, a useful trick is to use a clean old stocking (or cut an old pair of tights in half) and thread it through both sleeves. Then peg the stocking to the line (two pegs at the sleeve ends and one in the middle at the neck.

Or:

Hang on a rust-proof clothes hanger and peg the hanger to the line.

To line-dry dresses: Hang by the shoulders or hang on a rust-proof clothes hanger and peg the hanger to the line.

To line-dry pillowcases: Peg one side of the opening, so that the pillowcase sags open and can billow in the wind.

To line-dry sheets: Fold hem to hem; fold one hem over the line, peg using three pegs. Peg the two corners of the other hem just inside the first two, so that the wind can get inside the sheet. It should billow out like a sail.

To line-dry skirts: Peg one side of the waistband to the line and allow the skirt to sag open so that the wind billows though it. Or hang on a rust-proof hanger and peg the hanger to the line.

To line-dry socks: Hang by the toe, in pairs if possible.

To line-dry T-shirts: Shake T-shirts well before hanging on the line. Pull into shape and smooth seams. Peg, hems together, at both corners. Shake again when taking off the line before folding.

To line-dry towels: Shake towels well before hanging by the corners. Shake again when taking off the line.

182

To line-dry trousers and shorts: Peg at the waistband, letting the trousers sag open to catch the breeze.

To line-dry underwear: Peg big knickers and men's underpants at the waistband. Peg flimsy underwear such as thongs at the gusset. Hang bras in half over the line and peg in the middle.

DRYING LAUNDRY FLAT

Many garments should be dried flat, particularly woollens and stretchy knits which might lose their shape if hung on the line.

Shake the damp clothes well and pull gently into shape; fold in sleeves so that they do not hang down, and lay across the rungs of a drying rack. If you are worried that the garments may sag between the rails of the drying rack, lay a clean, dry, colourfast towel across the top and dry the garment flat on top of it. Put the drying rack in a warm, dry place, but not in front of direct heat.

Note: Never dry clothes directly on a radiator because they can shrink, become hard or turn yellow.

TUMBLE-DRYING

Tumble-drying dries clothes effectively, and is useful where there are no facilities for drying outside. It can also be set to go on when you are out at work or at night. Conversely, tumble-dryers are relatively expensive to run, not terribly environmentally friendly and can cause shrinkage of clothes. However, in a wet country like Britain, they are invaluable. You can reduce their environmental impact to some extent by using them only when you have a full load to dry – do not use for just one or two items.

Most things can be tumble-dried. If in doubt, look at the care label. As a general rule, do not tumble-dry: rubber, fine, delicate knits, most acetate, Lycra, delicate fibres and fabrics – including most wool unless the care label says otherwise.

Sort clothes for drying as you do for washing. Keep matched sets together, turn clothes inside out, remove belts, buckles and sashes which could tangle the clothes inside the dryer, put delicate and/or small items in mesh bags.

Non-colourfast items can bleed on to lighter colours in the dryer, so do not mix the two.

Separate slow-drying items such as towels, jeans and heavy cottons from quicker-drying items such as sheets and pillowcases, T-shirts, shirts and other lighter-weight cottons and linens. Synthetics dry even more quickly.

Separate clothes that shed lint such as towels from those that tend to attract it, such as garments made from polyester and fleeces. To avoid linting, turn garments inside out to dry.

If using fabric softener sheets, sort your drying loads into things that need them and those that do not. Things that need to be absorbent, such as tea towels and bath-towels, do not need them.

Dry clothes at a corresponding temperature to that at which they were washed (high temperature wash = high temperature drying and so forth).

The way to get the best out of your dryer is not to overdo it. Over-drying causes clothes to shrink and wrinkle. Sometimes light-coloured items can go yellow and synthetic items can be ruined.

When filling the tumble-dryer, shake out the clothes one by one then throw them into the dryer in a loose pile. Do not overfill – there needs to be room in the dryer for the clothes to tumble.

Always check the filter and remove any fluff and check that the water tray in condenser models has been emptied.

Do not aim to get things bone-dry. Linen in particular needs moisture to keep its suppleness, and over-drying towels can damage their fibres, making them harsh and hard. Remove clothes from the dryer when there is still a hint of dampness in the seams or at waistbands. Apart from reducing the danger of over-drying garments, it is easier to iron fabrics when they are still slightly damp.

Remove all clothes promptly. Do not leave piles of dried clothes lying in the dryer. They will get wrinkled, undoing all your good work, and you will need to iron things that would otherwise not need ironing.

Anything that is to be ironed should be rolled up and covered so that it remains damp until you are ready to iron. Otherwise, take out each garment, shake it and give it a snap so that it makes a whip-crack noise. Pull it gently into shape, smoothing out seams, straightening edges and so on, then fold neatly or put on a hanger and allow it to dry completely before putting it away.

Ironing

Some people claim to love ironing. One of the most charming of Beatrix Potter's characters is Mrs Tiggy-Winkle, who boasts that she is an 'excellent clear-starcher'. There is even a website devoted to the joys of ironing – the 'World Famous Ironing Cam', which promises a live webcam of a woman ironing. I came upon it by accident once when researching an article and it was with some trepidation that I went into the site. The internet is such an anarchic place, who knew what pervy suburban fantasies were being fulfilled?

In fact, the webcam was not working and the site turned out to be a perfectly clean, if slightly bonkers, celebration of ironing, with the express aim of bringing 'all the people of the world together, one crease at a time'.

In recent years the National Trust (which preserves historic UK homes) has tried hard to change its image as a charity for down-at-heel gentlefolk, and has begun to place as much emphasis on the parts of their properties once known as the 'offices' – such as the kitchens and the laundries – as on the antique-packed principal rooms upstairs. Although visitors like to see the priceless paintings and antiques, it is the 'downstairs' bits of the house that fascinate them.

In part, this popularity must be because generally we are looking at how our ancestors lived. Most of us, after all, would not have been the lord or lady living in the main part of the house; we would have led mundane, anonymous lives as the kitchen-maid, the laundry-maid, the footman or the gardener. We feel an empathy with these anonymous working people; a feeling that can only be heightened when one sees how laborious many common household tasks were in the past. Take ironing. At Dunham Massey, a National Trust property in Cheshire, there are iron laundry stoves, which were used to heat water for washing. On top of them heavy flatirons were propped to heat up. Judging the temperature was a matter of practice. To test if the iron was hot enough, the ironer licked her finger and lightly touched the surface: if it sizzled, it would do. Ironing was a particular chore in hot weather because the stove had to be kept going all day in order to reheat the irons.

To add to all this, there were no non-iron fabrics. Everything had to be ironed, and the Victorian love of frills, ribbons, smocking and other fussy adornments made the task even more difficult.

The rapid adoption of electric irons shows how much disliked ironing was. They began to appear after the First World War, and within ten years the old flatiron had disappeared. By 1929 a survey of 100 Ford employees revealed that 98 of them had the new electric irons in their homes. The first steam irons appeared in the 1940s.

Interestingly enough, even with the ease of modern equipment, ironing is still one of the most disliked household chores. In 2005 a survey by *Good Housekeeping* magazine showed that only one in six women admitted to liking ironing. Half of them did all the household ironing and only one in ten expected her husband to iron his own shirts. Pause for astonished silence …

Ever since I started keeping my own house, I have looked for ways to avoid ironing, because it is the one chore I absolutely loathe. I will spend an hour patiently cleaning one intricate piece of silver, but confronted with a pile of unironed clothes, I feel curiously depressed.

CHOOSING AN IRON

Steam irons have reduced the need for 'damping down' laundry (sprinkling it with water to get fabric in the best condition) though it will still sometimes need it – see p. 187. Steam opens the fabric's weave, allowing creases to be ironed out more efficiently, and the level and output of steam can be measured precisely for different fabrics. The higher the wattage, the greater the heat generated, so an iron of 1600W or above is suitable for general domestic use.

If you live in a hard-water area (and it's likely that you do), it is a good idea to pay more for an iron that incorporates features such as a self-cleaning function, which forces water and steam through holes in the soleplate to flush out any limescale deposits, and which has a high steam capacity.

Irons these days tend to be lighter in weight than they used to be, which makes the job less physically taxing. However, professional ironers think that a heavy iron is best. In the words of one: 'You need a little steam and a lot of lean.'

To clean the iron: There are several commercial cleaners available, which normally come in the form of a stick that you rub over a warm iron and then wipe off.

Alternatively, make a paste of baking soda and water and use it to brush the soleplate with an old toothbrush. Leave for a few minutes and scrub it off. Wipe with a damp cloth, then dry.

186

To descale a steam iron: Check the instruction manual for descaling irons with built-in anti-scale devices. Replace filters according to instructions. Anti-scale valves should be removed and soaked in vinegar. After the limescale has gone, rinse and put back in the iron.

For older-style steam irons, put some vinegar in the water tank, turn the iron on and let it steam for a few minutes. Empty, allow to cool, and rinse well with water.

HOW TO IRON LAUNDRY

There is no getting away from the fact that certain things simply must be ironed. They include:

All linens; damask tablecloths and napkins; silk; men's formal shirts; cotton bed linen – though you can get away with only ironing the pillowcases and maybe the tops of sheets if you prefer flat sheets and blankets to duvets. Poly-cotton bed linen will not need ironing, but is inferior to cotton and less comfortable to sleep in.

Most irons these days are specifically designed to be used with tap water. Using pure distilled water or softened water can actually damage the iron because they contain minerals that can build up inside, causing spitting, brown staining or premature wear and tear. Before beginning to iron, check that the steam holes are not blocked and that the soleplate is clean. If in doubt, test the iron on a clean rag. You can be sure that if you do not, you will get brown marks on your best shirt.

An ironing board should be easy to open and close, stable, sturdy and the right size for the ironer's height. It should also be well-padded. If the padding is not thick enough, buy a cover for it.

Cotton, silk and linen should be slightly damp to iron most effectively. Take clothes off the line or out of the dryer before they are completely dry. If not ironing them immediately, roll them up and put in a plastic bag until ready to iron and leave somewhere prominent so you do not forget about it and find a mildewed horror a week later. If clothes are bone-dry, dampen them with warm water, either by dipping your fingers in the water and flicking it over, or by using a spray bottle. You may also want to use a spray bottle if you go in for such folderols as scented linen water. These are scented waters (usually of lavender) that are sprayed on before ironing to scent the clothes or linens. Note that perfume can stain fabrics, so do not attempt to make your own linen waters.

After spraying, roll the clothes up and leave for an hour so that the entire garment becomes uniformly damp. Linen should be damper than cotton.

Tip: Instead of spraying, put the clothes in the tumble-dryer with a wet towel and tumble-dry for a minute or so.

Before you start ironing, have a supply of hangers ready for hanging shirts and dresses and clear a flat surface for placing folded items on.

Start by ironing things that require a cool iron first, gradually working up to the highest temperature. Check the care labels on garments for ironing instructions and, before you start ironing, close zips and hooks and eyes, but leave buttons undone.

If you suspect that the fabric may go shiny, iron on the wrong side and/or through a cloth, and always iron silk on the wrong side. To avoid shiny collars and cuffs, iron on the wrong side first, then give a quick once-over on the right side.

Avoid under-ironing: If you leave things too damp, they will feel rough and may develop a musty smell if you put them away damp. But ...

Avoid over-ironing: You can scorch fabrics or melt synthetics, while natural

187

fibres can go brittle or shiny. After ironing, the seams should still be slightly damp. Always air clothes before putting away.

After finishing ironing, empty the water chamber and store the iron in a dry place – not under the sink. Store upright, not flat on the soleplate.

To iron a shirt: This method was shown to me by Tony Luke, who has been in the dry-cleaning business for more than 40 years.

The secret with ironing shirts is the tension you place on the fabric. If you pull it tight, you will get a smooth, wrinkle-free finish.

First iron the sleeves. Do the cuffs, inside then out, and then do the main body of the sleeve, using a sleeveboard if available. Start at the bottom, pulling tight, so that you open up the pleat and do not make a line.

Next do the back yoke. Iron straight across it, rather than up and down to avoid wrinkling the seam. Do the bottom part and then turn over and iron the front. To iron around buttons, pull the shirt very tight and iron around them.

Finally, do the collar. Pulling the collar tight, start from the tip and iron towards the middle. Repeat with the other side.

> *Note: Never iron across the collar because it will wrinkle or get pulled out of shape.*

To iron gathers: Start at the edge and wiggle the point of the iron into the gathers.

To iron hems: Start at the edge and stop as soon as the slack material looks as if it might start to wrinkle. Do not iron over the seam, or there will be a seam mark on the right side.

To iron lace: Always iron through a cloth to prevent tearing the fabric.

To iron lined clothes: Turn inside out and iron the lining. Then do the outer shell.

To iron pleats: Lay or pin in place, then hold them tight and iron in long strokes from waist to hem.

To iron sequins: Place right side down on a thick towel to prevent damaging the sequins and iron through a cloth on the wrong side.

To iron sleeves: Use a sleeveboard if available. If not, roll up a towel and insert in the sleeve to iron. Creases in sleeves are undesirable. To iron puffed sleeves, roll up a washcloth and insert it in the sleeve to iron.

To iron flat sheets: Fold in quarters and give each side a quick once-over with the iron. Do not bother ironing fitted sheets.

To iron duvet covers: Fold in quarters, with the right side facing out, then quickly iron each side.

To iron pillowcases: Iron the flap inside, then iron the rest of the pillowcase. Do not iron in creases.

To iron a round tablecloth: Begin at the centre and work outwards, moving the cloth around the board. With large cloths, fold in half, wrong sides together, then iron.

To iron a square or oblong tablecloth: Fold in half lengthways and iron first on the wrong side, then refold and iron on the right side. Do not iron in creases. When ironing napkins, do not iron in creases.

189

To iron a lined skirt: Iron the waistband first on the right side, then turn the skirt inside out. Start by ironing the lining, then iron the outer fabric on the wrong side. Avoid pressing too hard on the seams, or they will mark the outside. If this does happen, lift the seam and iron underneath it to remove the crease.

PRESSING

When you iron something, you slide the iron backwards and forwards across the cloth. This is the technique used for ironing things such as sheets and shirts. In pressing, the iron is literally pressed on the cloth and lifted off. This technique is used when the fabric might be easily crushed, or the heat of the iron might make it go shiny or otherwise damage it – for example, on men's suits.

When pressing, it is a good idea to press through a dampened cloth – a clean white tea towel is ideal – to protect the fabric. Protect delicate items further by laying them on a thick towel before pressing.

Work only on the most wrinkled areas and, for preference, press on the wrong side. Apply the iron with a slight pressure, then lift off immediately. Be careful not to press too hard, or you might create shiny areas or seam marks on seams, lapels and pockets.

> *Tip: If a shiny patch does appear, brush the area with a clothes brush or a slightly dampened cloth.*

To press wool: Place on a thick towel to prevent seams making marks. Always press on the wrong side through a cloth using a medium temperature, because if the iron touches the surface, it can go shiny. Do not iron backwards and forwards, to avoid stretching the fabric. Iron until slightly damp, then fold. Air thoroughly before putting away.

To press silk: Place right side down on a thick towel and press through a damp cloth.

TO AIR LAUNDRY

Airing gets laundry completely dry. If clothes or bed linen are put away when still damp, they can start to smell musty, a smell that can permeate everything else stored with them, necessitating washing the entire lot. In some cases, mildew can develop.

Place folded articles such as sheets on a shelf in the airing cupboard if you have one. Otherwise, put on a table or shelf in a warm, dry place. Put dresses, skirts, shirts and trousers on hangers and leave in a warm, dry place to dry.

Once the ironing is completely dry, take out of the airing cupboard and put away. Do not store articles such as bed linen long term in the airing cupboard. The heat will cause yellowing and may even cause it to crack.

TO REDUCE IRONING

There are some things that never need ironing. They include: anything that says 'do not iron' on the care label; towels, washcloths and tea towels; underwear (unless you go in for silk camisoles and suchlike), socks and nappies; fleeces; most Lycra-based sportswear, swimsuits, bikinis; velvet, chenille, seersucker, and special crinkle-effect fabrics; fitted sheets (even cotton ones will smooth out magically as soon as you put them on the bed).

Drying laundry correctly is a good way to minimise ironing. If you hang clothes outside on a warm, dry, breezy day, the wind will billow out the fabric and remove wrinkles. When drying flat, pull the garment gently into shape before drying.

Further non-ironing tips: The tumble-dryer is the non-ironer's best friend. The trick is to shake out clothes before they go into the dryer, to start the de-wrinkling process. Do not allow them to over-dry and do not leave them in a heap in the dryer. Take them out immediately, then shake again and fold immediately, smoothing them with your hands as you do so.

Using this method, I have not ironed a T-shirt for about 20 years.

Bed linen really should be ironed (see above), but if you cannot bring yourself to do it, buy a beautiful bedspread to cover up the wrinkled sheets.

Crease-resistant shirts are increasingly available. They are made of cotton that has been treated with a special finish that makes them resistant to creasing while they are being worn. More important, they can be washed, hung on a hanger to dry and emerge unwrinkled.

191

Sending out the laundry

When I was a very young child, I can dimly remember our linen being sent to the laundry. It would be delivered back in cardboard boxes, starched and crisp, by a man in a blue van. More recently, the idea of sending out the laundry has been regarded as the height of luxury – something that only single, busy or very rich people do – which is weird when you consider the former luxuries, such as dishwashers, central heating and having more than one bathroom, that are now considered to be necessities.

Sending out the laundry is, however, becoming more popular again, especially in the larger cities. Men, in particular, have taken to it. In London, a common sight on Saturday mornings is to see men carrying a bundle of dirty shirts to the laundry and picking up a newly laundered set, all immaculately starched and folded in boxes.

Consider sending out at least some of the laundry, such as bed linen, if you are under pressure – say, when members of the family have been ill or you have had several people to stay at once, or you have young children and you just need to give yourself a break. The trouble is, it can become addictive. If you or your partner wears a lot of shirts and you argue about who does the ironing, send the shirts out instead.

Shop around for a laundry. Prices vary enormously, with some laundries charging virtually double the prices of others.

Send all parts of a set of bed linen, so that everything will wear at the same rate.

Make a note of what you have sent. If you are sending a lot at the same time, it is easy to overlook the fact that something may be missing. The best laundries still use iron-on labels that keep a record of what customers have sent, but many these days pin labels on, and they are more easily lost.

Mark your own laundry, either with your initials, or with your own iron-on labels (look in the clothes care departments of stores, or in sewing shops).

192

Be prepared for laundered items not to last as long as they would if they were washed at home. Professional laundering can be quite rough. Sheets and pillowcases with fancy embroidered or broderie anglaise hems will often get torn. If duvet covers have plastic snaps, they can melt in the heat of professional ironing machines. Avoid this by always doing up snaps before taking them to the laundry.

Dry-cleaning

Dry-cleaning is the reason that we can enjoy on an everyday basis fabrics that once were classed as luxuries because they were virtually impossible to clean. And it is the reason that heavy coats, suits and jackets can stay fresh and last longer; and that designers can make clothes using a mixture of fabrics that separately require a different washing technique, but which can all be dry-cleaned. This may not seem particularly startling until you read that the usual advice given for cleaning clothes made from more than one fabric 150 years ago was to dismantle the whole garment and wash each piece separately, before sewing it all back together again.

Dry-cleaning is the process of using something other than water – usually a solvent that does not distort fibres – to lift grease and therefore dirt from clothes. In fact, many traditional methods of cleaning use this principle. The technique of removing grease spots from clothes by sprinkling them with talcum powder (see 'An A–Z of fabric stains', p. 307) is a form of dry-cleaning.

Rather touchingly for such a prosaic activity, the origins of modern dry-cleaning are the stuff of legend – all the versions having something in common: that once upon a time someone accidentally spilt a volatile liquid on to fabric and was surprised when it came up clean. One story is that a French sailor accidentally fell into a vat of turpentine and when he emerged, he found that when his previously dirty uniform dried, it was suddenly clean. But it seems likely that the honour should go to a French tailor, Jean-Baptiste Jolly-Bellin in 1849. He noticed, after knocking over a lamp and spilling spirits of turpentine on to a cloth, that when the oil dried, the area of the cloth on to which it had spilt was cleaner. He then immersed the whole cloth in turpentine and – voilà! – the whole thing came up clean.

193

Turpentine had been used to spot-clean fabrics since the early 18th century, but Jolly was the first to see the commercial prospects of cleaning entire garments this way. He set up the first dry-cleaner, the Teinturerie Jolly-Bellin, with his son-in-law in the Rue St Martin in Paris in 1852. The first dry-cleaning establishment in Britain opened some 25 years later.

In addition to turpentine, early dry-cleaners discovered that several other solvents had a cleaning effect, including benzene, kerosene and gasoline. The problem with all of them was that they were highly volatile, inflammable and gave off noxious fumes. It was not until the 1920s that the first specific dry-cleaning solvent was developed. In the 1930s, perchloroethylene, a non-inflammable solvent, was introduced, and is still in use today.

Unfortunately, dry-cleaning often has a bad name, owing to disappointing results. The fault lies partly with badly trained dry-cleaners, anxious to make a fast buck, and partly with us, the public, because of our insistence that clothes be dry-cleaned as quickly as possible – we want overnight service, or even a four-hour service. What few people appreciate is that to dry-clean something properly takes time.

High-quality dry-cleaning should always start with removing stains. Dark garments and silks are put in a steam cabinet to bring up any hidden stains, and then each stain is spot-treated by hand. Dry-cleaning is essentially a grease-removing exercise, because most stains, not just the obvious ones, have a little grease or oil in them, and it is the grease that attracts the dirt. Once the grease is removed, the dirt will lift.

Stains have to be removed first because, even if the dry-cleaning process removes grease from a stain, there will be other residues that can get indelibly baked in when the garment has dried. Each stain-removing process can take about an hour to remove the stain and allow the garment to dry, so a badly stained garment with a multitude of stains can take four or five days.

After that, the dry-cleaning process itself is pretty straightforward. A dry-cleaning machine looks like a huge washing-machine. As with a washing machine, sorting of fabrics and colours is very important – a heavy fabric will, for example, act as a blanket to a more delicate one. The buttons are removed or covered with aluminium foil, and then the garments are tumbled in the solvent for a surprisingly short time – about four minutes. Any longer, and dirt starts being redeposited. The solvent is then spun out, taking the dirt with it.

TO DRY-CLEAN OR NOT

Dry-cleaning can be expensive, so if a garment can be washed, it should be. In general, the following items should be dry-cleaned. First, and most obvious, always dry-clean anything that says 'dry-clean only' on the care label (normally a circle with a P inside it; a line underneath is an instruction to the dry-cleaner). In practice, this means anything that might shrink with normal washing, or where dyes might run. Sometimes the outer part of a garment will be washable, but another part, such as the lining, will not.

If there is no care label – as is often the case with vintage clothing – or unless it definitely specifies otherwise, the following are usually dry-clean only:

Some acetates; beaded and sequinned fabric; brocade; some chiffons; chintz (if washed, the glazed surface is destroyed); some damasks; dralon; felt; flannel (as in suits); fur and some fake furs; gabardine; some jersey fabrics; metallic fabrics, such as lamé and some brocades; moiré; heavy silk satins; sheepskin; printed silks; silk taffeta; silk tulle; tweed; some velvets; some viscose; some wools, such as blankets. Anything with a trim that will not withstand normal washing, such as leather, diamanté straps, beads, sequins or fur, will also have to be dry-cleaned, as will over-printed fabrics, where the pattern might not withstand washing, and lined curtains. Upholstery fabrics, including slipcovers, will have to be dry-cleaned unless they are specifically labelled as washable.

THINGS THAT SHOULD NOT BE DRY-CLEANED

Anything that specifically says, 'do not dry-clean'; anything with a special finish that will be destroyed by dry-cleaning, such as waxed jackets and oiled sweaters; some plastics, including PVC, and some rubberised fabrics, both of which will be destroyed by dry-cleaning solvents. Feather and down duvets and pillows should never be dry-cleaned because they can trap toxic fumes from the solvents. Always wash them.

Never dry-clean fragile antique fabrics, unless you have taken advice.

DRY-CLEANING ESSENTIALS

Dry-clean your clothes regularly – little and often is best. Never clean just one part of a two-piece outfit. Both pieces will have a surface film of dirt and if one piece is cleaned but not the other, you will be able to see the difference.

If a garment is badly stained, get it cleaned as soon as possible – the sooner a stain is tackled, the better.

> Tip: If you are going out for a curry and know you are inclined to make a mess, wear something white – it will be easier to clean.

Do not expect miracles: sometimes the dry-cleaning itself will damage fragile fabrics – a case in point is printed silks, where one dye may be less colourfast than another.

If you do get a stain on silk, do not rub it. You will break the fibres, which leaves a white bloom. Even the gentlest rubbing damages the fibre. Blot the stain gently and then take the garment to the dry-cleaner.

Point out any specific marks and stains to the dry-cleaner – different stains need different handling. Take advice on whether it is possible to dry-clean the garment and how long it will take – if you are told that a badly stained garment will take less than four or five days, go elsewhere, because it probably means that the cleaner will not remove stains before cleaning the whole garment. For this reason, don't ask for an 'express' cleaning service because proper, high-quality dry-cleaning takes time.

Whatever you do, don't try to tackle the stain yourself – rubbing and scrubbing will damage the fabric and you may set the stain so that nothing will get it out.

Take all clothes out of the dry-cleaner's plastic bags when you get them home to allow them to air. And never store clothes in plastic bags – the polymers in the bags can transfer to the clothes, causing indelible staining and yellowing.

CHAPTER 7
The Study

We went to his study for coffee, a jolly room full of books and trophies and untidiness and comfort. I made up my mind that if I ever got rid of this business and had a house of my own, I would create just such a room.

John Buchan, The Thirty-Nine Steps

Poor Richard Hannay, on the run and in danger of his life from German spies, dreamed of a tranquil, book-lined study – a Victorian viewpoint that saw the study as an essentially masculine room, an escape from the often suffocatingly feminine domestic sphere, a room where a chap could talk to other chaps and could smoke, read and do business. Women didn't need a study. If they were rich and leisured enough, they read for pleasure; if not, they were occupied with house and children.

So ingrained is the notion that studies are a male domain that they are still often decorated in a self-consciously masculine style, with dark colours and comfortable chairs, and personal mementoes such as school photographs and framed certificates on the walls.

It is unlikely that much work ever went on in the traditional study. In the modern home, however, especially if someone works from home or if there are children who need a quiet place to do homework, the study has become one of the busiest rooms in the house – a mixture of computer room, office and library.

A study or a home office is becoming increasingly important. According to the most recent available figures, more than three million people in the UK work from home, an increase of over a million since 1997. Of these, more than two-thirds are teleworkers – in other words, they need a computer and a telephone in order to do their work. But even the most computer-literate will find that an office can never be entirely paper-free.

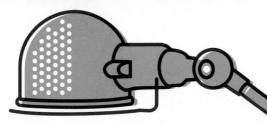

If you can turn a room in the house into a study, it will be one of the best decisions you will make. Computers, printers and the other essential paraphernalia of the study – or home office – are not lovely things to look at, and the papers and filing with which the modern home is inundated take up a lot of room. And if you work from home, siting the computer in the corner of the living-room or the bedroom is unsatisfactory because it means you can never get away from work. Rooms to consider turning into a study are the dining-room, if it is not used very often, or a spare bedroom. Alternatively it may be possible to make clever use of the space in a spare corner of the landing or the hall.

The essentials

If you are working from home, it is important that your office is set up in the most efficient way possible. It makes sense to buy a proper computer desk, which can accommodate a printer or has a special pull-out stand for the keyboard. Although they look modern and slick, avoid glass desks: resting your arm on the cold surface when doing mouse-work is extremely uncomfortable after a while. An adjustable office chair is a must, to enable you to sit at the computer in the most comfortable and efficient way. Repetitive strain injury (RSI), in which muscles and nerves become damaged by repetitive movements at the keyboard, can be avoided by sitting at the computer with correct posture and at the correct height. Good storage is essential – there should be bookshelves or a bookcase and preferably a filing cabinet for important papers, or at least room for box files to be stored. Therefore, in a study, the priorities are tidiness, storage and keeping electronic equipment in good working order.

Electronic equipment

Nowadays, even the most rudimentary home office has at least a computer, a printer and a phone, with often a scanner and a fax as well. When cleaning, the main problem is dust. Apart from looking unsightly, dust is bad for electronic equipment because it can affect its performance.

The equipment itself requires attention. In 2004 a report appeared entitled 'Lifting the lid on computer filth', which showed just how dirty offices can be.

This study by a microbiologist called Dr Charles Gerba, of the University of Arizona, found that 'work stations' – or desks, as normal people call them – can contain nearly 400 times as many microbes as a lavatory seat. Most of them lurk on telephones (25,127 microbes per sq in), keyboards (3,295) and computer mice (1,676). By comparison, the average toilet seat contains 49 microbes per sq in. Cold and flu viruses on keyboards can survive for up to 72 hours. If you touch any of these things and then touch your skin or put your fingers in your mouth without washing your hands, you will transfer the microbes. Similarly, if you eat lunch at your desk, crumbs and spills can harbour bacteria. Cleaning of desks and equipment was found to reduce bacteria by 99 per cent.

Although the report applied to office workers, there are lessons there for the home office, too.

TO CLEAN THE COMPUTER

To clean the computer screen, use a lint-free, antistatic cloth, or special antistatic, non-smear wipes designed for computer screens. These are quite expensive. A good home-made alternative is a used conditioner sheet. Spray very lightly with water and use to clean the screen.

Unplug the mouse and wipe over with a damp cloth and a little household disinfectant (or use an antibacterial wipe).

To clean the keyboard, use a small, stiff, flat brush to clean between the keys – an old, clean eyeshadow brush will do – and then wipe over with a cotton swab dipped in a disinfectant, and squeezed until almost dry (you do not want to get any moisture into your keyboard). Wipe over with a barely damp cloth.

Avoid eating and drinking at your desk. Crumbs can get into the keyboard, and if you spill a drink over it, you will probably have to get a new one. A small spillage can sometimes be contained, but act quickly. Switch off the computer and unplug the keyboard. Tear paper towels into strips and dip just the edge of the paper into the pools of liquid, letting the towel soak it up by capillary action. Do the same between the keys. As the paper becomes soggy, replace it. Be patient and don't dab the water or you may spread it. Leave to dry upside down in a warm, dry place. Do not plug back in unless the keyboard is completely dry.

TO CLEAN THE TELEPHONE, FAX MACHINE AND MOBILE PHONE

Unplug the phone before cleaning. Use a damp cloth and a little disinfectant (or an antibacterial wipe) to clean the handset, paying particular attention to areas that come in contact with your skin. Then clean the cradle – there is no point ridding the handset of microbes, only to put it back on to a dirty surface – and the rest of the phone. To clean between the keys, use a cotton swab dipped in a little disinfectant and then squeezed dry.

Clean the fax machine in the same way.

201

> *Note: Cats like sleeping on fax machines because they are warm. Inevitably, they shed fur and dust all over the machine and will eventually damage it. Keep cats out of offices.*

Mobile phones also need cleaning, which can be a bit fiddly. Switch off the phone, then clean with antibacterial wipes. Clean between the keys as above.

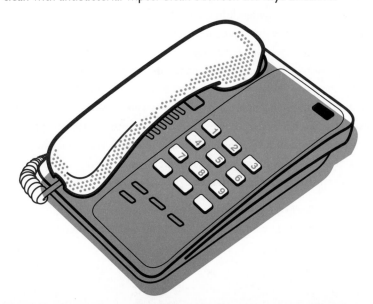

Paperwork

It is all too easy for the modern home to become inundated with paperwork. Even with the rise of online banking, most official documentation is still paper-based. Filing is a chore, and easy to put off, but is done more easily if it is not allowed to accumulate.

TO ORGANISE PAPERWORK

If you work from home, it is important to keep work and domestic paperwork separate, but the following method works equally well for both.

Buy several large box files or a small filing cabinet for long-term storage. Divide into sections, keeping like with like. For example, do not have a separate file for gas bills and another for electricity bills, etc. Make one file marked 'Utilities' and then sub-divide that into electricity, gas, telephone, TV, water and so on. Similarly, keep all documents relating to your car together, such as registration documents, insurance certificates and garage bills.

At the start of a tax year (April), start a file for the new tax year and put anything that you know you will need for next year's return in it as you receive it.

To avoid losing bills and anything else that needs filing, keep one box file somewhere convenient – for example in the hall where letters arrive. Divide it into 12 sections, one for each month. Put papers in the pockets for the relevant month, and store them here until you have time to place them in the long-term files; this way you will always know where they are.

When filing, put the most recent papers at the front. A useful rule is that for every new one that goes in, a redundant old one should be taken from the back and thrown away (excluding important tax documents, of course).

When throwing away private papers, either tear them up, burn them or invest in a shredder. Shredders are inexpensive and available from office supply stores and some hardware outlets. Although identity theft is rare, it is good sense to destroy anything sensitive or confidential. This includes unsolicited junk mail (see below) such as credit card offers, or anything that has your name, address or any other personal details.

Tip: Online fraud is also rare, but if you are worried about buying online, keep one credit card for online transactions only and ask the card

202

*company to put a very low limit on it – say $500. That way, if your card
is used fraudulently, the fraudsters cannot buy very much with it.*

To stop unwanted mail: To stop the flood of junk mail that flows through our
letterboxes in ever increasing quantities, register with the Mail Preference
Service (www.dmachoice.org), which will pass on your details to relevant
companies. They must then stop sending out unsolicited mail, but it may take
up to four months before you notice a significant reduction.

Similarly, registering with the National Do Not Call Registry (www.donotcall.
gov) will stop that other bane of modern life, the unsolicited telemarketing
call. It is worthwhile noting that it is now unlawful to make unsolicited direct
marketing calls to people who have said they do not wish to receive them. The
service takes a month to take effect.

KEEPING OFFICIAL DOCUMENTS

There are some papers that should be kept for a lifetime – either yours or the
lifetime of the asset. These include birth and marriage certificates, Social Security
documents, court orders and decrees, Medicare of Medicaid documents, house
and other deeds, copies of wills, bond certificates, motor vehicle documents,
driver's licence, mortgage papers, insurance certificates, passports, share
certificates, professional certificates, educational qualifications, loan agreements.
Common sense dictates what is and what is not important.

203

Bank statements and bills: There is no actual requirement to keep bank and
credit card statements, unless they relate to your tax return. In practice,
however, banks or building societies often require bank statements going back
several months if you are taking out a mortgage or loan. If you need copies of
statements, they may charge you for them.

To play safe, keep them for a year. Keep chequebook stubs, cash machine
slips and credit card receipts until all the transactions have appeared on your
bank statement, and then throw them away (unless they should be ketp for tax
purposes).

Similarly, with utility bills, although there is no requirement to keep them,
you need to show recent bills to a bank or building society if taking out a
loan. It is also useful to have an idea of what you have been paying in case you
are suddenly landed with an unusually large bill and want to compare it with

previous bills, or if you want to get an idea of average use before deciding whether to switch utility providers. Keep for a year, or longer if you are self-employed and they relate to your tax return – see below.

Tax returns: **By law you must retain financial papers relating to your recent tax returns. These include the W-2 statement from your employer; statements of interest from a bank or building society; share dividends; details of any other income, such as rental income, inheritances or freelance payments; pension payments; details of capital gains; expenses, and so on.**

How long you keep these papers after you have filed the return depends on whether you are employed or self-employed. If employed, you must keep your W-2 and other documents for at least three years after the end of the relevant tax year. If the IRS believes you underreported your income by 25 per cent or more, it has six years to audit you, so you may want to keep records longer.

The IRS itself advises you to keep your records indefinitely if you don't file a return – or if you file a fraudulent return. For more information on what papers to keep and for how long, see the IRS website.

204

Whether employed or unemployed, any papers relating to assets that may generate capital gains or losses should be retained indefinitely. Similarly, anyone who has been the subject of an IRS audit should hang on to all relevant documents for several years. If in doubt, always contact the tax office for advice – they are generally extremely helpful.

Guarantees, receipts, etc: **Receipts for goods that are still under guarantee should be kept for the life of the guarantee along with the relevant financial record, such as a credit card statement. Other receipts for expensive goods, such as pieces of art or antiques or jewellery, should be kept for as long as you have the item – you may need it as proof of ownership for insurance purposes, for example. Also keep receipts/contracts for continuing services such as mobile phone contracts or gym memberships as well as the manuals that came with electrical appliances. Throw all other receipts away.**

Books

When I was a child, the whole family went to the library every Saturday to get our books for the week. We did not have a huge number of books in the house, because the library fulfilled most of our needs. My mother had a lot of poetry books, and my sister and I had the usual quota of children's classics and Enid Blyton, but we had nothing like the numbers of books that people routinely have these days.

Books are being bought in greater numbers than ever now, thanks to the introduction of competitive pricing and the new chains with their special offers, and the convenience of the internet. It is all so easy that one can quickly get carried away and buy far more than one actually needs. But there is a genuine excitement about books these days. I, like virtually every woman over 30, am a member of a book club. Once a month we meet at someone's house for supper and conversation about the book, which could be anything from a classic to a newly published novel to a biography. Book clubs have had a bad press because they are seen less as an occasion for serious conversation – which is deemed 'good' – than as an excuse for a social gathering – which is, apparently, very, very bad. Why? I think this puritanical attitude is due to that fact that despite the vast numbers of books that many people have, they are still regarded with a reverence bordering on superstition. We live in a throwaway age, when the concept of repairing something is regarded as laughably quaint. But mention that you are thinking of getting rid of some of your books and people react as if you are planning a Nazi-style book burning.

It is most perplexing, because I am sure that the average motley collection, consisting largely of thrillers, out-of-date reference books, unreadable novels – bought because they won a prize but never opened – and cookery books that have never been used, could withstand pruning without bringing about the collapse of Western civilisation.

TO CARE FOR BOOKS

Because they are made of fragile paper, books are unsurprisingly rather vulnerable. They are susceptible to light and air pollution, both of which cause yellowing of the paper and, in the case of sunlight, fading of the spines. Dust damages books, as do rodents, and insects that are extremely partial to them include furniture beetles, death-watch beetles, carpet beetles, moth larvae and silverfish.

Books dislike both low and high levels of humidity – too dry, and the pages of books can become brittle and crack; too damp, and they can develop a musty smell and become mildewed. Damp, mouldy books will mean a lot of mould spores flying about the house, which is not a pleasant prospect: moulds are unhealthy and should not be breathed in. Oddly enough, newer books deteriorate more quickly than old ones. The paper, made from wood pulp, is less durable than the rag pulp paper used until the middle of the 19th century.

One of the easiest ways to shorten a book's life is to handle it roughly – for example, bending it back so that the spine breaks, or even pulling it off a shelf. Never pull a book by its spine because you risk damaging it. The correct way to remove a book from a shelf is to reach right over the top of the book and down behind it and pull it forward.

If there is no space above the book, push the books on either side forward so you can get a firm grip on the one you want, or press your fingers down firmly on the top of the book, about an inch from the spine, and draw it towards you.

> Note: This may seem rather a fussy way to handle the garden variety books we all own, but even (in fact especially) ordinary paperbacks benefit from gentle handling. And the right way is as easy as the wrong way.

When replacing a book, push the two on either side apart so you can slide the book in easily.

TO CLEAN BOOKS

The best way to keep books clean is to read them. When you take them off shelves, dust is dislodged. Otherwise, use a lambswool duster to whisk dust off every now and again – once a month is ideal, once a quarter more realistic. Do not use a feather duster, which will just throw dust around and the hard spines may catch on books and tear them.

Once a year, take all the books off shelves. As you do so, dust the top of each one with the upholstery attachment on a vacuum cleaner on a low setting or with a soft brush (such as a shaving brush with natural bristles). Hold the book tightly so that dust does not slip down between the pages. Whisk the brush quickly along the top, from the spine outwards, into a duster or, if very dusty, into the nozzle of a vacuum cleaner. Then clean the covers and the spine. Turn back dog-ears, unless the pages are very brittle.

Very crumpled pages can be restored to a semblance of their former selves with a steam iron on a low setting. Put another piece of paper on top of the page to protect it.

Examine for insect damage. To kill insects and larvae, wrap the book in acid-free tissue paper, put in a polyethylene bag and freeze for seven days. Allow to return to room temperature slowly.

> Note: Consult an expert before trying this with old and/or fragile books.

Brush mildew off in the same way, but track down the source of the damp that has made the book mouldy in the first place. Take care not to breathe in mould spores. In fact, unless a mildewed book is old or precious, toss it.

After taking all the books down, vacuum the shelves thoroughly, using the crevice tool to get into all the corners. If necessary, wipe with a barely damp cloth. Wipe dry and ensure no trace of moisture remains before replacing books.

Use this annual cleaning as an opportunity to cull your books. As you put each book back, ask yourself if you will ever read it again. If the answer is 'no', put it on a pile. If there are a lot of them, a second-hand bookseller may buy them from you. Take the rest to the charity shop.

TO STORE BOOKS

Books are surprisingly heavy, so ensure that shelving is strong enough to support them without sagging. A series of short shelves, built side by side, is less likely to sag than one long one. Rare or old books are beyond the realm of this book but should probably be stored behind glass. Antiquarian booksellers should be able to advise on storage and cleaning.

If you have a lot of books, consider some sort of order on the shelves. Putting them in alphabetical order makes the most sense. If you choose another method, such as storing them by size (biggest books on the bottom shelves) or by colour, store them alphabetically within the system.

Shelves and bookcases should be full enough for the books to support each other, but not so crammed that you cannot remove them easily.

Store books upright on shelves, but large books such as albums need to be stored flat because they cannot support their own weight (do not let them overhang shelves).

Do not push books right to the back of bookcases. Instead, line them up so they are flush with the front of the shelves. That way, you allow air to circulate behind them and do not have an irritating little ledge in front of the books, which will need dusting.

If storing books long-term, keep them somewhere clean, dry, dark and well-ventilated. Cellars, garages and outhouses tend to be damp.

Part II

THE
TECHNIQUES

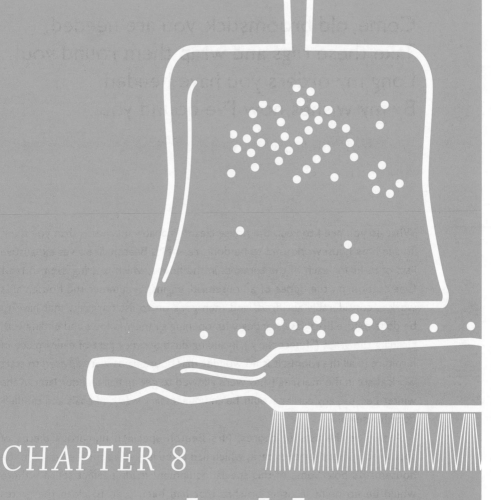

CHAPTER 8

Household Equipment

Come, old broomstick, you are needed,
Take these rags and wrap them round you!
Long my orders you have heeded,
By my wishes now I've bound you.

Johann Wolfgang von Goethe, The Sorcerer's Apprentice

What do you need to keep the house clean? Probably much less than you think. To see how housework used to be done, read Mrs Beeton. She gives exhaustive lists of tasks for each of the servants in the house, which is tiring even to read. One section, on the duties of a housemaid, begins, 'In summer the housemaid's work is considerably abridged,' and then goes on to list ten tasks that have to be done before breakfast, starting with opening all the windows and ending with cleaning the grate ('if necessary'), including dusting every part of every piece of furniture in all the rooms. It is no wonder that housemaids were advised to start work at six in the morning (they were allowed to get up half an hour later in the winter because any earlier would 'be an unnecessary waste of coals and candle'). Poor housemaids.

Alongside the lists of chores, Mrs Beeton specified numerous pieces of special equipment for each task, which had to be lugged about the house in the housemaid's box. Some of this special equipment made perfect sense – there would be no point in using brushes that had been used to clean the grates anywhere else, but why could a stair brush be used only for brushing stairs and no other carpet in the house?

Times have not changed that much since 1861 in one respect at least: with an eye to their profit margin, manufacturers are very keen to suggest that we need to buy all sorts of specialist equipment, or new 'improved' versions of it. You can tell they are 'improved' because they are often called 'Wonder' this or 'Super' that and they cost twice the price of the old versions.

Most department stores have a homeware department, as do DIY superstores. In general, the range is predictable. You will not find specialist things in these outlets; so, if your town has an old-fashioned hardware store, track it down. For some reason, my part of London is peculiarly blessed with these establishments. Hardware stores stock things that the large department stores do not sell. Because they specialise in hardware and everything to do with the home, they will beat any department store hands down. They tend to be run by slight obsessives, which means you can spend ten minutes discussing, for example, replacement lever arms for toilet tanks (apparently, there is often a run on them in January, because they tend to break in cold weather), but it is always a pleasure to talk to someone who knows his job.

The internet is another great source of specialist or hard-to-find household equipment. Sites come and go all the time, but a quick Google search (don't be afraid to start with a broad topic and refine your search to exactly what you're looking for) will likely find your product.

Basic cleaning equipment

Researching this book has led me to streamline my own household equipment in the same way that I have reduced the number of household chemicals I use. It is easy to be seduced into thinking that every task requires some special, unique equipment – special cloths for this, or brushes for that.

In fact, a few pieces of equipment will do most jobs. The list below is not intended to be prescriptive. It is actually the list of things that I use to clean my house, the things that over the years I have found most useful, efficient and time-saving. The idea is to have as few pieces of equipment as possible and to use them, rather than to fill the cupboard under the stairs with equipment that never leaves its packet. As my mother, who hates housework, says, 'It doesn't matter how many dusters you have if you never use them.'

DRY BRUSHES

Brushes are the most effective way to dust small items, or to apply polish to carved furniture. Build up a small collection of old, well-washed blusher brushes and shaving brushes. Or go to an artists' suppliers and buy a few. Soft brushes are for dusting. Stiff hogshair brushes are the ones to use to apply polish.

Other brushes that are particularly useful are clothes brushes, lint-removing brushes and shoe brushes (including brushes for polishing leather shoes and a wire suede brush). Also, do not throw away old toothbrushes. Keep a few for fiddly cleaning jobs.

As brushes get dirty, wash them briefly in warm water and mild detergent. Rinse well and allow to dry naturally.

Broom: Stiff bristles whisk dust up into the air, so choose one with soft bristles and, if possible, an adjustable handle, to save your back. Natural bristles hold the dust better than synthetic.

Wash bristles in warm, soapy water, but do not immerse the wooden head. Rinse and shake the broom head thoroughly to get rid of the excess water. Allow to dry naturally. Store brooms upside down to avoid crushing the bristles. Drive two nails into a wall, about 2 in apart, and hang the broom upside down on them.

Dustpan and brush: Rubber or plastic dustpans are better than metal, which can rust. They also have no hard edges to mark floors. Wash the dustpan occasionally in warm soapy water. Wash the brush as above.

WET BRUSHES

Bristles on brushes for wet work need to be short and stiff. Choose natural bristles rather than nylon because they are less likely to scratch surfaces or catch on fibres.

Toilet brushes: Buy cheap ones and replace them often. After using the brush, run it under the flush to clean it. Put a little undiluted toilet cleaner in the brush container. Replace brushes often.

Scrubbing brushes: A useful selection is a large scrubbing brush for the floor; a small nailbrush for the laundry (e.g. for scrubbing collars and cuffs); and a softer brush to clean silver. In all cases, natural bristles are preferable to synthetic. This is particularly important when choosing a brush to clean silver.

DRY CLOTHS

In other words, cloths needed for dusting, polishing and shining dry surfaces. The main thing to remember is to have plenty and to keep them clean. Otherwise, you are just pushing dirt around.

Dry sponge: Made of a special rubber, dry sponges are useful for cleaning surfaces where water cannot be used – for example, on lampshades. They do not work on grease but are one of the few things that can clean porous brick. When dirty, throw away. Dry sponges cannot be washed.

Dusters: Avoid the traditional yellow dusters. They shed lint, their dye runs when they are wet and their loose hems can catch on things, such as splinters in wood. Instead, look for white or light-coloured flat-hemmed dusters.

215

You need plenty of dusters – at least a dozen. Wash dusters frequently in the machine and launder without fabric softener because it can impede the duster's natural absorbency. Dry naturally or tumble-dry.

Flat duster mop: For cleaning wooden floors. Use dry for sweeping or damp for mopping. Choose natural fibres to prevent scratching the floor. Avoid mops that are impregnated with wax. Wash as necessary in warm, soapy water. Allow to dry naturally.

Fluffy dusters: These long-handled dusters deal with dust in high and awkward places (pictures, cornices, behind radiators) and are the best thing to clean books. They hold on to the dust, rather than whisking it round the room. Choose natural lambswool over synthetic, which can scratch. Wash as necessary in warm soapy water, rinse well and allow to dry naturally.

> *Note: Avoid feather dusters. They do not hold the dust and their quills can scratch furniture.*

Specialist polishing cloths: For polishing metal. A silver polishing cloth is probably the most useful product for buffing up lightly tarnished silver, because it contains a tarnish inhibitor. Cloths are also available for copper, stainless steel, etc. To clean, follow the manufacturer's instructions.

WET CLOTHS

For all heavy-duty cleaning involving detergent and/or disinfectant, use plain white traditional cotton dish cloths (also use for cleaning dishes). They are naturally absorbent and do not shed lint, while their loose weave gives a natural friction, which makes for good all-round cleaning power. They are also cheap, so buy plenty.

When cleaning cloths are dirty, wash them without fabric softener. Replace frequently.

> Note: Do not use sponges. They create too much lather, making it difficult to rinse things quickly. They also harbour bacteria within their depths, and are impossible to clean.

Chamois leather: This is traditional for windows but is particularly good for cleaning jewellery and polishing pearls.

After use, rinse the chamois in warm water. Chamois is cured with oil, so detergent will strip it and make it go hard. Rinsing in water should be enough, but if it gets very dirty, it can be cleaned with ordinary soap. Lather with soap and rinse well in warm water. Lather with soap again and squeeze dry without rinsing. Leave to dry naturally away from direct heat. The soap keeps the chamois soft.

Dish mops: A little old-fashioned, but string dish mops are the best thing for washing glasses.

After use, rinse out well. Wash as necessary in the dishwasher on a low-temperature wash, standing the dish mop in the cutlery holder. Or wash by hand in hot, soapy water, rinse and allow to dry naturally.

Mark and stain eraser sponges: These sponges are made of melamine foam that, when moistened with water, breaks up dirt and grime on a surface without use of chemicals. They are especially useful on ground-in dirt on walls, scuff marks on surfaces, grimy paintwork and uPVC garden furniture. The sponges break down as you use them. Once worn to a rag, discard.

216

Microfibre cloths: These are a modern miracle. They are made from a special synthetic cloth containing millions of fibres that pick up dust and dirt and, when wet, will clean grime and grease too. The miracle is that they clean only with water – no detergents are necessary. They are particularly good for getting a shine on stainless steel, bathroom fittings, mirrors and tiles. Use for all cleaning jobs that do not require disinfecting (i.e. not in the toilet). There are many brands, and some manufacturers claim that you can cut chemical usage by 80 per cent. They are relatively expensive but last for ages.

After use, machine wash with no fabric softener. Allow to dry naturally.

Mop: Old-fashioned cotton mops are cheap, last a long time and are good for heavy work, but they can be cumbersome and heavy and take ages to dry. Instead, choose a synthetic mop such as the Vileda Supermop, which is a traditional mop head made from strips of Vileda cloth. It is light and whisks into corners in a flash.

Wash the mop head as necessary in warm, soapy water. Rinse and allow to dry naturally. Hang on a hook to store, making sure the mop head does not drag on the floor. Replace mop heads frequently.

> *Note: Sponge mops should be avoided. They are virtually impossible to clean, which means you are just spreading dirt and germs around the floor.*

217

Scourers: Nylon scourers and soap-filled metal pads such as Brillo will get to grips with ground-in dirt and burnt-on food on saucepans. Cut soap-filled pads in half to make them go further.

Rinse nylon scourers out after use. Wash occasionally in hot, soapy water, rinse and allow to dry naturally. Replace frequently. After using soap-filled pads, squeeze them out very well and leave to dry naturally; if left wet, they will rust. Wrap in aluminium foil. Once the soap has gone, discard them.

Squeegee: The best tool for cleaning windows – also shower screens, mirrors and tiles – is a squeegee. This is the metal or plastic tool with a rubber blade that professional window cleaners use. Squeegees are available from hardware stores, home stores and car accessory stores. After use, rinse and wipe dry.

OTHER EQUIPMENT

Use the list of equipment above as the basis for the household cleaning armoury. It will still, however, need to be supplemented with a few other things.

Bins and laundry baskets: Have a waste bin in every room in the house. If there is space in the bedrooms, have a laundry basket in each as well.

Wash and disinfect the kitchen and bathroom bins once a week. Wash other bins occasionally in hot, soapy water.

Blind cleaner: This consists of prongs covered with a synthetic furry fabric. The prongs fit over slats in Venetian blinds and you run it along them to clean them.

Wash in hot, soapy water after use. Dry naturally.

Buckets: You need three buckets: one mop bucket to enable you to wring out mops efficiently when cleaning floors, plus two more. With two buckets you can wash and rinse at the same time, without constant refilling. Plastic is cheaper and lighter than metal.

After use, rinse out and allow to dry.

Cotton swabs: For fiddly jobs, such as cleaning silver polish from nooks and crannies, or for swabbing antique or delicate china.

Gloves: Cotton gloves are useful for dry, dirty jobs, where you do not want to leave finger marks, such as cleaning silver or polishing furniture. Rubber gloves should be used for all wet jobs involving chemicals or where you need water to be hotter than the hand can bear. Disposable latex gloves are useful for grim jobs, such as clearing up sick.

Wash cotton gloves in the machine. Rinse rubber gloves after use and allow to dry naturally. Throw latex gloves away after use.

Plastic bowls: As well as a washing-up bowl, have a selection of small bowls of different sizes for jobs such as stain removal, cleaning jewellery, or anything else where only a little detergent is needed.

Wash the bowls as normal. After washing-up, remember to wash the underside of the washing-up bowl, which can get greasy and gritty.

Plastic spray bottles: For spraying home-made cleaners or water when using microfibre cloths, or spraying ironing that has got too dry. Buy several from a garden centre – they are usually used for spraying houseplants. Wash as any other plastic.

219

Electrical equipment

It is salutary sometimes to remember that until the invention of electrical machines to help clean the house, housework was one of the most physically arduous jobs there was. We still rely on them, but perhaps take them so much for granted that we forget what a boon and a blessing they are.

THE VACUUM CLEANER

The first vacuum cleaner was invented in Chicago in 1865. It was hand-powered and did not catch on. Neither did the cleaner patented 36 years later by a British engineer called H. Cecil Booth, which was so large that it had to be drawn by horse and parked outside a house to clean it. Nor did another hand-operated machine patented by a Birmingham engineer, Walter Griffiths, in 1905. It was powered by a bellows, which had to be compressed 'by the ordinary domestic servant' in order to suck up the dust.

The first electric vacuum cleaner was invented a year later by James Murray Spangler, a caretaker from Ohio, who rigged up a machine consisting of a fan, a box and a pillowcase, plus a rotating brush to loosen dirt. He patented the idea and sold it to his cousin's Hoover Harness and Leather Goods company. Which is why people talk about doing the 'Hoovering', and not doing the 'Spanglering'.

The Hoover company is very keen that 'Hoover' is not used as a synonym for 'vacuum cleaner', except in relation to the company's own products. I think that is rather a shame. I would be delighted to have contributed something to the English language. But 'vacuum cleaner' it will have to be.

CHOOSING A VACUUM CLEANER

Some research that Hoover (now part of the Hoover Candy group) sent me threw up some interesting facts about our vacuum cleaner habits. Seventy per cent of British people vacuum every two to three days. We like vacuum cleaners to be lightweight but efficient, even though the more powerful a motor, the heavier it has to be. And, surprisingly, we like our vacuum cleaners noisy.

When choosing a vacuum cleaner, it is the dust pick-up capacity that is important. The bigger the motor, the better the pick-up, but the heavier the machine. For anyone with asthma or dust allergies, the filter efficiency is of paramount importance. Choose a vacuum with a bag, for preference, and one that has a HEPA (High Efficiency Particulate Air) filter. This way, everything will be contained – the filter will capture anything that leaks from the bag. For more on this, see 'Household pests', p. 322.

After that the main choice is between an upright model and a cylinder one, either with bag or bagless. Both have their passionate advocates, but sales for both are about the same.

If you have large expanses of fitted carpet, an upright may be more useful, although cylinder models often have a turbo brush for cleaning large areas. Cylinder models are smaller and less cumbersome than uprights, making them easy to store (useful if there is restricted space) and easy to manoeuvre on stairs. They have a wide range of attachments for cleaning upholstery, etc. On the other hand they are less efficient at picking up dirt from pile carpets unless they have a turbo attachment, and their dust bags need replacing more frequently.

Nowadays, all but the most basic upright models have the same range of attachments as cylinder cleaners, and can be adjusted to clean wooden floors as well as carpets. They clean large areas of carpet efficiently, their upright position is considered to be more comfortable for most people, and their large capacity means the bag has to be emptied less often. However, they often do not reach right to the edge of carpets, they can be heavy, an important consideration if there are a lot of stairs, and bagless models are noisy.

Bagless cleaners, as popularized by James Dyson, use centrifugal force to suck up the dust and dirt into a central chamber in the machine, which is then emptied. For a long time Dyson cornered the market, but other manufacturers now make bagless models too.

Conventional vacuum cleaners tend to be quieter and lighter and the dust is enclosed in a bag, making them suitable for those with asthma or dust allergies. Bagless models have a greater capacity. I have not found them any more efficient at picking up dirt, and find them heavy, cumbersome and ugly.

USING THE VACUUM CLEANER

Apparently, only 10 per cent of people ever look at instruction manuals. Take time to do so and you will find that the vacuum cleaner becomes one of the most useful tools in the house.

If your vacuum has adjustable suction, make use of the variable settings on the cleaner; do not just set it to maximum. Maximum power is likely to weaken the fibres of a fitted carpet and do serious damage to old or valuable rugs (especially fringes). The heavy suction will also make vacuuming harder work. In general, the best advice is to use medium power on fitted carpets, low power on rugs and maximum power on hard floors.

Do not make work for yourself. To clean a carpet, use medium power and do not press down hard. Float the head across the floor and let the machine do the work.

If you have them, use the different heads. The standard head is fine for carpets, but can rub grit into hard floors. For those, use the large brush head.

Use the vacuum cleaner to help with your other cleaning. For example, on something that cannot be vacuumed direct, brush the dust off and into the vacuum cleaner, on low power. This way, you are taking the dust out of the house, instead of whisking it up in the air, ready to settle over everything again.

Keep the vacuum cleaner clean. The wheels can pick up dirt, which marks carpets, and grit, which damages wooden floors. Wipe the wheels occasionally with a damp cloth. Check the heads and attachments for trapped fibres. Pull away trapped fibres from carpet heads and beater bars. Use the vacuum cleaner and the crevice tool to get out any other dust and dirt. Empty the bag or lift-off canister and change filters regularly.

Use all the attachments. They can do many of the jobs that require a duster or a brush in half the time. They include:

Crevice tool: Probably the most useful of all the attachments, especially if the cleaner has a long tube attachment. Use it to clean the edge of carpets – no cleaner can reach right to the edge – as well as behind radiators, along the tops of baseboards and to remove cobwebs. It can also be used to get dust out of intricate plaster moulding, but go easy if the plaster is old or crumbling.

Upholstery brush: This looks like a smaller version of the large brush attachment. Use it for stairs, also for upholstery. It is amazing how crumbs and other detritus accumulate down the back of the sofa. Vacuum upholstery once a week and occasionally use the crevice tool to get into all the nooks and crannies. Also use this attachment to vacuum the mattress once a month (see 'Household pests', p. 322). With the power turned low, use the upholstery brush on curtains and fabric blinds.

Dusting brush: The best way to clean Venetian blinds. Also use this soft brush to clean dusty shelves and, on minimum power, the television screen, lampshades, the tops of books, even ornaments (go easy on that Ming vase, though).

THE STEAM CLEANER

Steam cleaners are very popular in Europe, and are increasingly being used in Britain and the United States. They generate super-heated steam (300°F, which cools to 250°F when it leaves the machine) to clean all hard surfaces: ovens, cookers, carpets, upholstery, even windows. They require no chemicals – the steam is what removes dirt.

Typically steam cleaners are supplied with a large brush for carpets and floors, a smaller brush for upholstery and tiles, a narrow steam jet, extension tubes, cleaning cloths and a window cleaner. To use, fill the tank with tap water (in hard-water areas, a chemical water softener is added), and heat up (it takes ten minutes or so).

A switch on the handle releases the steam. The idea is to direct the jet at whatever is being cleaned. The steam loosens the dirt, which can then be wiped off with a cloth.

Steam cleaners are particularly useful in bathrooms and kitchens, because the heat loosens grease and other ground-in dirt, including tricky-to-remove things like paint spatters on baths and basins.

They can also be used for carpets and upholstery, but it is rather a slow process and the results can be variable. Really filthy carpets should be professionally cleaned, and the steam cleaner can then be used once a month to ensure they do not become filthy again.

223

OTHER CLEANING GADGETS

The following are not strictly necessary or fall into the class of luxury, but are worth considering.

Central vacuum systems: A vacuum unit is installed in a garage or similar and hidden pipes lead from it to each room in the house, where there is an inlet hole. A vacuum hose is attached to the inlet hole and the dust is sucked straight out of the house and into the vacuum unit. These systems are very efficient and neat, and because dust is taken straight out of the house, they are good for asthma sufferers. But they are expensive and cannot be installed in houses without stud walls.

Three-in-one vacuum cleaner: These machines wash carpets and upholstery as well as vacuuming. They can be a bit cumbersome.

Robot cleaners: These small cleaners use intelligent navigation systems to cover every inch of the carpet, going round and under furniture, and returning to a recharging station to top up the power. They promise effortless cleaning and are particularly good for older people, or for those who cannot lift ordinary vacuum cleaners. But they are expensive and it is a bit of a nuisance to set them up. They are also very slow and cannot negotiate stairs.

Handheld vacuums: These small hand-held cleaners are useful for dealing with spills in the kitchen, for vacuuming the interior of the car, or for doing the stairs if you cannot manage a full-size cleaner. They do not have a large capacity and tend to be very noisy.

Hard-floor cleaner: These machines vacuum and wash all hard floors, including vinyl and other non-porous finishes, such as ceramics. They are useful if you have a lot of hard floors to wash. Otherwise, a mop and bucket will do most average kitchens and bathrooms.

Floor polisher: A floor polisher is worth considering only if you have acres of parquet, because the machine is heavy and can be cumbersome. Polishers can be used to apply floor polish or to buff up an existing finish.

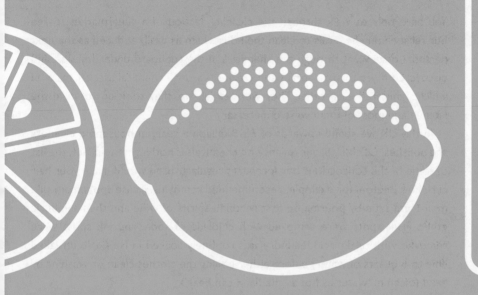

CHAPTER 9
Household Chemicals

Soap is civilisation

Unilever company slogan

You have only to walk through the cleaning section of a supermarket to see our reliance on chemicals to clean the house. I am as easily seduced as the next person. I once went through the chemicals in the cupboard under my sink, and discovered more than 30 sprays and creams – a small chemical arsenal, many of which duplicated each other. They were expensive, they took up room in the kitchen and most of them were unnecessary.

In the UK we spend upwards of £518 million a year on household cleaners and polishes. Of course, our reliance on chemicals is nothing new. In fact, the list of some of the concoctions our forebears regularly used would make your hair curl. Mrs Beeton, for example, recommended removing grease spots from silk, moiré and satin by pouring on first rectified spirits of wine and then sulphuric ether. Fruit spots were removed with chloride of soda, and ink spots were removed with oxalic acid. Laundry was routinely soaked in lye (½ lb unslaked lime to 6 quarts of water) before either boiling the clothes clean or washing by hand (often in 'water as hot as the hand can bear').

But while our ancestors were not afraid of using hazardous chemicals with what now seems now like admirable sang-froid, they were not exposed to anything like the chemicals that we are.

In 1930 the global production of chemicals was 1 million tonnes. Today, that figure has risen to 400 million tonnes. In the same period, the number of chemicals produced and marketed has risen from around to 30,000 to up to 100,000, of which 17,000 are used in household products. Some 100,000 different substances are registered in the EU market, and every day we ingest a cocktail of chemicals through the air we breathe, the water we drink, the food we eat and through our skin. Little is known about the effects on our health of prolonged contact with these products, not to mention the effect on wildlife and the environment.

There is also an increasing body of research that links frequent use of household cleaning products and other chemicals in the home to the increase in childhood asthma. In a study of 14,000 children by Bristol University in

2004, researchers found that in the 10 per cent of families who used household chemicals such as bleach, carpet cleaners and air fresheners most frequently, children were twice as likely to experience wheezing as those in the families where they were used least.

The trouble is that it is almost impossible for the consumer to make an informed choice because manufacturers are not legally bound to declare a full list of contents. European Commision recommendations suggest that products containing specified substances at a concentration greater than 0.2 per cent should be listed, along with those containing enzymes and preservatives. But it is all rather vague. A label may say 'phosphates', for example, but not how much or what they are. Sometimes, labels seem deliberately obfuscatory – why list 'aqua' at the top of a list of ingredients, for example, as some manufacturers do, when most people would more readily recognise it as 'water'?

I do not believe that all chemicals should be banned from the home. Modern household cleaners have made a major advance in our lives. But we should limit their number and the amount we use. When we do use them, we should use as little as possible of the product, and very strong chemicals should be used sparingly, if at all. Chemicals we should use sparingly include bleach; ammonia (found in window cleaners); Triclosan, an antibacterial found in multi-purpose cleaners and detergents; sodium or potassium hydroxide, found in oven cleaners; and benzenes (also found in oven cleaners).

But in the modern world, one has to be realistic about these things. Throughout this book, I have sometimes recommended chemicals that are extremely toxic – generally when nothing else will do. But I have tried to do this as rarely as possible and have always suggested using the minimum amount of product to get the job done.

GREEN CLEANING
It is possible to carry out many cleaning procedures without chemicals at all – by using, for example, a steam cleaner, or microfibre cloths and mark and stain eraser sponges, which clean using only water. There are also growing numbers of eco-friendly cleaning products, which though they contain chemicals, are based on natural ingredients that are more easily broken down in the environment than synthetic chemicals. Many of the new luxury household products also contain low-impact, gentle, natural ingredients.

227

Other natural products with less environmental impact include such traditional favourites as vinegar, lemon juice and baking soda. These also have the advantage of being versatile and cheap.

Technically speaking, of course, these 'natural' products could be considered to be toxic. Lemon juice and vinegar, for example, are both strong acids. Very high concentrations of salt can kill you. In general terms, though, they are safe for humans to ingest, absorb or breathe. They also readily break down in the environment. Non-toxic cleaners also include those whose chemicals are generally understood – for example, dish soap is most definitely a chemical, but it biodegrades readily and while you would not want to eat it or rub it all over your body, you are not likely to end up in casualty if you do. Get used to reading the back of bottles of household cleaner: if something is described as poison, toxic, hazardous or corrosive, use it with caution.

The basic household cleaners

On a day-to-day basis, I suggest you use as few chemicals as possible around the house – for all the reasons given above. The good news is that it is possible to keep a house perfectly clean with just a handful of products.

DISH SOAP

I use dish soap for almost everything. It is particularly good for cleaning old, fragile items, or anything that is sensitive to detergent, such as limestone or marble. It is very good for windows and mirrors – add just a drop to water – and for cleaning wooden floors.

Use the gentlest dish soap possible – anything eco-friendly, unperfumed or designed for sensitive skins is best. Throughout this book, whenever I mention dish soap, this is the kind I mean.

ALL-PURPOSE DETERGENT

For heavier cleaning jobs, you need a good all-purpose liquid detergent. Yes, this is a chemical, but don't beat yourself up about it. Use it sparingly to clean kitchens, bathrooms, floors and paintwork. One basic cleaner will do most jobs. Supermarket brands are generally cheaper than proprietary brands, but I confess I have a fondness for Mr. Clean because it is what my mother used. Do not be seduced into buying different cleaners for specific areas of the house – a bathroom cleaner, a kitchen cleaner and so forth. Manufacturers want you to think that you need different cleaners because then you will buy more. Do not line their pockets.

TOILET CLEANER

I am afraid you do need to use a chemical to clean the lavatory. There are pumice toilet cleaners out there, but they will eventually scratch the surface of the toilet bowl, so toilet cleaner it will have to be. You could use bleach, but bleach will not remove limescale.

> Note: Use either toilet cleaner or bleach, not both, and certainly not both together. Mixing bleach with any substance other than water can potentially produce toxic gas.

229

FURNITURE POLISH

Use a good paste, high-beeswax polish. Beeswax polishes are expensive, but you will only be using them once a year, so they are worth the outlay. Do not use silicone polishes and sprays. Unlike wax polishes, they do not fill in scratches on the wood, but leave a hard, shiny surface layer, which builds up over time and ruins the appearance of the piece of furniture.

METAL POLISH

Again, do not buy different polishes for specific metals, with the exception of silver, which does need its own cleaner (other polishes will react with it). For silver, use either a cream polish or a dip; do not use wadding, which is too abrasive.

For brass, copper, chrome and stainless steel, I use a general-purpose metal cleaner from a car accessories shop. Autosol is a good all-round brand.

OTHER BASIC HOUSEHOLD CLEANERS

In addition to the above, you will need detergent for laundry and possibly fabric softener as well, plus a few proprietary stain removers (De-Solv-It, a solvent cleaner, White Wizard and Wine Away). If you have a dishwasher, you will need dishwasher detergent, rinse aid and possibly salt.

I also keep scouring powder or paste for heavy-duty cleaning jobs (for a recipe for home-made scouring powder, see p. 237), washing soda (for heavy-duty deodorising and drain cleaning), a non-caustic drain cleaner and a non-caustic oven cleaner for emergencies (though if you follow the tips for oven-cleaning given on p. 9, this should not be necessary). For keeping a protective shine on marble and metals, I use a microcrystalline wax. The best-known brand is Renaissance, but John Lewis now has its own brand.

Baking soda

Bicarbonate of soda, a.k.a. sodium bicarbonate, a.k.a. baking soda ($NaHCO_3$), a.k.a. bicarb is, in my opinion, one of the best and safest substances you can use around the home. You can even use it to clean your teeth in an emergency, though it doesn't taste very nice (baking soda is one of the main ingredients in proprietary whitening toothpastes). It is cheap, non-toxic and efficiently broken down in the environment. Use it to clean ovens, fridges, drains and much more. Buy it in bulk, rather than the tiddly little boxes sold in supermarkets. It must be admitted that, used on its own, baking soda is not strong enough for very heavy cleaning jobs. If your worktop or fridge is really filthy, you will probably have to resort to stronger cleaners. Baking soda works best on averagely dirty surfaces, or in conjunction with other chemicals, particularly vinegar. I have described many uses for baking soda throughout this book. Please turn to the index for specifics. In addition, try the following.

TO USE BAKING SODA ON KITCHEN SURFACES

Decant baking soda into a large shaker. Sprinkle over worktops and other surfaces to clean them. Stains, such as the ink from price stamps, tea bags left on the work top and fruit juice, can be removed by making a paste of baking soda and water and rubbing the stain until it disappears.

Sprinkle baking soda on a damp cloth and use to scrub wooden chopping boards. The baking soda will help remove odours such as onion or garlic.

Or:

Sprinkle the board with baking soda and spray with vinegar. The mixture will fizz furiously. Let the bubbles subside, then scrub the board. Rinse and dry.

Sprinkle baking soda in stainless steel sinks. Its slight abrasiveness will clean the sink without scratching.

Sprinkle baking soda into rubber gloves to deodorise them and to make them slide on more easily (if your skin is too sensitive for this, just turn rubber gloves inside out to store).

TO USE BAKING SODA ON POTS AND PANS

To remove burnt bits from saucepans, fill with 2 inches of water and bring to the boil. Add a teacupful of baking soda and leave the pan overnight. The next day, the burnt bits should have lifted.

Clean white enamel saucepans by boiling a generous amount of baking soda and water in them for 10 minutes.

Remove stains and odours from non-stick pans by adding 2–3 tbsp baking soda to half an inch of water. Bring to the boil and simmer until the stains have disappeared (be careful not to let it boil dry). You may need to season the pan again with oil.

Clean copper pans by sprinkling half a lemon with baking soda and using it to scrub the metal.

TO USE BAKING SODA ON COOKERS AND OVENS

Clean glass stove tops by sprinkling with baking soda and adding a little water to make a paste. Rinse and wipe dry to a shine.

To remove burnt-on food splatters on stove tops, wet the area first, then sprinkle liberally with baking soda. Let it sit for an hour, then clean off (make sure there is enough water and baking soda to soak into the burnt-on bits). See also 'To clean conventional ovens', p. 10.

TO USE BAKING SODA IN THE FRIDGE

See 'To clean the fridge', p. 17.

TO USE BAKING SODA IN DRAINS

See the sections on cleaning and unblocking drains, p. 49.

Vinegar

Like baking soda, vinegar is a cheap, efficient, non-toxic and environmentally safe cleaner. Vinegar – distilled malt vinegar, although the brown variety will do – is the best descaler, and is wonderful for cleaning windows, is a good deodoriser and a gentle cleaner. It is especially good for descaling kettles and giving a shine to glass.

Vinegar, which means literally 'sour wine', results when wine or another alcoholic liquid is allowed to ferment a second time by exposure to bacteria in the air. Eventually, the fermented liquid will become vinegar – acetic acid ($C_2H_4O_2$). Vinegar can be made from the juice of many sorts of fruit and grain, including barley (to make malt vinegar), apples (to make cider vinegar) and grapes (to make wine vinegar). The Japanese make vinegar from rice; the Filipinos make it from coconut. White distilled vinegar is often made from wood.

Vinegar is extremely useful for housekeeping. It deodorises, cleans, restores colours and is the best descaler. It will also kill germs.

For housekeeping purposes, the best vinegar to use is white distilled malt vinegar. Its smell seems to linger less than brown malt vinegar, though this can be used very successfully. Do not, however, use vinegar on any porous surface or anywhere you suspect it might stain. Never use vinegar on marble, alabaster or unglazed pottery.

Buy vinegar in bulk to save money.

TO USE VINEGAR AROUND THE HOUSE

I have described many uses for vinegar throughout this book. Please turn to the index for specifics. In addition, try the following:

Remove water marks from worktops and kitchen surfaces
by cleaning them with a paste made from
2 tbsp salt and 1 tbsp vinegar.

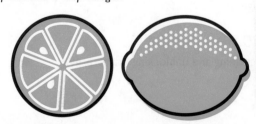

Spray full-strength vinegar on a chopping board last thing at night and allow to dry; do the same on worktops, to keep them smelling sweet.

If you want a stronger vinegar (say, to tackle very heavy limescale), bring to the boil and simmer until reduced by about a third. Allow to cool and use.

Instead of adding vinegar to final rinse when washing glasses (see p. 148), spray newly washed glasses lightly with vinegar before drying immediately.

As well as the lemon and baking soda mixture mentioned on p. 231, copper pans can be cleaned with a paste of equal quantities of vinegar and table salt. Rinse and polish to a shine.

Dark stains on aluminium pans can be cleaned by adding equal quantities of vinegar and water and boiling.

A small dish of vinegar will attract fruit flies keeping them away from fruit.

Although the best way to clean windows is with dish soap (see p. 247), you can stretch commercial liquid (not cream) window cleaner by combining it with vinegar and water (to one third commercial cleaner, add one third water and one third vinegar.

Disinfect the doorknob and toilet handle in the bathroom by spraying with undiluted vinegar and wiping dry.

Note: Water and electricity do not mix. For light switches, spray the cloth very lightly, then use it to wipe around the switch.

Another use for vinegar: Vinegar was the saviour of my misspent youth. When I drank too much, as you do in your twenties, I would invariably get hiccups. Then someone told me that a teaspoon of vinegar is an instant cure. I tried it. It worked. It works every time.

Lemon juice

Lemon juice is actually quite a strong acid. With a pH value of 2.3, it is stronger than vinegar (pH 2.8). It can therefore be substituted in any household procedure where vinegar is used. The cost, however, would be prohibitive. Vinegar is much cheaper and comes in the large quantities required for housekeeping. Keep lemon juice for smaller jobs or use up lemons that have been used for cooking. Lemon juice is excellent for cutting through grease, hence its inclusion in many dish soaps and detergents. It has excellent bleaching abilities, it makes the house smell fresh and it is entirely harmless.

TO USE LEMON JUICE AROUND THE HOUSE

Lemon juice is mentioned throughout this book (see index). Here are some more ideas:

> Half a lemon dipped in salt will remove rust stains from vinyl floors. Rub into the stain, then rinse with clean water and dry.
>
> Place a squeezed-out lemon half on top of a rusty screw head (making sure the flesh is in contact with the metal) and leave overnight. The next day, enough rust should have gone to enable you to get a purchase on the screw. Alternatively, soak a paper towel in lemon juice and cover the rusty screw.
>
> Remove rust stains from clothing by soaking in a little lemon juice and water. Rinse, then launder as usual.
>
> Use lemon juice as a substitute for vinegar when descaling. Stick a lemon half on the end of a limescale-encrusted faucet and leave for a couple of hours.
>
> Boil squeezed-out lemon halves in a stainless steel saucepan to remove a light build-up of limescale.
>
> Run lemon rinds through the waste disposal to clean and freshen it.
>
> Half a lemon dipped in salt can be used to clean copper and brassware.

234

Other household cleaners

There are one or two other products that you might consider using. I rarely use them myself, but the following are all things that some people swear by.

ANTI-BACTERIAL CLEANERS

In recent years a number of anti-bacterial products have come on to the market, many of which contain Triclosan, a chlorophenol that is suspected of causing cancer in humans. Phenol can cause a variety of skin irritations, is a poison if ingested, and can be stored in the body. Ask yourself why you think you need anti-bacterial products in your house. It is not a hospital. Unless someone in the house is seriously ill, with a compromised immune system, normal levels of cleanliness, common sense and soap and hot water will keep a house clean enough for family life. What is more, there is some evidence that people who use anti-bacterial products tend to rely on them, while neglecting basic rules of hygiene. It is, for example, no use spraying a worktop with an anti-bacterial spray and then wiping it over the surface with a dirty cloth.

AMMONIA

Make no mistake, ammonia is a highly toxic substance. It is corrosive and gives off choking fumes. But it is probably worth keeping a bottle for for heavy-duty degreasing jobs – for example, for cleaning grill pans (see 'To clean grill pans', p. 13).

BLEACH

There are two main types of bleach for household use – chlorine bleach and oxygen bleach. Oxygen bleach contains sodium percarbonate or hydrogen peroxide. It is used mainly in the laundry, where it is a useful chemical because it can be safely used on coloured fabrics (see 'Bleach', p. 161).

235

The bottle of bleach found under virtually every kitchen sink is chlorine bleach, a solution containing sodium hypochlorate with its familiar suffocating smell. It is an effective sanitiser and deodoriser. It brightens laundry and whitens whites. It is extremely cheap.

On the other hand, it is highly toxic. It should not be allowed to splash on skin or into eyes, and it is potentially deadly if swallowed. Mixing chlorine bleach with other chemicals, especially acids or ammonia, will produce dangerous gas and/or an explosion. Bleach cannot be used on all fabrics, and over-bleaching can damage them. It can also damage copper, aluminium, silver and non-stainless steel and marble. Do not pour chlorine bleach down the drain if you have a septic tank. Since I started writing this book, I have almost completely ceased to use chlorine bleach, and now use it only when absolutely necessary.

TO USE BLEACH AROUND THE HOUSE

Plain chlorine bleach can be used for a variety of cleaning and disinfecting chores, but should be used sparingly. Do not use bleach as a matter of course, but save it for occasions when a disinfectant is necessary, such as when a member of the family has been ill or when cleaning up after pets. Make a solution of 8 fl oz bleach, I gallon warm water and I tbsp washing detergent and use to clean and disinfect hard surfaces, such as worktops, sinks, floors, tiles and bathrooms. Wash the surface, leave the solution on for about five minutes, rinse and let it dry.

To sanitise and disinfect cat-litter trays and dustbins, make a solution of I fl oz bleach per I pint of water. Empty the bin or tray, wash it with hot soapy water and rinse with plain water. Wash again with the bleach solution and leave for five minutes. Rinse again and leave to dry.

Bleach is the best and cheapest mould remover (see 'Ventilation', p. 95). In fact, it is the main component of most proprietary mould removers.

Mildewed shower curtains can be brought back from the dead by soaking in a solution of bleach (one part bleach to four parts water) for 10 minutes or so before washing in the machine.

HOUSEHOLD WIPES

Wipes – that is strong paper or synthetic sheets impregnated with cleaning fluids – are extremely popular. There are wipes to clean bathrooms, to clean kitchens, to degrease cookers, to clean windows and flushable wipes to clean toilets. At the time of writing, they cost on average $6.00 for a packet of about 60.

If you live in a tiny house or flat with little or no storage space, wipes have their uses. But they offend my frugal soul. A large bottle of all-purpose cleaner costs around $5.00 (less if you buy a supermarket brand) and a bumper packet of cleaning cloths will set you back the same – or cost even less if you buy them in bulk from janitorial suppliers, or cost nothing at all if you cut up old T-shirts or sheets and use them as cleaning cloths.

Even if you slosh the cleaner on to the cloth with abandon, it has to be cheaper than using a wipe that is designed to be thrown away after one use – adding to Britain's growing mountain of rubbish.

People like wipes because they seem more convenient than the conventional cloth-and-bottle-of-cleaner option. As someone said to me, using a kitchen wipe on worktops does not really feel like cleaning.

Making your own household cleaners

If you have run out of a cleaning product, make your own. It is good to have a small repertoire in case of emergency, added to which, making your own household cleaners, like making jam or bread, satisfies the inner housewife. Generally, home-made cleaners use fewer chemicals than manufactured products and are cheaper and more environmentally friendly.

TO MAKE A GENERAL CLEANER

To 1 gallon of hot water, add half a teacup each of baking soda, vinegar and household ammonia. Use as a general household cleaner.

TO MAKE A FLOOR CLEANER

To 1 gallon hot water, add a squirt of dish soap and 1 teacup of vinegar. This can be used on all floors, including wooden ones, but make sure the mop is wrung out until barely damp.

237

TO MAKE A CLEANER FOR BATHS, BASINS AND TILES

Put 4 oz baking soda into a small bowl, add 1 tbsp dish soap and add enough vinegar to make a creamy liquid. If you like, put it into a squeezy bottle, but it will not keep, so use it up quickly.

TO MAKE A SCOURING POWDER

Mix together equal quantities of baking soda, borax and cooking salt. Store in a large shaker and use as any scouring powder.

TO MAKE A CARPET AND UPHOLSTERY CLEANER

If you have a spill on a carpet and no carpet cleaner to hand, the following home-made cleaners work very efficiently and are good to know in case of emergencies:

Make a solution of water and mild, unperfumed, uncoloured dish soap in a deep bowl. Swish the water round with your hand vigorously to create a mass of foam. This will be your cleaning agent.

Take a white cloth and scoop up some of the foam with it. Work the foam into the stain. When you are satisfied that it has gone, rinse with a solution of half and half water and white vinegar, and blot well. Then rinse with plain water, and blot well with a white paper towel to remove excess moisture. Place white paper towels on top, weight them down and allow to dry. When dry, vacuum or brush to bring up the pile.

Another carpet cleaner: On wool carpets, use a gentle detergent designed for wool. The proportion is 1 tsp detergent to half a pint of barely lukewarm water. Work inwards on the stain to avoid spreading it. Do not rub, but blot well as you go. Once you are satisfied that the stain has gone, spray the area with a solution of four parts water to one part white vinegar. Place plenty of white paper towels on top of the damp patch and place a weight on top. Leave overnight. When dry, vacuum to bring up the pile.

238

TO MAKE A WINDOW CLEANER

Most commercial window cleaners are made from a mixture of ammonia, alcohol and water. Think how cheap these products are and how much you are therefore paying for a fancy bottle, label, advertising, marketing and so forth.

Hold that thought, and when your bottle of commercial window cleaner is empty, refill it with a mixture of 45 per cent water, 45 per cent rubbing alcohol and 10 per cent household ammonia. Shake well before using.

This is particularly good for interior windows and mirrors.

TO MAKE A FURNITURE POLISH

Grate a block of beeswax into a pan. Pour over turpentine to cover and leave in a warm place (not over direct heat because turpentine is highly inflammable) until the wax has dissolved. Stir very thoroughly. Pour into a jar to store.

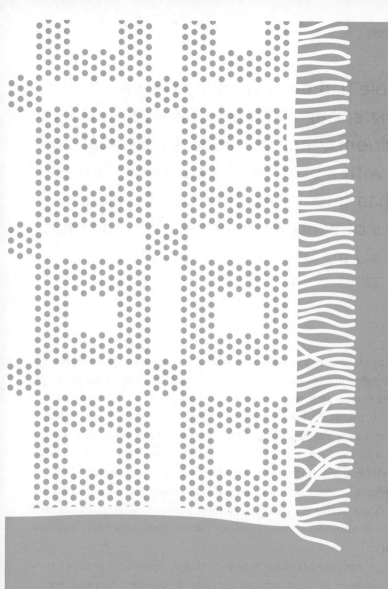

CHAPTER 10
How to Clean

The mole had been working very hard all morning, spring-cleaning his little home. First with brooms, then on ladders and steps and chairs, with a brush and a pail of whitewash; till he had dust in his throat and eyes, and splashes of whitewash all over his black fur, and an aching back and weary arms.

Kenneth Grahame, The Wind in the Willows

A few years ago, I was invited to a lecture on dust, for conservators and cleaners of historic country houses. It turned out to be an intriguing morning. You might have thought that there is not enough to say about dust to fill one and a half hours. Nothing could have been further from the truth. Dust, it appeared, is not just dust. It can be 'embedded', 'corrosive' and 'abrasive'. It can attract insects, and yet also filter out light, thus making it 'pragmatic'. More lyrically, dust is 'part of life', it is 'dirt in the wrong place', a matter of hurt pride to cleaners who feel that dust reflects on their housekeeping skills. And dust is always with us: it is 'Schrodinger's cat' in that it always has a potential existence, but does not exist until it has been observed. What we did not discuss (that came later) was how to get rid of it.

This chapter not only addresses how to dust, but explains the best and least time-consuming way to clean virtually everything you might find in a house, with special techniques for the different materials.

'If a job's worth doing, it's worth doing well' is one of those sayings that is full of common sense, but has a curiously lowering effect upon the spirit. It sounds smug and scolding and implies that doing something 'well' also means that it's going to take an inordinate length of time. It makes more sense to say that if you're going to do something, you may as well learn to do it properly – not for its own sake, but for the advantages it brings.

Just as a schedule makes a house run more smoothly, the right technique and the right equipment prolong the life of whatever it is that is being cleaned. The wrong way of cleaning can damage an object beyond repair – for example, wood will be ruined by water or the incorrect polish; and a stain in a carpet can be set indelibly with the application of the wrong chemical. Conversely, the right way to clean something will keep it in the best condition for as long as it is needed or wanted. We spend so much on our houses and the things that go in them that it seems perverse not to learn how to look after them. This is particularly important in times of a downturn in the property market. Remember the property boom of the 1980s, when you moved house as soon as the oven got dirty? When the property market slows, people tend to stay put, so maintenance becomes a priority if we don't want the house to become shabby.

But more important than any of the above is the time that cleaning takes. Even I, who have written a book on housework, do not enjoy it for its own sake. Housework is just something that has to be done – as quickly and efficiently as possible, so I can get on with the rest of my life, even if that merely means that I can lie on the sofa and watch telly.

241

The essentials

When it comes to cleaning houses, the only way is down. In other words, the correct technique is to start at the top of the house and work down. This way, you will know that the whole house is clean and that you haven't gone over anything twice – something that can happen if you take a haphazard, scattergun approach, doing a little bit here and a little bit there.

But the kitchen is likely to need the most work, so a little preparatory work is in order. Before starting to clean the rest of the house, go into the kitchen and check what needs doing. Now is the time to put anything very dirty in to soak in hot, soapy water such as the grill pan or oven shelves. Squirt some liquid detergent on the stovetop and leave it to work.

Now carry on with the rest of the house. Turn to the relevant chapters within this book for ways of tackling specific problems in specific rooms.

The reason to start at the top is that you bring all the dust down with you. Begin with the bedrooms, then go on to the bathroom(s). As you finish each room, shut the door. Finally, clean the landing before starting on the stairs, which should be cleaned from top to bottom, meaning you will always be standing on a dirty step and cleaning towards you.

Now start on the downstairs rooms, working in the same methodical way. Clean the living-room(s), dining-room and study, along with any other rooms such as a cloakroom or utility room. As you finish each room, shut the door to prevent dust flying in. Clean the hallway before finally tackling the kitchen – which will be much easier to clean after the initial preparations.

To clean a room

The rules for cleaning a room are left to right, top to bottom and back to front. The idea is to get back to the door, knowing that each part is clean and than you have not gone over the same area twice.

It saves time to gather together your equipment before you start, to avoid having to stop and go and get something half-way through the job. The amount depends on the level of cleaning you plan to do, but at the very least will include dusters (and possibly brushes for dusting), cleaning cloths, some sort of cleaning fluid, a bucket and mop for wet work, a broom or vacuum cleaner for floors, and any specialist cleaners for specific jobs. Also arm yourself with a black plastic trash bag for emptying waste-paper baskets and any other rubbish.

Cover your clothes with an apron or overall and wear rubber gloves if necessary.

The first job is to open all the windows, which has the double effect of airing the room as it is being cleaned and also dispersing dust and chemicals in the air, which would otherwise be breathed in.

Don't start cleaning straight away. First, stand at the door and give the room a good, hard look. Look not for what needs doing, but for what does not. Your aim is to make as little work as possible.

Any big jobs, such as the windows, should be done first. Then tackle the rest of the room in an orderly fashion. Start at the door and work round the room in a clockwise direction, and from top to bottom. This might involve brushing cobwebs from the ceiling first, going on to dust shelves and their contents, starting at the highest, dusting furniture from top to bottom, and ending up at the bottom by dusting baseboards. Tidy as you go, putting any rubbish into the trash bag.

When you get back to the door, you know the whole room is done.

Finally, sweep, mop or vacuum the floor, depending on its type, working from the back of the room to the door. As you finish, close the door behind you.

TO DUST

Do not flick at things with a duster – all you will be doing is spreading dust round the room, ready to settle on everything you have just cleaned. Make a pad of the duster, tucking in the hemmed edges so that they do not catch on anything. This applies particularly to traditional yellow dusters with loose-hemmed edges; for preference, buy flat-hemmed dusters (see 'Dry cloths', p. 215).

First dust the contents of shelves. Take each piece off its shelf and dust it, putting it somewhere out of the way. It is easier to dust intricate pieces of china with a small soft brush – an old, well-washed blusher brush would be ideal.

Use the duster for large, flat surfaces. Press down on the dusty surface and pull the duster gently towards you. As you dust, keep turning the duster so that you are always using a clean surface. Dust from top to bottom and from front to back. If the surfaces are very dusty, sweep dust into the nozzle of the vacuum cleaner. Wash dusters regularly.

For skirting boards, high shelves and out-of-the-way places like behind radiators, it is quicker to use a fluffy lambswool duster, which catches the dirt in its fibres. Do not use feather dusters, which flick dust about. Their sharp quills can also damage objects.

TO WASH A CEILING

Don't. If a ceiling is so dirty that it needs washing, paint it instead. The most you should do is dust the corners for cobwebs. Use a fluffy duster, or lift them with a broom and vacuum using the long nozzle. Plaster ceiling roses around lights can also be vacuumed, using the brush attachment and a long nozzle. Intricate moulding can attract a lot of dust. Vacuum occasionally, using the brush attachment.

243

Once a year, get up on a ladder and clean the moulding. Use a hogshair brush to get all the dust out and, as you go, brush into the nozzle of the vacuum cleaner.

TO WASH A WALL

Marks on walls can make a room look shabby, so tackle them as they occur. The problem with removing marks is that if the surrounding area is dirty, the patch where the mark has been removed will show up lighter than the rest. On these occasions, you may think of washing the entire wall. But it is a chore and the results can be patchy. It is often much quicker and easier to give the room a lick of paint.

However, if you are determined to wash the wall, here is how to go about it. If one wall is cleaned, it is likely that all the others will have to be done too because the cleaned wall will look different from the rest. First make a clear pathway for yourself by removing all furniture to the centre of the room. Take down curtains and put dustsheets on the floor. Take down pictures, but leave picture hooks in place.

Have two buckets of water, one plain and one containing a little detergent, plus cloths for washing, rinsing and drying.

Start at the wall to the left-hand side of the door. Dust all over with a lambswool duster, then start washing.

Unlike other cleaning jobs, this is one that is done from the bottom to the top. The reason for this is that if you start at the top, drips will streak the dry, dirty areas below and are very difficult to remove. You might say that if you work from the bottom, dirty water will fall on to the newly washed areas, but it is simple just to wipe these marks off and they don't seem to leave streaks in the same way.

Dip the cloth in the bucket containing detergent and then wring well before washing. The latex paint generally used on walls may be water-soluble, so use as little water as possible. A well wrung-out cloth stops getting the walls too wet and also prevents water dripping down your arm and down the walls.

Work in patches (mentally dividing the wall into squares helps), and when one patch is clean, rinse it with water from the other bucket and then dry it. It helps to have someone else to help with the rinsing and drying.

Work round the room in a clockwise direction, until you get back to the door.

In practice, it is usually bathroom and kitchen walls that are washed most frequently, and the paint used here will probably be oil-based and therefore easier to wash. Another advantage is that these tend to be smaller than other rooms in the house, but there is no denying this is a truly dispiriting task. And wall painted with latex paint can only take a couple of cleanings before its surface deteriorates and it will need painting again anyway.

To wash a wallpapered wall: Don't. The only wallpaper that can be washed is vinyl, and even then you must go carefully. Use a very well wrung-out cloth and do not scrub.

Other wallpapers can be vacuumed. Do this once a quarter or so, using the upholstery brush and a gentle suction. Marks can sometimes be removed with a rubber eraser – use a white one so as not to transfer dye on to the wallpaper.

To tackle marks on an latex-painted wall: The problem with removing marks from a wall is that if the surrounding area is dirty, the patch where the mark has been removed will show up lighter than the rest.

When tackling marks, extra care needs to be taken with latex-painted walls. Latex paint is a water-based paint. If it is washed too hard with detergent, the paint can come off on the cleaning cloth, leaving light patches on the wall. Use a mark and stain eraser sponge (these are particularly good at removing crayon). Do not attempt to rub marks off with an eraser – it can leave a greasy mark on emulsion paint.

245

> *Note: To discourage children from writing on all the walls in the house, you could paint one area with blackboard paint (from DIY stores) and make this the designated wall-writing area. However, another school of thought says that this will only encourage them to think that walls are for writing on.*

TO WASH PAINTWORK

By 'paintwork', I mean all the painted bits that aren't walls or ceilings – the baseboards, window frames, doors, picture rails, wainscoting, staircases and banisters. They are painted with oil-based paints (gloss or eggshell), which are much more hard-wearing and easier to clean than latex. And the results are certainly more satisfactory.

To tackle marks on gloss paintwork: This hard-wearing oil-based paint is the easiest to clean. Most marks will respond to ordinary household detergent and elbow grease. If not, use water and a mark and stain eraser sponge. These sponges are particularly good at getting scuff marks off skirting boards, and removing crayon marks, ingrained grime (e.g. on painted banisters), ingrained dirt on window frames before washing windows, and finger marks on paintwork.

To tackle marks on eggshell paintwork: Although oil-based, eggshell paint is not as hard-wearing as gloss. As well as the usual marks, it can sometimes get what look like silvery pencil marks. These usually appear on doors where people have brushed past carrying something like a sports bag, or when wearing silver jewellery.

Because eggshell paint is more porous than gloss, marks can leave stains (crayon is a particular culprit), and excessive rubbing can damage the finish.

Start with an ordinary pencil eraser (the white plastic art erasers are best because coloured ones can make their own marks). If that does not work, use an eraser sponge, as above. But go easy – you can damage eggshell. If light patches appear, wash the rest of the paintwork with a detergent designed for paintwork, such as trisodium phosphate and water.

246

Windows

Windows are like a house's eyes. Clean windows let in light; they lift the spirits, and they make a room seem more welcoming. It is not surprising that when people are selling a house, one of the first things they are instructed to do is to clean the windows. Conversely, it doesn't matter how clean the interior of a room is, if the windows are dirty, it always seems depressing and grubby. Luckily, windows are very easy to clean – except where they are difficult to reach. How often you clean them depends on where you live. In a town, which is likely to be dusty and grimy, once a month is ideal, but once a quarter is more realistic. In the country, twice yearly in the autumn and spring will probably be all you need.

TO WASH A WINDOW

Try to clean windows on a cool, cloudy, windless day – not too hot, not too cold. Sunshine, wind and hot weather dry the glass too quickly, causing streaks. Washing windows in freezing conditions is an exercise in masochism, and if the washing water is too hot, you could cause the panes to crack through thermal shock.

Use warm water (for your own comfort – it makes no difference to the windows), to which you have added the merest drop of dish soap. This is what I normally use for exterior windows, because I feel I need water and detergent to cut through city grime. But if windows are not too dirty, plain water and a slug of vinegar will do just as well.

For interior windows and mirrors, try the home-made cleaner on p. 238.

Before cleaning the glass, wash the window frames and sills with hot water and detergent. This will avoid transferring dirt on to your clean window panes.

Sometimes black mould grows in the corners of windows. To remove, make a weak mixture of bleach – 1 tsp to a cup of cold water – dip an old toothbrush in it and use to remove the mould. Then wipe with a clean damp cloth before proceeding with the windows.

247

Now wash the window panes. Work from top to bottom to avoid dripping water on to just-washed glass. After washing, use a squeegee on the glass (this is the rubber-bladed tool that professional window-cleaners use). Work from top to bottom (or side to side – see below) in a figure-eight movement and wipe the blade between swipes.

Finally, wipe off any small streaks and give the glass a final polish with a clean, dry, lint-free cloth. If washing the outside and inside of the windows at the same time, squeegee the outside panes vertically and the inside panes horizontally. This makes it much easier to see if there are any streaks – and which side they are on.

> Tip: Fly spots on windows can be removed with a little straight alcohol – vodka does very well.

To wash a sash window: Sash windows are lovely. They look elegant and they are an extremely effective way to ventilate a house (always open them at both top and bottom to ensure a good exchange of air). But they can be difficult to clean, especially if they are inaccessible by ladder.

To clean the outsides of sash windows from the inside, first pull down the upper sash, lean out and clean as much of it as you can safely reach. Push up the lower sash, sit on the window sill and clean the rest of the upper sash.

Reverse the sashes. Pull the upper sash down as far as it will go and push up the lower sash. Clean as much of the top of the lower sash as you can. Close the upper sash and, again sitting on the window sill, clean the rest of the lower sash.

This can be a nerve-racking procedure, especially on upper floors, which is often made more difficult if the windows are old and rickety, or if they stick. Be sensible: dirty windows are preferable to lying broken and bloody on the pavement.

To clean a vinyl window: These plastic frames are supposed to be low- or even zero-maintenance, but they can get very grimy, with ground-in dirt that is impossible to remove with detergent. Instead, use a mark and stain eraser sponge. These are the best things I have found for cleaning all plastic, including plastic garden furniture.

WINDOW-CLEANING PRODUCTS

Glass is particularly easy to clean, and by far the best cleaner for it is the water/dish soap mixture mentioned above. If you insist on using a commercial window cleaner, use one of the liquid cleaners. Avoid cream cleaners, which always leave streaks.

Always use a lint-free cloth, or you will be trying to pick bits of fluff off the cleaned windows. Use one for washing, one for drying. Lint-free linen cloths (available at better home goods stores) are better than sponges, which hold too much lather.

Many people swear by the traditional chamois leather, but I dislike its slimy feel, and it seems to take an awful lot of rubbing to get rid of the last streaks. Save your chamois leather for polishing your pearls (see 'Jewellery', p. 81).

A traditional method of cleaning windows is to use vinegar and water and then to wipe the glass with old newspaper. The ink in the newsprint is reputed to give a protective screen. On the contrary, I have found that the ink makes everything filthy – the glass, the newly washed window frames and sill, my hands, my rubber gloves, anything, in fact, that it touches.

SELF-CLEANING WINDOWS

A few companies have developed glass that cleans itself. The best known is Activ by Pilkington.

The glass has an extremely thin coating, 15 nanometres thick, of microcystalline titanium oxide, a compound that is used in, among other things, toothpaste and sun creams. The coating reacts to ultraviolet rays in normal daylight, causing a reaction that breaks down and disintegrates organic dirt on the glass, even things like birds' mess.

The coating is also 'hydrophilic', meaning water does not bead up on it. Thus, when it rains, instead of forming the usual raindrops on the window pane, the water 'sheets' down the glass, carrying away the dirt. It also dries evenly, so the glass is not marked.

In dry conditions, simply hosing down the windows will produce the same effect. At the time of writing it cost around 10 per cent more than ordinary glass.

It is worth considering for skylights, conservatory roofs and for any inaccessible windows. As well as being convenient, it has environmental credentials in that it does not require any harsh chemicals to clean it – just water.

249

Floors

There is a scene in my favourite film, *When Harry Met Sally*, where Sally tells Harry what went wrong with her relationship with Joe, her boyfriend of five years, from whom she has recently split. One of the problems, she says, is that she and Joe had always said they were much better off than their married friends because they could make love on the kitchen floor whenever they wanted. But now they are no longer together, she realises that they had never actually done this. 'Not once,' she says. 'It's this cold, hard Mexican ceramic tile.'

Perhaps Sally's sentiments struck a chord with me, because I used to live in a house that had terracotta tiles on the kitchen floor. They were freezing cold underfoot, and were hard on the legs and feet. They seemed to drain all the heat out of the room in winter, and anything dropped on them stood no chance. And, no, I never made love on them either.

On the other hand, they were fantastically hard-wearing. I think they had been laid some time in the 1970s and, with a good scrubbing, looked as good as new. The choice of hard flooring is always this compromise between practicality and comfort.

Take wooden floors, the acme of modern design. As one, it seemed, the British nation ripped up its carpets and sanded and varnished the floorboards underneath. People quickly realised the drawbacks. Floorboards in most houses were not meant to be uncarpeted. With top-quality boards, you could get away with it. But in Victorian houses – the main victims of this trend – floorboards were often made of cheap, knotty softwood, which over the years had shrunk, leaving great gaps between them.

Bare boards, people discovered, are draughty; dust flies up between them, and it sounds as if a herd of elephants is on the move whenever someone gets up to make a cup of tea.

Despite this, they were seen as healthier than carpet, particularly for the allergy-prone. I would contend that this is only the case if the floor is kept as dust-free as possible. Otherwise, the dust and the dust mites it harbours fly round in the air (see 'Household pests', p. 322).

Whatever the reason – health, aesthetics, fashion – taste for the modern, clean look of hard floors continues. As well as traditional wood, stone and tile, there is a vast range of synthetic floor coverings that replicate the look of natural materials but are cheaper and easier to care for. They have helped fuel the taste for hard flooring as something beautiful in itself, and not just a necessity for places like kitchens and bathrooms. Hard floors are here to stay, so it pays to know how to keep them in good condition.

TO CARE FOR FLOORS

The following points apply to all floors, including stone, wood, laminate and carpet:

Take your shoes off. All over the world, people remove their shoes on entering a house – except in some Western countries, where it is seen as unacceptable. It is bad manners to insist that guests remove their shoes, but your family is another matter. By taking off their shoes, they will track much less dust and dirt into the house.

All carpets and flooring will be protected by a doormat. Put one at the entrance of every outside door. For more on types of doormat and how to care for them, see 'The hall', p. 138.

Put caster cups or felt pads (widely available) on the legs of furniture to prevent scratches on hard floors and dents in carpets.

Use rugs to protect areas of heavy traffic, such as in hallways, throughways from room to room and at the bottom of stairs (but not, for obvious reasons, at the top).

> Note: Dye from handmade rugs can stain light woods and carpet.
> Furthermore, sunlight can fade carpet and wooden floors, so you are
> likely to have darker patches where the rugs have been.

TO CLEAN HARD FLOORS

The following points apply to all hard floors, including wood, stone, laminate and vinyl.

Sweep or vacuum hard floors at least once a week, more often in areas of heavy traffic (kitchen floors will probably need sweeping once a day). Mop hard floors once a week. Before cleaning, attend to any spills or stains.

If you have large areas of floor, consider buying an electric floor cleaner. Modern models are lightweight and easy to use. They can be used on vinyl, ceramic and any sealed floor surface but because they deposit quite a lot of water on the floor, should not be used on any unsealed surface or wood block, which could swell.

> Tip: Always vacuum or sweep before using an electric floor cleaner.
> If there is any grit on the floor, the scouring action of the brushes
> can scratch the surface.

TO SWEEP A FLOOR

Use a soft-bristled brush, which will not lift the dust. In a large room, start at the back of the room in one corner and, working left to right, sweep the dust towards you until you reach the door. Use long, smooth strokes – you want to do as little work as possible. Finally, sweep the dust into a dustpan and brush or vacuum it up.

251

In a small room, start at each corner and sweep the dust to the centre in front of the door. Sweep the dust into a dustpan or vacuum it up.

TO VACUUM A FLOOR

Always vacuum a room last, after dusting, cleaning and any other tasks, such as making the beds. That way, you will get rid of all dirt and dust that you have knocked on to the floor. Adjust the vacuum cleaner to the type of floor you are vacuuming. To vacuum hard floors, use the brush attachment (cylinder models) or set the beater bar high (uprights). Reset the power to maximum. Work from the back of the room, ending at the door. Work from left to right, going across the room in strips. Hard floors are much quicker to vacuum than carpets, so you can do this speedily.

Note: Many people find vacuuming hard work. This is because they press down too hard on the floor. Don't make it difficult for yourself. Float the suction head across the floor – using only enough pressure to guide it where you want it to go. See also 'The vacuum cleaner', p. 219.

TO MOP A FLOOR

Move everything out of the way and off the floor. Have two buckets, one containing water and a little detergent or mild dish soap (just a dash – you do not want too many suds), the other bucket containing only clean water. Start from the back of the room. When mopping, the trick is not to use too much water. Dip the mop in the first bucket and wring it out as much as possible.

Mop the floor in a figure-eight pattern, pushing the mop right into the corners of the room. Once you have finished cleaning one section, dip the mop into the second bucket, wring the mop until almost dry and rinse the section you have just cleaned.

Proceed in this way, working from left to right across the room and from the back of the room to the front, until you reach the door. Replace the water in both buckets as it gets dirty. If you keep the mop as dry as possible, the floor should be almost dry by the time you have finished.

If a floor is very dirty, sometimes your only recourse is to get down on your hands and knees. Many people are reluctant to do this because of its connotations of skivvydom, but it is as quick as mopping, especially in a small room, and gets the floor much cleaner. While you're down there, you may as well take the opportunity to clean the baseboards at the same time.

Have two buckets, as above, and use a lint-free cotton floor cloth. Wring the cloth out until it is barely damp and clean from the back of the room to the front, rinsing as you go (again, with a barely damp cloth).

> Note: Some manufacturers recommend using only plain water for cleaning certain types of hard floor, particularly laminates. But water alone will not clean well enough. If in doubt, use a very small amount of a neutral pH detergent, such as mild dish soap, and make sure the mop is wrung almost dry. Rinse with plain water.

253

CORK FLOORS

Cork flooring is not seen much these days – its hey-day was in the 1970s. It is cheap, soft and warm underfoot, but because it can swell and crack if it gets wet, it is not suitable for bathrooms or kitchens. Most modern cork tiles come ready-sealed.

Care and cleaning: Sweep up as required – at least once a week. Mop with a barely damp mop and mild detergent (see above). Try to prevent water seeping into the cut edges of cork tiles.

In case of a flood, mop up as much water as possible, then open the windows and turn on the central heating to dry it out as quickly as possible.

LAMINATE FLOORS

A lot of 'wooden' floors are actually laminate, that is, made from a high-density fibreboard core, on top of which is a layer of photographic paper with an image of wood or stone and a top layer of melamine laminate. Some newer floors replace the photographic paper with a very thin slice of wood. Laminate usually comes in the form of strips or tiles that are designed to be locked together.

Modern laminates are extremely versatile and durable and come in a wide variety of styles. They are cheap, easy to lay and warm underfoot, but they can be affected by moisture or humidity, so check whether they are suitable for bathrooms. If they get badly damaged, dents cannot be sanded away.

Care and cleaning: Although modern laminate floors are extremely hard-wearing, they can be dented, scraped and scratched. High heels, dog and cat claws and furniture legs are the main culprits. To minimise damage, use caster cups or felt pads on furniture and put rugs in areas of heavy traffic. Place plants on stands, never in direct contact with the floor, even if you use drip trays.

Sweep or vacuum regularly to keep dust down. Mop once a week (more for kitchens), using mild detergent and a well wrung-out mop (see above). Never flood laminate floors with water when cleaning and avoid getting them too wet. Special laminate cleaners are also available.

Laminate floors have their own protective coating so should not be waxed. In fact, polishing is not only unnecessary, but can also make floors slippery or dull the finish. However, if the surface has become dulled, specialist laminate gloss coatings are available, which give a protective, non-slip gloss coating.

254

LINOLEUM FLOORS

Although it resembles vinyl (see below), linoleum is made from natural materials such as linseed oil, pigments and pine resin on a jute backing. Linoleum has been around for 150 years and was immensely popular because of its water-resistance and ease of cleaning. But linoleum manufacturers did not keep up with fashions and it fell out of favour from the 1960s in the face of competition from vinyl. Recently, it has had a bit of a revival, with new designs, and is now the fashionable choice for trendy urbanites who like its durability and the fact that it is a relatively natural product. It is slip-resistant, so is particularly suitable for kitchens and bathrooms. But it is expensive and needs to be laid professionally. Linoleum is sold in the UK as Marmoleum.

Care and cleaning: Vacuum and sweep regularly as required. Damp-mop once a week using a mild detergent. Specialist cleaners are also available – check with the supplier when buying the lino.

RESIN FLOORS

Resin flooring, which comes in tiles or strips, is made from a PVC resin compound compressed under high pressure and temperature. As with laminates (see above), a photographic image gives the look of a wide range of natural materials, including stone, wood, terracotta and metal: the effect is extremely lifelike but also warm underfoot and water-resistant. Resin flooring is non-porous so it is very suitable for kitchens and bathrooms. It can, however, be expensive when compared to other floorings, such as vinyl, and generally needs to be fitted professionally. Amtico is the best-known make.

Care and cleaning: Use caster cups or felt pads under furniture legs. Sweep regularly to prevent dust and grit scratching the surface. Damp-mop once a week or as necessary, using a mild detergent. If you like a slightly shiny surface, apply a specialist dressing (available from your supplier). The floor must be clean when the dressing is applied, and any excess dressing must be removed with a specialist product, also available from your supplier.

One flat I used to live in had Amtico floors in the shower room and kitchen. Instead of Amtico dressing, I used a natural liquid floor wax. It was made from carnauba wax and was extremely easy to apply. After cleaning the floor, pour a small amount of wax (the recommended amount is 1 eggcupful for 2 square metres) and spread it evenly over the floor with a damp mop or cloth. Allow to dry without polishing. It gives a protective coating and a semi-gloss finish. The reason I prefer it is that it is easily removed with hot water – no need for specialist removers.

255

RUBBER FLOORS

Increasingly popular in urban settings, rubber flooring is water-resistant and non-slip and is therefore particularly suitable for kitchens and bathrooms, although it can look a bit clinical. It is available in a wide range of colours and textures. As rubber ages, it hardens and improves.

Care and cleaning: Sweep and damp-mop as above. Occasionally use a specialist rubber cleaner (consult the supplier for advice).

STONE FLOORS

Natural stone floors are extremely fashionable and not the luxury item they once were, owing to cheap imports and modern methods of production. The most popular stone floors are limestone, marble, travertine and terrazzo (cement inset with marble chips), granite and slate. Natural stone is very heavy, so check the strength of the floor underneath before fitting. Timber sub-floors on upper storeys may need strengthening.

Stone floors are hard-wearing, luxurious and perfect for areas of heavy traffic, such as bathrooms, kitchens and hallways. They also combine well with the increasingly popular underfloor heating, which is a bonus because otherwise they are cold and hard underfoot. They still tend to be expensive, and anything that drops on them is likely to break.

Care and cleaning: Though stone floors appear hardy, they can be damaged by incorrect treatment. Protect areas of heavy traffic with rugs. Be aware that dyes from handmade rugs can stain stone floors, so do not lay rugs directly on the floor; use an underlay. This also prevents the rug from slipping (see 'Rugs', p. 264).

Most modern stone floors are sealed and polished, but they can be scoured by dust and grit. Sweep or vacuum regularly. Wipe up spills promptly. Mop once a week or as necessary, using mild detergent and a well wrung-out mop. If a floor is very dirty, with layers of built-up dirt and grease, use a specialist stone cleaner. Normal strong detergents and acids can damage stone, especially unsealed limestone and marble. Specialist stone sealants are also available and are particularly useful for sealing and protecting stone and other porous materials such as unglazed terracotta or quarry tiles.

TILE FLOORS

Ceramic tiles are one of the most hard-wearing floor surfaces, and especially useful for kitchens, bathrooms, utility rooms and conservatories. But they can chip or crack if anything heavy is dropped on them and are cold and hard underfoot. Be sure to buy tiles that are designed for floors; wall tiles are not hard-wearing enough.

Unglazed floor tiles, such as some quarry tiles or terracotta tiles, are porous so need to be sealed.

Care and cleaning: Glazed ceramic floor tiles are super-simple to keep clean. Sweep and damp-mop as required. Wet tiles can be very slippery, so always dry them afterwards. Unglazed tiles will need sealing with a specialist product. For more on ceramic tiles, see 'Stone', p. 267.

Note: For some reason, if you use a sponge mop to clean ceramic tiles, water always seems to collect in the grout.

VINYL FLOORS

Modern vinyl floors offer the widest varieties of colours and textures for flooring. Vinyl is tough, water-resistant and therefore particularly suitable for bathrooms and kitchens. It is available in sheets or tiles and comes in a variety of thicknesses and a wide price range from cheap to surprisingly expensive. It is very easy to clean, but can go yellow over time.

Care and cleaning: Vinyl is extremely easy to clean. Sweep or vacuum as necessary and wash floors at least once a week, using household detergent. If you want to give a protective shine, especially on white floors, use a liquid self-polishing floor finish.

WAXED FLOORS

Most hard floors can be waxed. Wax protects the surface and gives a soft, attractive shine. But it is extremely important to use only specialist floor waxes which are designed not to be slippery. For details on how to wax a floor, see below.

Care and cleaning: Sweep and mop solid waxed floors, including parquet and stripped floorboards as outlined above. To remove the dust and at the same time bring up the shine without waxing, an old-fashioned but extremely effective method is a paraffin cloth. To make, soak pieces of old blanket or heavy-duty cotton cloth in a mixture of half and half paraffin and malt vinegar. Hang them out to dry. To use, tie the cloth round the head of a dry mop and use to dust the floor. Store in airtight plastic boxes or bags when not in use.

TO WAX A FLOOR

Do not wax floors more than a couple of times a year. Not only will you be making unnecessary work for yourself, but polishing more frequently will cause the polish to build up and become smeary. Not only will this show up every mark, but eventually it will have to be removed, which is a dirty job.

Use a polish specially designed for floors. Many of these products require buffing after application. Use a small amount of wax (following manufacturer's recommendations). Using more is of no benefit; in fact, you will just be making

257

more work for yourself. Spread thinly but evenly over the floor with a cloth tied round the end of the mop. Buff either by hand or preferably with an electric floor polisher.

To maintain the shine in between waxings, use the paraffin cloth mentioned above, or buff up with the electric polisher, using clean felt pads and no polish.

Some modern waxes do not require buffing up after application. Of these, one very reliable (and easily found) make is One Step Floor Wax from the SC Johnson Company.

To use: pour a small amount of wax (the recommended amount is 1 eggcupful for 2 square metres). Spread evenly over the floor with a barely damp cloth or mop (or tie damp cloth to a mop head). Allow to dry.

Floors with a urethane finish do not need waxing, but see 'Wooden Floors in Bathrooms', below.

> Note: Never use furniture polish on wooden floors. It can give a lethally slippery finish.

258

WOODEN FLOORS

There are many different types of wood flooring. First, and most expensive, is solid wood flooring – solid pieces of wood, normally floorboards, nailed to a wooden sub-floor. It is not to be confused with 'real wood flooring', sometimes also known as 'wood construction flooring', which consists of planks made from two layers of solid wood with pieces of wood at 90° sandwiched in between. 'Engineered wood' flooring is made from a cross-ply backing with a veneer of solid wood on top. Wooden flooring can be nailed or glued down, but more often comes in tongue-and-groove planks that slot together to form a floating floor on top of a layer of underlay. Parquet flooring is made from blocks of hardwood laid in a pattern.

Wooden floors are the modern choice because they are warm underfoot, hard-wearing and beautiful, but they can be dented, scraped and scratched, and can swell or warp if they get too wet. For this reason, wood flooring is not recommended for kitchens or bathrooms (but see below).

Care and cleaning: Try to discourage people from walking on wooden floors wearing high heels. Cats and dogs can also do a surprising amount of damage by scratching floors with their claws. Put down rugs in areas of high traffic, but be aware that if sunlight fades the wood, you will be left with darker patches where the rug was lying. Always use an underlay or liner (this also stops rugs from slipping). Use caster cups or felt pads on legs of furniture.

The way you look after a wooden floor depends to an extent on the surface finish. This may be a waxed finish or – more likely with engineered or wood construction flooring – a urethane surface finish.

Wood and water do not mix, so wipe up spills immediately (beech is particularly susceptible to water staining).

If you have inherited a wooden floor and are not sure what type of surface it has, try the following on an inconspicuous area of the floor:

Scratch the floor with a coin and rub the scratched material between your fingers. If it feels waxy, it is probably a waxed surface.

Drop two drops of water on to the floor and leave for ten minutes. If white spots appear on the floor under the water, it is a wax finish. (Remove the spots by rubbing a little floor wax into them with grade 000 wire wool.)

Wooden floors in bathrooms: Most manufacturers and retailers do not recommend wooden flooring in bathrooms. In households where there are very messy bathers (for example, small children), that is probably sensible, but in an all-adult household it is possible, as long as you take a little care. I have had wooden flooring laid in a bathroom with great success. It was light beech 'real wood flooring', laid in tongue-and-groove planks. I bought a very large bathmat – the largest I could find – to prevent excess water splashing on to the floor. It was cleaned once a week using the damp-mop method outlined above. I think the secret to its success was using a natural wax floor polish every few months. This sealed any little gaps between the wood strips, making the floor more water-resistant and dried to a semi-gloss finish. In the two years I lived with that floor I had no problems either with water seepage or with swelling or warping of the wood.

259

TO CARE FOR A WOODEN FLOOR

Dust scours all wooden floors like sandpaper. Vacuum them frequently. Before vacuuming, check that grit has not lodged in the wheels of the cleaner (this seems to be more of a problem on upright models).

On cylinder models, use the brush attachment and sweep with the grain of the wood. On upright models, lift or turn off the brush, because it can damage wooden floors. Similarly, if you prefer to sweep, avoid hard bristle brooms (in any case, these will throw dust around, rather than sweeping it up).

TO WASH A WOODEN FLOOR

Wooden floors – whether waxed or with a urethane finish – can be washed. Use water and the merest smidgen of mild detergent, such as dish soap.

> Note: Although I would always recommend following manufacturer's instructions for cleaning wooden floors, I have found that some say that only water should be used. This does not get floors clean. I have washed floors with mild dish soap for years with no problems. But, if in doubt, test on an inconspicuous area of floor first. Or use a special cleaner designed for urethane floors.

Wring the mop until it is nearly dry. Rinse with clean water and an almost-dry mop and wipe dry if necessary with a dry mop or cloth (an old towel on the bottom of the mop is ideal).

Solid floors can also withstand sanding. If they are very dirty, do not try washing them. Hire a sander and prepare to get really filthy. After sanding, either wax or apply a varnish designed for floors. On balance, I prefer the soft sheen of a wax.

> Note: Engineered and wood construction flooring cannot normally be sanded, because the top layer is too thin. A very few makes can withstand one or two sandings during the floor's lifetime, but consult the manufacturer/supplier first and, if in doubt, do not sand.

Carpets

For a large part of the 1990s and right into the current decade, carpets have been decidedly out of fashion, having been ousted by wooden floors, which were seen as modern, cleaner and healthier. In particular, carpet had a reputation for harbouring dust mites, which are a major cause of asthma (see 'Household pests', p. 322). But the tide of fashion has been turning, as people begin to tire of the noisy, unforgiving hardness of wooden floors.

Carpet is warm and soft underfoot. It is particularly suited for bedrooms. Who wants to get out of bed on a cold winter morning and have to scuttle across a cold wooden floor?

As well as feeling better underfoot, carpets provide protection and insulation. Several years ago, I returned home very late one night to find that the cold-water tank had burst. Water was pouring through the ceiling, inundating the sitting-room below. Luckily, the carpet soaked up most of the flood and confined it to my flat, so that my neighbours were not flooded too. It took a while to dry, and the flat smelled like a wet dog for weeks, but a wooden floor would probably have had to be replaced.

Buy the best carpet you can afford and buy the correct carpet for the level of wear it will receive. The better the quality of fibre, and the more densely it is woven, the harder-wearing it will be. Do not economise in high-traffic areas of the house, such as the hall, stairs and living-rooms.

A cheap, low-quality carpet will look good when it is first laid, but will quickly wear out and, in the long run, prove more expensive.

> Tip: A quick test of durability is to press the pile; the quicker it springs back, the better.

Never put carpet in kitchens and bathrooms or lavatories, not even a carpet designed for these areas (normally a man-made fibre with a water-resistant backing). In kitchens, crumbs and other food spills are inevitable and can never be completely removed from a carpet. In bathrooms, carpets get wet even if you use a bathmat; make-up and other cosmetics can bleach and stain carpet, and if there are men or boys in the house … well, need I say more?

261

TO CARE FOR CARPETS

Remove shoes. It is generally assumed that high heels damage all floor surfaces. In fact, it is hard floors, particularly cheap laminates, that are damaged by high heels. On carpets, the shoes that do the most damage are rubber-soled shoes such as trainers, because of the way they twist the pile.

Protect carpet at entrances to outside doors by always using a doormat. Similarly, use rugs on carpets in areas of heavy traffic and put protective caster cups or felt pads under the legs of furniture. To wear carpets more evenly, move the furniture occasionally. Worn patches occur in places such as in front of chairs and where people walk through from one room to another. But when moving furniture, lift it, do not drag it across the carpet (this protects the furniture as much as the carpet). Have carpets professionally cleaned occasionally.

> *Tip: To remove indentations in a carpet made by furniture legs, place an ice cube in the indentation and leave overnight. Alternatively, place a damp cloth over the mark and very lightly hold a medium-hot iron over the mark. Do not press too hard, or you will have an iron mark in place of the indentation. Or hold a steam iron over the mark and, as you feel the pile begin to lift, rake up the pile with your fingers being careful not to burn them.*

TO VACUUM A CARPET

Vacuum all carpets as frequently as they need it – two or three times a week is about right, more if there are small children or pets in the house, less if you live on your own. Vacuuming removes the dirt and grit that collects at the base of the pile, and helps keep the pile upright. In addition, regular vacuuming is the best way to keep carpet beetles and moths at bay, and (if a cleaner fitted with a HEPA filter is used) can keep levels of dust mite allergens down.

Before starting on the main body of the carpet, vacuum around the edges and other hard-to-reach places using the crevice tool (alternatively, use a stiff hand brush). Although some vacuum cleaners are better than others, none of them reaches right to the edges of carpet.

While you are about it, vacuum along the tops of the baseboards too (alternatively, have a long-handled fluffy lambswool duster handy, and whisk it along the tops of the baseboards as you are vacuuming the carpet).

Set the brush head low or use the turbo function/power brush as appropriate for your cleaner. Do not set on maximum power, because excessive suction can pull the pile out of carpets.

Vacuum from the back of the room to the front, ending at the door. Work from left to right, going across the room in strips, rather than making lots of little backwards and forwards movements, and vacuum more slowly than you would over a wooden floor, to give the machine a chance to do its work.

> Note: Loop-pile carpets, such as Berbers, should not be vacuumed using the brush head or power brush, because they can make the carpet look felted. Use the suction brush only.

New carpets can be vacuumed as soon as they are laid. For the first few months they will shed copious amounts of fibre. The main thing to remember is that the vacuum cleaner bag or dust container will need to be changed more frequently.

Other problems include pilling, which occurs in mixed-fibre carpets, and loose tufts, particularly in loop-pile carpets. In both cases, the remedy is to cut them down to the level of the surrounding pile.

263

TO CLEAN A CARPET

Have carpets deep-cleaned as often as they need it, depending on the level of wear – every two to five years is about the average. The cheaper, if more energetic option is to do it yourself with a hired machine. However, in my opinion, professionals do a better job because their machines are more powerful and they have specialist cleaning products.

If you choose to go down the professional route, ask friends for recommendations for good carpet cleaners, and choose stable and well-established companies. Work-for-hire cleaners are less likely to have developed reasonable standards and a complaints procedure should things go wrong. The most common methods for cleaning are shampooing, hot-water extraction and chemical cleaning (compounds brushed into the carpet and vacuumed up). A reputable contractor should recommend the most suitable method.

Remove smaller marks, stains and spills yourself. See 'An A–Z of carpet stains', p. 316.

Rugs

Though some of the finest Persian and Turkish rugs can cost a fortune, there are plenty of cheaper rugs around – and there is no simpler way to beautify and add colour to a room. A rug can also be used to disguise worn or shabby carpets, or to give warmth and softness underfoot to a hard floor.

But it should be remembered that rugs are for walking on. One reason that old rugs fetch high prices at auction is that buyers value the well-worn look that only years of use can bring. But there is 'well-worn' and there is 'beaten-up'.

TO CARE FOR RUGS

Move rugs around so that they get even wear. Constant wear in the same place – say, from people walking on it – will result in holes appearing. Leaving a rug in the same place also makes it more vulnerable to sun damage and insect attack. When moving the rug, check its condition.

Never place a rug on top of a hard floor without a liner or pad. Hard floors can be uneven, which results in uneven patches of wear on the rug. If a rug is laid directly on to floorboards, dust can rise up between the gaps.

Dust and grit can work into the pile. Though small, these particles have razor-sharp edges and the effect is like thousands of tiny knives cutting into fibres. Often, too, the particles are acidic, another cause of damage to fabric, especially wool and silk.

Rugs are also vulnerable to insect attack. The two main culprits are likely to be moths and carpet beetles. If you see the familiar holes, do not panic; there are remedies. For more on dealing with these creatures, see 'Household pests', p. 322.

The dyes in rugs are very vulnerable to fading. Either the whole rug fades or dyes fade at different rates, leaving uneven bright patches of colour. If the rug is in direct sunlight, move it. If light levels are uniformly high, draw the curtains or close the blinds when the room is not in use.

TO VACUUM RUGS

Unless a rug is very old or valuable – in which case, seek specialist advice on its care – it should be vacuumed regularly, at least once a week. Use a medium to low suction and turn off brushes on upright cleaners. Vacuum both the back and the front, and move the vacuum head parallel to the short side to prevent the rug being pulled out of shape.

When vacuuming, pay attention to the fringes. They are an integral part of the weave and are easily broken off. Try to avoid vacuuming the fringes at all, but if you must, use a low suction. To avoid the fringe getting sucked into the nozzle, put an old stocking over the nozzle.

> *Tip: If fringes are getting damaged, turn them under and sew webbing to the edge of the rug.*

To stop rugs creeping: Rugs creep across carpet because the pile of the carpet lies in the opposite direction from the rug's pile. As a result, whenever anyone walks on the carpet, the pile moves and causes the rug on top to move too.

Do not use a large piece of furniture to anchor the rug, because over time it will pull the rug out of shape. Instead, use one of the several products on the market that prevent rug creep. The best I have found is a synthetic fleecy material that is cut to fit the back of the carpet. It stops rug creep on carpets and hard floors and, because it is cushioned, also acts as a pad.

To store a rug: A rug that is being stored – for example, when a room is being decorated – should be rolled up, not folded. Roll with the pile facing outwards and roll in the direction of the pile. As you roll, layer in sheets of acid-free tissue paper and cover in an old, clean sheet. Larger rugs should be rolled on to a large tube for support. Ask at a carpet shop for old cardboard tubes, or you could always buy a length of plastic drainpipe.

> *Tip: To find the direction of a rug's pile, stroke the rug. Like a cat's fur, the pile will feel smooth when stroked in the right direction and rough when stroked the wrong way. Roll up a rug in the direction of the pile.*

TO CLEAN RUGS

Over the years, however much you vacuum, dust and dirt can become embedded. Rugs used to be washable, but modern dyes are less stable than old ones. Too much cleaning can weaken the fibres, so have a rug cleaned professionally only every five to ten years. If a rug is old or valuable, find a specialist cleaner by asking friends or your local phone book.

Before you clean, you might consider the old-fashioned method of beating the rug to remove ingrained dust and dirt. Do not hang it over a line to beat it, because you might stretch it, fray the fringe or loosen the fibres. Instead, lay it face down on an old sheet and beat it methodically, starting at the top and moving down the rug from left to right. This is hard work, but the amount of dust that is dislodged is extremely gratifying.

> *Tip: To revive the colours of a rug, brush with a mixture of ¼ pint vinegar to 4 pints water.*

Natural fibre floor coverings

Natural fibres became a fashionable alternative to carpet in the 1990s. Indeed, their ubiquity has turned them into a design cliché. The most common are coir, a coarse fibre made from coconut husks, which is very scratchy underfoot; jute, a light, soft fibre obtained from two plants of the linden family; seagrass, a smooth, hard-wearing fibre made from a grass-like water plant; and sisal, a tough, hard-wearing fibre made from various species of agave cactus.

> *Note: Natural fibres are often mixed with other fibres such as wool to give durability plus versatility.*

TO CARE FOR NATURAL FIBRE FLOOR COVERINGS

Though natural fibres appear hard-wearing, they are much more delicate and less hard-wearing than traditional carpets. Do not expect much more than five years' life from sisal, and slightly less from seagrass and coir. Jute should last two to five years. All these vegetable fibres also stain easily and react badly if they get wet. Sisal shrinks, and coir expands but then shrinks back, often causing the seams to break. They are all prone to water marking and can develop mould in a damp atmosphere, so should be used with caution in kitchens and bathrooms.

Have the carpet professionally treated with a stain repellent such as Scotchgard. Water and other spills will mark the carpet. Vacuum regularly, using the suction brush only. Mop up spills as they occur and do not rub into the fibres. Washing and shampooing are not recommended on natural fibres. Dry chemical cleaning is possible, but ask the advice of a professional carpet cleaner who is used to dealing with these fibres.

Stone

Stone has been used for building and decoration in houses since time began. People have always loved stone because it is beautiful, durable, can support a lot of weight and is extremely hard-wearing. It can be polished to a high shine, carved into intricate forms and can be painted or gilded. It is plentiful and sustainable and, if looked after correctly, will last for years.

In Britain stone was traditionally used for fire surrounds and tiles and occasionally for floors in larger houses. It was expensive and, until the coming of the railways, difficult and expensive to transport. Local stone was used and, aesthetically, this still makes sense and explains why a new stone floor can sometimes seem 'wrong' in a house. In a cold, damp country like Britain, stone can make houses seem even damper and colder, so on the whole we have not gone in for stone or marble floors except in the areas of the house that took a lot of hard wear, such as entrance halls, kitchens and work-rooms.

In recent years, stone has become very fashionable. Limestone, marble and the like fit in perfectly with the taste for minimalist interiors. No high-end kitchen is worth its salt unless it has granite worktops. No updated bathroom is complete without its limestone floor (preferably with underfloor heating). Though stone has always been – and continues to be – an expensive luxury item, imports from China and Eastern Europe have brought it within the reach of increasing numbers of people. And with cheap transport and modern production methods, a whole range of different types of stone is now available to us. I said that stone is expensive – it is, but if you are thinking of whether you can afford to lay a stone floor, you might be surprised to find that it is often cheaper than high-quality carpet.

Because stone is literally 'rock hard', we assume that it is indestructible. In fact, it varies widely in hardness, porosity and durability. Some stone is extremely porous, which means it is easily stained. Once something has gone into it, it will not come out, which is a good reason not to have a limestone worktop or kitchen floor. Other types of stone are so soft, they will not withstand anything but the gentlest handling (alabaster, for example, can be marked with a fingernail). Some stone is brittle and can be easily broken or chipped. Others can cause cleaning problems because of their very composition. Marble is a good example. In hard-water areas, the inevitable limescale will be difficult to deal with because it has the same composition as marble. Therefore any chemical that dissolves limescale will also dissolve marble.

All of this is actually good news for the housewife, because when it comes to stone, the less you do to it, the better. Yet another reason to have it in your house.

268

TO REMOVE GREASE STAINS FROM STONE AND UNGLAZED TILES

Make a poultice of fuller's earth (available at pharmacies). Add enough water to make a thick paste and spread it over the stain. Cover with cling film and leave overnight. The next day, scrape up the poultice and the grease should have been absorbed.

TO CLEAN GROUT

Clean with a solution of bleach and water (three parts water to one part bleach), using a scrubbing brush (wear rubber gloves). Rinse with clear water and dry.

TO REMOVE HEEL MARKS FROM STONE FLOORS

Rubber heels can leave marks on stone floors that are difficult to remove. The following mixture, sometimes called V&A mixture, will clean them off and can also be used for cleaning all stone, including marble.

Put 12 fl oz mineral spirits, 12 fl oz water and 1 tsp mild, unperfumed dish soap in a jar and shake well. The mixture will form an emulsion and then separate out into a white emulsion with clear liquid below. Use the white emulsion for cleaning.

To use, dip a clean white cloth or piece of cotton wool into the solution, squeeze nearly dry and swab the marks. Work from the outside towards the centre of the mark so as not to spread it. As the cloth gets dirty, fold it so that you are always using a clean part (or change the cotton wool swabs). Once the mark has gone, rinse with clean water and dry.

GRANITE

A crystalline igneous stone, composed of quartz, feldspar and mica, granite comes in a range of colours, from pale grey and pink to darker greys, reds and black. It is extremely hard and durable and can be carved and polished to a high shine. It is the first choice for worktops.

Cleaning: Most modern granites are treated before leaving the factory to prevent staining because granite is quite porous. Even when it has been polished, it remains porous and is susceptible to staining by oil and grease, wine and fruit juices. It is therefore important to wipe up spills as they occur, especially if they involve strong-coloured food or drink, acids or oils.

Clean regularly with a damp cloth and a neutral detergent (mild dish soap for preference). Do not use abrasive cleaners or scouring pads on granite. Do not use bleach. After cleaning, wipe dry to prevent water marks.

If the surface dulls over time, special granite polishing creams are available to restore the finish.

LIMESTONE

A sedimentary rock composed mostly of calcium carbonate, limestone varies in density, texture and porosity and comes in a range of colours from cream to grey to brown. Bath stone, travertine and Portland stone are all types of limestone. It makes beautiful tiles and floors, but is not suitable for kitchen worktops because of its porosity and subsequent susceptibility to staining. Never consider anything other than sealed limestone for bathroom surfaces and floors.

Cleaning: Because limestone is porous, it can pick up grease and dirt easily and will stain. It is also easily damaged by acids, such as lemon juice or vinegar.

Most modern limestone is sealed to make it less susceptible to staining and often polished to a high protective shine.

Wipe up spills as they occur, especially if the spill is acidic and/or highly coloured (such as fruit juice or wine) or greasy (cooking oil). Cigarette burns will also stain limestone.

Modern sealed and polished limestone is easy to deal with. Wash using water and a neutral detergent (such as mild, unperfumed dish soap). Rinse and dry. Do not use harsh abrasives or acidic products.

Older unsealed limestone (such as limestone floors in older houses) needs to be treated with more care. Dust regularly so that dirt does not get ground in. Mop regularly. Wring the mop almost dry – do not swamp the floor with water, rinse with clean water and dry. Do not use abrasives or strong cleaners, and never allow limestone to come into contact with any acids.

Tough marks, such as shoe scuffs, can be removed using the V&A mixture (see p. 269).

MARBLE

Marble is a hard, granular, crystalline form of limestone (calcium carbonate), created through the action of heat. True marble is usually white or grey, but there are decorative marbles in black, green, yellow and red. Marble can be carved, is often polished to a high shine, making it ideal for mantelpieces, floor and wall tiles, table tops, and the tops of vanity units in bathrooms. It is not suitable for kitchen worktops because it is porous and stains easily.

Cleaning: Like limestone, marble is susceptible to being damaged by acids, such as fruit juices, lemon juice and vinegar. Newly worked and polished marble is relatively impervious to moisture, but older marble tends to be more porous and can stain easily – the ring made by a glass of wine on a marble tabletop, for example, will soon be indelible.

Dust frequently – dirt soon gets ground into marble. Any small grease spots will attract dust, which can then be drawn into the fabric of the stone. For dusting, a brush is better than a cloth, which tends to smear dirt into the surface.

If you think marble needs washing, always dust it first. Clean as for limestone, using water and a gentle detergent, such as mild, unperfumed dish soap. Wring the cloth out well, rinse with another very well wrung-out cloth and plain water, then dry with a soft cloth. Specialist marble cleaners are also available at specialty stores.

Do not use harsh abrasives or strong, acidic cleaners. Never use any sort of acid on marble in order, for example, to remove limescale. The acid will dissolve the marble along with the limescale. Inappropriate use of harsh cleaners can cause marble to crumble.

Protect the surface with a microcrystalline wax. The best-known make is Renaissance (available at specialty stores and on the internet), which is used by conservation experts to revive and protect not only marble and other stone but also furniture, leather and metals. On marble, it freshens colours, gives a soft sheen and can help protect the surface from spillages, such as wine or fruit juices. Its colour remains true and will not go yellow. Waxing is particularly recommended for marble in bathrooms to protect it from water staining.

To use, apply a small amount of wax to the marble in a circular motion and immediately polish off (the wax hardens very quickly, making it difficult to polish off). Work in small areas, polishing as you go. In bathrooms, pay particular attention to the areas that are liable to staining, such as around the base of taps. You should not need to apply the wax more than once a year.

271

> Note: Apply wax only to clean marble. Otherwise, you will seal in existing stains.

SLATE

A fine-grained metamorphic rock that splits into thin, smooth layers, slate ranges in colour from dull blue through to grey, purple and green and is used for floors, fire surrounds and table tops.

Cleaning: Slate is easily chipped and broken. It is also porous, so tends to pick up oil, dirt and grease (though modern slate tiles are usually sealed).

Dust, sweep and wet-clean as for marble.

TILE

Ceramic tiles are not strictly stone, but are made from fired clay and come either glazed or unglazed. They can be made in almost any colour or pattern and, if glazed, are extremely hard-wearing and tough (unglazed tiles are porous and can stain unless sealed with a protective coating). They can take vigorous cleaning, and their only drawback is that they can chip or crack if something heavy is dropped on them. They are the ideal choice for splashbacks in kitchens and bathrooms; worktops, walls and floors.

Cleaning: Clean once a week using a dilute solution of household detergent and a soft cloth. Tiled worktops may need heavy-duty cleaning with something stronger, such as an abrasive cream cleaner. Rinse and dry with a soft cloth so that hard water does not leave dull patches of limescale on the tiles. See also 'To clean really filthy tiles', p. 102.

Even if you mop up spills as they occur, grouting can become stained. Coffee, tea, fruit juices, red wine and spices such as turmeric are the worst culprits. Most stains will respond well to a mixture of three parts bleach to one part water. Scrub well with an old toothbrush to get into the grout, then rinse and dry. (The same method can be used to remove mildew from tiles in bathrooms and showers – use equal parts bleach and water.)

A grout sealant (available from DIY shops) will help protect grout, or grout pens can be used to freshen up dirty or discoloured grout.

Treat unglazed tiles such as terracotta as any porous stone. They are easily stained, so wipe up any spills quickly (they are particularly prone to stains from grease or oil). To prevent this, seal unglazed tiles with a penetrating sealer (available from DIY shops).

> *Tip: Spray ceramic tiles lightly with vinegar and polish dry with a soft cloth to remove any limescale and make tiles extra shiny.*

Wooden furniture

How often do you polish your furniture? Once a week? Once a month? Does waxing wood fill you with a warm glow, making you feel like a genuine domestic goddess (or god, come to that)? There is nothing like the smell of furniture polish to make one feel that a room has truly been cleaned, and it is a favourite trick among less assiduous cleaners to spray polish liberally around to disguise the fact that they have skimped on any actual cleaning.

In fact, when it comes to furniture, your mantra should be 'less is more'. Of course wooden furniture should be polished. The thing is, you do not have to do it that often. A few years ago, I interviewed the housekeeper and conservation cleaners at Blickling Hall, the magnificent Jacobean house in Norfolk that is now owned by the National Trust. One of the highlights of the house is its intricately carved double staircase. It gleams with a soft, mellow glow and yet it is waxed only once every five years. In the long periods in between waxings, gentle buffing of the surface retains its sheen. You would think that a housemaid attended to it every week of its life.

Of course, very few of us own a place like Blickling, but many people have pieces of antique furniture that they have bought or inherited. Yet more have bought expensive pieces of modern furniture. A few years ago, I commissioned two bedside tables from a Cornish furniture designer. They cost about as much as similar tables from a London store such as Heal's or the Conran Shop, but I did not have to compromise on size or materials. They are exactly the right height for my bed and are made from cherrywood with a black walnut veneer trim. I know they are unique and I view them and other pieces of modern furniture I have bought as tomorrow's antiques. Here is how to look after all types of wooden furniture.

273

TO CARE FOR AND CLEAN WOODEN FURNITURE

Dust furniture once a week. On flat solid surfaces such as table tops and pieces with no handles, carving or protruding or loose bits (such as raised veneer), use a flat-seamed duster (see 'Basic cleaning equipment', p. 213). Dust with the grain, buffing lightly to bring up the shine.

Occasionally, take drawers out and dust them all over. Also dust the runners and the bottom of the drawer. If a drawer is sticking, dust will make it worse.

On carved pieces or where there are loose bits that could catch on a duster, such as raised veneer, dust with a brush. Brush along the grain of the wood. You can, if you like, brush it into the nozzle of the vacuum cleaner as you go (the preferred method in conservation circles). Brushing is just as quick as using a duster and is better for getting dust out of cracks and crevices.

If you use a brush, cover the metal ferrule with tape to avoid scratching the furniture.

Do not wash wooden furniture, but if the surface is sticky, a wipe over with a barely damp cloth will not do any harm. Use water only, without any cleaning products. Go very carefully if there are loose bits of veneer. If any moisture gets underneath, it could cause the wood to swell and further loosen the veneer.

TO POLISH WOODEN FURNITURE

Furniture does not need polishing any more than once a year. With a new piece of furniture wait at least a year before polishing or oiling it.

Virtually the only product needed for wood is polish, preferably one containing a high proportion of beeswax. (To find out how to make your own, see 'Making your own household cleaners', p. 237). Do not use a spray polish. Apart from the fact that spray polishes often contain silicone, which does wood no good at all, you cannot regulate the amount used, they do not fill small scratches as wax does, and they can make the surface very slippery. Never use silicone spray polishes. They are the death of wood. They give a hard, bright shine, which is inappropriate on anything but modern synthetic finishes. If you then try to polish over it, no wax can penetrate the silicone layer, but sits on the surface of the wood, giving a curious fish-eye effect. It also remains sticky, which attracts dust. Silicone sprays bond to the wood, making them almost impossible to remove. Unlike traditional finishes, they cannot be softened. The only recourse is to rub the surface back, and that is best done professionally.

Apply wax with a soft cloth or hogshair brush, working well into the wood. Use as little as possible: if you can see that the surface has gone matt, that will be enough. Using a lot of polish will not give a better shine; it will just make more work.

Let the polish dry a little and then buff the surface using either a clean dustcloth or a clean brush. The idea is to remove the excess polish, so fold the duster over as you work, so you are always using a clean piece of cloth. Otherwise, you will be rubbing in polish you have just taken off. Do not polish over or near places that are cracking or lifting.

If using brushes, mark one brush 'Polish On' and the other 'Polish Off', so they do not get mixed up.

Contrary to popular belief, wax does not 'nourish' wood. Rather, repeated coats of wax fill in tiny scratches and build up a protective coating on the surface of the wood. Beeswax gives a soft, mellow shine.

If the surface of the furniture seems to be losing its lustre between polishings, buff it up with a duster when you do the dusting: it will quickly recover its shine.

TO OIL WOODEN FURNITURE

Furniture oil gives a soft, subtle glow rather than a shine. It is a look that is particularly suited to modern furniture.

On furniture finished with a furniture oil (such as Danish oil or tung oil) the same oil can be used to refresh the finish. These oil spoils, so buy in small amounts. Flood the surface with the oil and then immediately wipe it off with soft cloths (cut-up pieces of old T-shirt are ideal). Never let oil dry before wiping it off. It will go sticky and be very difficult to remove. Wipe off as much as possible, working in the direction of the grain and well into the wood. Leave 24 hours before applying a second coat of oil. Leave another 24 hours before applying a final third coat of oil.

TO PREVENT SUN DAMAGE

There is no reliable way of preventing sun fade on wooden furniture – which can happen within the course of a month in a bright room – except to draw the curtains and blinds whenever possible and to move objects around so that the same parts of them are not constantly being exposed to shafts of sunlight. If furniture is not being used, cover it with dustsheets. For a fuller discussion of the subject, see 'Sun damage', p. 115.

> Note: Do not cover furniture with polyethylene, which can trap moisture, or plastic sheeting. The plasticisers it contains can migrate to the wood and stain it.

Modern pieces and modern finishes are more sensitive to light than antiques. Damage to antiques can be treated, but it is a job for a professional restorer.

TO PREVENT CARELESS HANDLING

Furniture gets knocked, things get spilt on it, and it gets scratched. Lifting it incorrectly can weaken it, as can dragging it across the floor. Children climb on it. Cats sharpen their claws on it.

Position furniture where people will not bump into it. If you need to move furniture, do not drag or push it, but lift it by the most solid part of the frame.

Do not lift tables by the tops, or chairs by the back or arms, or anything by the handles or any projecting or decorative part. When lifting a chest of drawers or a desk, remove the drawers before lifting it by the frame.

Do not overload furniture. It is all too easy to push the bottoms out of drawers and damage hinges, doors and backs of wardrobes.

TO PREVENT DAMAGE FROM HEAT AND A DRY ATMOSPHERE

Modern heating systems dry a house out. This is not too much of a problem with new furniture, which is designed for a dry house. But with antiques, or furniture that is imported from other parts of the world, sudden transportation to a dry atmosphere can cause the wood to dry out and crack.

I have direct experience of this: several years ago, I was given a large rosewood carving from Singapore, a country where the relative humidity never drops below 76 per cent. Within a few months of being moved to the dry atmosphere of a centrally heated house, it developed a large crack. Luckily, it was on the back, so I filled it with a dark wood filler that was the same colour as the wood and polished it, and it looked like new.

Sometimes the problem occurs when old houses are damp-proofed; levels of moisture in the house change and, as it dries out, so does the furniture.

The remedy is to keep the house at a constant low temperature, rather than subjecting furniture to the fluctuations of temperature that come from the usual habit of turning the heating on and off throughout the day. Consider keeping the heating on throughout the day at a low temperature, boosting it if necessary. This is a good habit to get into for other objects (see 'To care for paintings', p. 127).

Do not place furniture in front of direct sources of heat, such as radiators, and don't put hot plates or cups of tea directly on to a wooden surface – they can scorch or mark the surface. Use mats or a cork or cloth table protector. Even these may not be enough with very hot dishes – such as a casserole taken straight from the oven. Remember that when mats are described as 'heatproof' – often up to 500°F – it means that the mats themselves will not be scorched or damaged, not the surface on which they are resting. Even with heatproof mats, heat can be transferred and can leave a mark on the furniture.

TO PREVENT DAMAGE FROM MOISTURE

Perversely, too much moisture is not very good for furniture either. Problems often occur when furniture is put into storage in somewhere damp and cold such as a garage or a cellar – a common victim is the rarely used extra leaf for a dining table.

In very damp conditions, wood can swell or become mildewed, and glue can break down on veneers, causing it to lift off the surface. In addition, woodworms love damp conditions (see below).

Do not store furniture in attics unless they are very well insulated: they tend to be too cold in winter and too hot in summer and also experience wildly fluctuating levels of humidity.

If furniture has got damp, move it to a warm, dry place and allow it to dry out over time. Before moving it into the house, check for woodworm (see below).

Do not put vases of flowers directly on wooden surfaces. Even if you have been careful filling the vase, moisture often condenses on the outside and forms a ring at the base. A cloth will not offer much protection because the moisture will soak through and stain the surface beneath. Damage can occur surprisingly quickly – within a couple of hours. If you must put vases on wooden surfaces, always use a large, waterproof mat.

The same goes for glasses. Always use mats or coasters to protect the wood. If water does spill on to a wooden surface, mop it up immediately.

277

TO PREVENT WOODWORM

Woodworm, also known as the furniture beetle, is more precisely a wood-boring weevil. The brown, hairy adult beetles are rarely seen – they are only 3 mm long. Most people do not even know they have woodworm until the familiar small holes appear in furniture and woodwork.

The beetles are active in the summer, when they mate. The female deposits her eggs (around 50) in cracks and crevices in wood. The eggs hatch after about a month and the larvae immediately start to eat the wood. They remain there until they are fully grown, which can take between two and five years. Finally they pupate, and a few weeks later the adult beetles emerge by eating their way out of the wood. They fly away, leaving the familiar holes.

Woodworm thrive in cold, damp conditions. The good news is that with the heat and dryness of most modern houses, woodworm are less of a problem than formerly. Problems arise when an infested piece of furniture is brought into the house, or when furniture is stored.

If renting space in a self-storage facility (see 'Self-storage', p. 334 for more on this), check that storage rooms are warm and dry if you are planning to store furniture for any length of time. It is not unusual for people to put things in storage and not look at them for a year or more – by which time, the damage is done.

Painted wood is not invulnerable to attack, because woodworm will lay eggs in cracks around the joints. The same applies to lacquerwork, which, unless the piece is lacquered inside and out, is purely decorative.

Give anything that comes into the house a thorough inspection inside and out. Look for loose bits of wood and at the insides of drawers. Pay particular attention to cracks in the wood and areas around the joints, and look at pieces of end grain, shining a torch on them if necessary. The familiar round exit holes are not necessarily a sign that the woodworm is active. The thing to look for is a fine dust, called frass – the best sign is a little bit of dust just by a flight hole.

TO TACKLE WOODWORM

There are various effective chemical treatments for woodworm available from DIY shops. However, they only treat woodworm as they emerge, not the unhatched eggs or larvae, so treatment has to be repeated.

> Note: These chemicals are harmful, so always follow the safety directions and instructions for use.

For bad cases of infestation, consult a furniture conservator/restorer. If you are having difficulties locating such a company, contact a local museum. Though most have their own conservators, they likely would have local recommendations.

The professionals will often treat woodworm by environmental methods, either by controlled heat and humidity or by freezing. Small pieces, such as boxes, can also be frozen at home.

Put the item in a bag to exclude air and then place in the freezer for a week (the temperature needs to be 0°F – which is the temperature of most domestic freezers). Take it out after a week, bring it back to room temperature and then freeze again for another week. The initial freezing will kill larvae but not the unhatched eggs. It is the second freezing that kills them.

Note: Be cautious when freezing, especially if the object is made of other materials as well as wood, particularly metal against the grain of the wood, and glass. These both expand and contract at different rates from wood and may cause it to crack. For valuable pieces, consult an expert.

TO REMOVE WHITE STAINS

The rings left by glasses are difficult to remove. Here are three effective remedies:

Mix olive oil and cigarette ash and rub it gently into the stain. This takes time and patience, but it does eventually work.

Make a mixture of half and half boiled (not raw) linseed oil and pure turpentine. Shake well. Rub into the stain with grade 0000 wire wool. Boiled linseed oil is available from DIY shops.

Apply a proprietary burnishing cream. There are various brands available, but Liberon is a good make.

TO REMOVE SCRATCHES

Waxing wood will disguise light scratches. To disguise them further, apply a darker polish. Be aware, however, that you will have to polish the entire piece to keep the colour even.

To remove scratches on light wood, rub the scratch with half a walnut kernel (cut in half and rub firmly in). This has a fairytale ring about it, but works very well. For darker woods, use a Brazil nut kernel.

TO LIFT DENTS

The traditional remedy is to place a damp cloth over the dent and place a warm iron over the cloth. The warmth and moisture should swell the grain. If the dent does not disappear straight away, apply the cloth several times over the next few days to raise the dent gently.

Note: The combination of wood, heat and moisture is never a good one. Do not try this on valuable, delicate or antique furniture. Far better to give the piece of furniture a good polish to disguise the dents slightly and learn to live with them.

To stop a wooden drawer from sticking: Take the drawer out and dust well. Also dust the runners. Take a candle and rub it along the bottom edge of the drawer and along the runners. This old-fashioned remedy works extremely well. Another trick, which I have used to very good effect, is to polish the runners and bottom edges of the drawers with Renaissance wax.

To clean metal handles on wooden furniture: Metal polish applied carelessly when cleaning handles will damage wood. It is best to remove them for cleaning, but this is not always possible.

In fact, very bright brass fittings look wrong on furniture. Do not attempt to clean them with metal polish but buff them every time the furniture is dusted. If you want to give them a shine, use Renaissance wax, which will keep the brass bright and will not harm the wood if any gets on the surface.

Metal

Metal may be strong, but it is not invulnerable. Although a metal object may not break if you drop it, it can get dented or scratched. Metal tarnishes; it corrodes; it rusts; it falls apart.

To confuse matters, not all corrosion is bad. Sometimes it is called a patina, and is highly prized. I remember an edition of *The Antiques Roadshow* where a couple had brought a bronze to show the experts. Because they were house-proud, they had used metal polish to clean the bronze before they went to the show, thus removing the patina. Uncleaned, it would have been worth a great deal of money. As it was, they had reduced its value to virtually nothing.

So if you own a brass, bronze or copper objet d'art, think carefully before you get the metal polish out.

With the exception of antiques, however, metals benefit from care and attention, to prevent rust or tarnishing. Most metal objects can be cleaned by dusting with a slightly damp cloth. If the metal is prone to tarnishing or rusting, dry it with a soft dry cloth. Polish only when it becomes tarnished. Brass, iron, copper and silver are prone to tarnishing. Gold, platinum, stainless steel and chrome are not. When bronze changes colour with age, the coating that develops is not tarnish, but patina (see above), which is much admired.

TO POLISH METAL

With the exception of silver, which should be cleaned only with silver polish (see 'Silver', p. 149), you do not need to buy separate polishes for each type of metal. Chrome, copper and brass can all be cleaned with Autosol (available from car accessory shops), which is the polish recommended by the National Trust and used in all their properties.

Use a soft cloth to apply the polish and another to polish it off.

For flat surfaces, use a flat-seamed cotton duster, which is less likely to catch on the metal, and fold it into a pad. All metal polish works by removing the top layer, so polish in straight lines, rather than circles, to avoid getting patterns of wear. As you polish, fold the cloth over so that you are always working with a clean surface.

Avoid letting polish build up in chased or patterned pieces. Use a hogshair brush to get into all the crevices and remove all the polish. Leaving polish on the metal can itself cause corrosion.

281

ALUMINIUM

A light, silvery metal, aluminium is used – in a domestic setting – for cooking utensils, particularly saucepans.

Care and cleaning: Do not keep foods in aluminium pans for any length of time because aluminium can be stained by certain foods, such as acids. For this reason, wash as soon as possible after use, using warm, soapy water. Remove burnt-on bits with a soap-filled pad. Do not use bleach or a product containing bleach on aluminium because it can cause pitting.

To brighten dull aluminium, fill the pan with water, add 2 tbsp cream of tartar or 8 tbsp white vinegar or lemon juice and boil for 10 minutes. Tip out the water, wash the pan and dry it.

An alternative to the cream of tartar or vinegar is to boil up some apple peelings. The result is the same.

> Note: Aluminium washed in the dishwasher will turn black. Always wash aluminium pans and utensils by hand.

BRASS

An alloy of copper and zinc, prized for its bright yellow colour, brass is used for a variety of household objects, like fire-irons, curtain poles, faucets, door furniture and decorative handles on furniture. Brass tarnishes quickly, so it is often lacquered.

Care and cleaning: Lacquered brass should only need dusting with a soft cloth. Using brass polish will destroy the lacquer and expose the metal to air, causing tarnishing. If this does happen, remove the lacquer with a proprietary remover, clean and polish the brass and reapply a lacquer designed for metal.

Unlacquered brass will require polishing. Use a quality metal polish, following the instructions above. After polishing, apply a coat of Renaissance wax to retard tarnishing. A coat of wax should protect the metal for at least a year.

Note: Chlorine bleach and acids can corrode brass.

To clean really filthy brass: The following is only to be attempted on solid objects that are not precious or antique.

Do not attempt to clean very dirty brass with metal polish alone. Brass is quite porous, so dirt can get polished into it and the ingrained grime is difficult to remove. Remove as much of the surface as possible using warm soapy water and, if the object is not precious, a soap-filled pad. If the object is solid, you can immerse it in water, but hollow objects with filled bases (such as brass candlesticks) should not be immersed because you will never get the water out. Instead, you will have to swab it clean.

If the brass has corroded, make a paste of equal parts salt, flour and white vinegar. Apply and leave to harden and dry. Rinse off, then polish.

Another method is to boil the object (as long as it is hollow) in a solution of equal parts water, vinegar and salt.

Yet another method, which also works on copper, is to coat the object in a thick layer of tomato ketchup or brown sauce. Leave several hours and then rinse off.

After polishing, apply a coat of Renaissance wax to prevent further tarnishing. Do this only on solid objects.

To clean brass handles on furniture: Very bright brass looks out of place on furniture, especially antiques. A soft, dull glow is much more in keeping. Therefore, do not polish brass handles with metal polish, because it will not look right and you are very likely to damage the wood. Instead, buff up with a soft cloth when dusting the furniture and give a coating of Renaissance wax, which will protect the metal but not harm the furniture.

To clean brass faucets: These are usually lacquered, so merely need dusting with a soft cloth. If the lacquer wears off, or if you have old brass faucets, consider the amount of work involved before you decide to polish them. Most people are content to let them stay dull.

To clean brass curtain rods: These are usually lacquered, so merely need dusting with a soft cloth.

To clean brass fire-irons: These get very dirty. Scrub well with a stiff brush, using a solution of water and dish soap, to remove sooty deposits. Then, if you like, apply the flour and vinegar paste mentioned above, before polishing. However, before you polish, consider whether you want bright, gleaming brassware – too much can make a place look like a pub. A better alternative is to rub with steel wool or very fine sandpaper to bring up the metal to a dull gleam, without getting the high shine of polished brass.

283

To clean brass door furniture: Modern door handles and fingerplates are usually lacquered, so should be dusted with a soft cloth. Older handles may need polishing, but often the friction from people's hands is enough to get a satisfactory shine. If you want to polish door handles, place a piece of cardboard over the painted surface of the door to protect it from the polish. After polishing, apply a coat of Renaissance wax to prevent tarnishing.

To clean brass preserving pans: Clean the outside with metal polish, but never use it on the inside of the pan (it is poisonous). Clean the inside with a paste of vinegar and water.

BRONZE

An alloy of copper and tin, bronze is highly prized for the patina that builds up with age. It is usually made into decorative objects.

Care and cleaning: Bronze needs to be kept as clean as possible. Dust is not only unsightly, it is also corrosive and can scratch the surface of the metal. Dust regularly with a soft cloth and use a soft brush to flick any dust out of crevices. If you like, flick the dust into the nozzle of the vacuum cleaner, to get rid of as much as possible. Bronze should never be washed or it might corrode. And it should never be polished with any sort of metal polish. However, it can be protected with Renaissance wax. If the bronze is old or precious, do not apply anything without talking to an expert.

If bronze develops light green spots or patches, it might be suffering from 'bronze disease'. This is a rapid form of corrosion that occurs when chlorides and oxygen combine in a damp environment and attack the metal. Outdoor sculptures are particularly susceptible. Bronze disease is treatable, but is not a job for an amateur, especially if the piece is valuable. Contact a metal conservator: your local museum may be able to help.

Modern bronzes are usually lacquered. Dust occasionally with a soft cloth.

CAST IRON

Cast iron is an alloy of iron, carbon and silicon that is cast in a mould. It is hard and brittle and is found in the home in cast-iron pots and pans and door furniture.

Before using a cast-iron pan for the first time, season it. To do this, heat the frying pan over a low heat until it is hot enough to make a drop of water sizzle. Pour in enough clean cooking oil to cover the base. Remove from the heat and allow to cool, and then wipe out the excess oil with a paper towel.

Care and cleaning: Wash as normal after use, using hot, soapy water. Do not put a hot pan in cold water, or it may crack. Always wash cast iron by hand, not in a dishwasher, otherwise it will rust. After washing, dry immediately and coat lightly with vegetable oil.

Note: Rust is not harmful if ingested.

Over time, as the pan is used, it will blacken and develop a coating that eventually becomes virtually non-stick.

CHROME

Chromium is a soft, silvery metal, much prized for its beauty and the fact that it can be polished to a high shine. Chrome, as it is often called in a domestic setting, means chrome-plated metal, usually brass or steel. It is used for bathroom and kitchen fittings, such as faucets, fittings on household appliances and light fittings, as well as for the trim on cars. It does not tarnish and is resistant to corrosion.

Care and cleaning: Chrome fittings in a house will not normally get very dirty. Clean by wiping with a soft damp cloth to remove fingermarks and so forth. Polish with a dry cloth. If more is needed, use a paste of baking soda and water, rinse and dry with a soft cloth. Avoid using any harsh abrasives, which might scratch the chrome and mar its beautiful surface. You should not need to polish it, but if you feel the urge to do so, use a metal polish, as above.

COPPER

A moderately hard metal, reddish-brown in colour, copper is believed to be the first metal used by man. It polishes to a deep shine, but tarnishes and corrodes. It is used for decorative objects and cooking utensils. Copper conducts heat quickly and evenly, which is why it is still regarded as the premier material for saucepans. A copper bowl is also reputed to produce the snowiest and most voluminous whisked egg whites. But copper readily forms a greenish layer of tarnish, called verdigris, which is poisonous. It can also react with acids and other compounds in foods. As a result, copper pans are coated with another metal, usually chrome, tin or stainless steel.

Care and cleaning: Wash copper saucepans as usual, in hot, soapy water, and dry. Polish the outside with metal polish, as above, or use one of the following methods:

Sprinkle half a lemon with salt and clean the copper with it. Rinse and dry with a soft cloth.

Make a paste of vinegar and salt and rub into the copper with a soft cloth to clean it. Rinse and dry with a soft cloth.

Douse the copper with brown sauce or tomato ketchup and leave for an hour or so. Rinse off the sauce and dry with a soft cloth.

If the lining wears through, the pan must be relined before it is used for cooking. Kitchen equipment shops will often have a list of people who can do this.

STAINLESS STEEL

Stainless steel is steel (an alloy of iron), to which chromium (minimum 10.5 per cent) has been added. The chromium prevents the steel from rusting. Though it is rust-proof, it can be pitted and stained by salts and acids. Stainless steel is used throughout the house, from cutlery to sinks, from bathroom fittings to large and small household appliances. Stainless steel is an increasingly fashionable, hard-wearing and beautiful material for worktops and splashbacks.

Care and cleaning: Vinegar, tomatoes, eggs, fruit, table salt and the mineral salts in tap water can damage stainless steel if left in contact with it for any length of time. Knife blades are particularly susceptible to staining and pitting, because they are made from hard steel that gives a good cutting edge but is less resistant to corrosion. Very hard tap water can leave a white film on stainless steel. Detergents, heat and very hot grease or oil can cause a characteristic 'rainbow' staining that is difficult to remove. Sometimes you see little spots of what looks like rust – generally small pits of corrosion in the metal.

Heat, grease and limescale can mark stainless steel. To remove, wipe over the surface with undiluted white vinegar (or, in the case of cutlery, soak for a short time in a little vinegar). Wash, rinse and dry as usual. Although vinegar can pit stainless steel, it will not cause damage if it is only in contact with cutlery for a short time.

Stainless steel cutlery: Ideally, cutlery should be washed up immediately after use. If this is not convenient, at least rinse it. A brief soak will not do any harm, but a longer one will. According to CATRA (Cutlery Allied Trades Association), leaving stainless steel cutlery in tap water overnight causes as much corrosion as three or four months of normal use.

You can, however, if washing up immediately, stand the cutlery in a jug of hot, soapy water to get it started before you get round to washing it.

When washing by hand, cutlery should be the second thing to be tackled, after glasses. Do not just throw everything in together and then fish out the cutlery from the bottom of a bowl of soupy-looking water. All that rattling round will scratch the cutlery, and if you have used steel wool to clean other things, such as roasting tins, minute fragments could stick to the steel, causing rust marks.

Use hot water and a little dish soap. Wash with a soft cloth or a dish mop, rather than a brush, and never use harsh abrasives or scourers. Always rinse cutlery to avoid rainbow stains developing, then wipe dry immediately to avoid water marks.

When using the dishwasher, first check that cutlery is dishwasher-proof – in other words, that it can be washed at up to 150°F. Again, wash it immediately. Do not leave it sitting in the wash and hold cycle. Use the cutlery basket, placing knives with the blades point downwards for safety. Once the dishwasher cycle has finished, take the cutlery out and immediately wipe dry with a soft tea towel to avoid water marks.

Regular washing in a dishwasher can cause rainbow detergent stains. These can be removed by rubbing with half a lemon. Rub in well, then rinse and dry with a soft tea towel. Other marks can be removed with a proprietary stainless steel cleaner, such as Bar Keepers Friend Liquid. While it is perfectly OK to wash knives and forks in the dishwasher, kitchen knives should always be washed by hand (see 'Knives', p. 40).

> Note: It is prolonged contact with acids that pits stainless steel. When lemon is used to remove marks, the acid is not in contact with the metal long enough to cause damage, and, in any case, is rinsed off.

Stainless steel appliances: Kettles, toasters and so forth, should be cleaned with a damp cloth to remove marks. Dry to a shine with a soft cloth. If they are very marked, try a stainless steel cleaner, such as Bar Keepers Friend Liquid. Use this also to clean large appliances such as cookers and fridges. To remove any streaks left after cleaning, pour a tiny amount of baby oil on to a soft cloth and wipe in well. (See 'To clean stainless steel worktops', p. 45).

Or use a microfibre cloth to remove marks and bring up a shine.

Stainless steel worktops and splashbacks: Use a microfibre cloth and water. Or, if the metal is very marked, use a small amount of cream cleaner, such as Bar Keepers Friend Liquid, on a soft cloth. Wipe in the direction of the surface grain. Rinse with clean water and polish dry with a soft cloth. Shine with baby oil, as above.

Stainless steel sinks: Use a gentle cream cleaner, not harsh abrasives. Bar Keepers Friend Liquid is my preferred product. After cleaning, rinse with clean water and wipe dry with a dry cloth. Splash marks should not be a problem on sinks if you dry the sink after cleaning it.

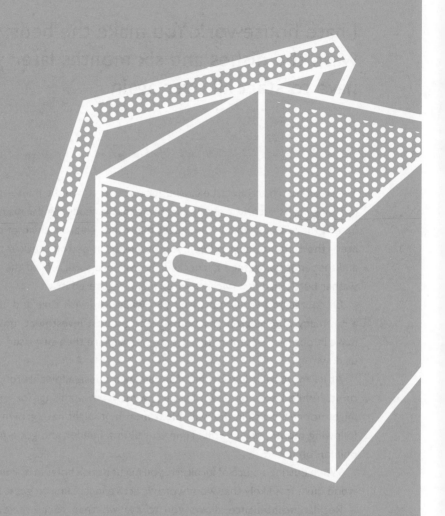

CHAPTER 11
Schedules

I hate housework. You make the beds, you wash the dishes and six months later you have to start all over again.

Joan Rivers

The great French architect, Le Corbusier, once described the house as 'a machine for living in'. As such, it is hardly surprising that it needs regular maintenance. To extend the analogy, would you expect that other great machine of the modern age – the car – to keep going if you never put in petrol, checked the oil level and topped it up, washed it, checked the tyre pressure, refilled the windscreen washer bottle, had it serviced, insured it and registered it?

Of course you would not. And yet, while we lavish care and attention on a car, many of us neglect our house – the greatest investment most of us will make in our lives – for months, if not years and are then surprised when it lets us down.

At its most basic level, then, maintaining a house allows us to keep an eye on it. While knocking down spiders' webs from a ceiling, for example, we might notice a crack in the wall. Next month, it might have grown bigger; the following month, bigger still. Time to call in a builder and get a professional opinion on it.

When dusting a piece of furniture, you might notice holes in it, which produce wood dust. It is likely that woodworm is active in it. Time to get it treated.

Regular maintenance allows you to see whether your precious things – which you have probably worked hard to earn the money to buy – are still in good condition. Have moths attacked your cashmere jumpers? Is the sun fading that picture?

Put quite simply, housekeeping is easier when you have a timetable than when you do not. By sticking to a schedule, you know whether there is food in the fridge for dinner; what needs cleaning and when; whether you have fresh clothes for tomorrow; and countless other details that contribute to the smooth running of the house and – by extension – family life.

The point is not to make more work for yourself, but less. By devising a system – by which I mean the best system for you, not hard and fast rules and regulations imposed from the outside – you know the house is ticking over at the level of acceptability for your family and that the wherewithal is in place for comfortable living.

Everyone has standards, below which they will not fall. One couple I know will never sit down for a cup of coffee after dinner unless the washing up has been done. As I have said, I never leave the house without making the bed.

The following, therefore, is not meant to be prescriptive. Rather, it is a series of suggestions on how beginners or the totally confused might like to tackle housekeeping. As you become more experienced, you will want to discard some tasks, or add others that are more suitable for your own house and family. There is a concept in psychoanalytical circles, formulated by D.W. Winnicott, of the 'good enough' mother. She stands in contrast to the 'perfect' mother, who immediately satisfies all her baby's needs, thus preventing normal development. The 'good enough' mother tries to satisfy her baby's needs but in a way that gradually allows normal tensions and frustrations into a baby's life, which he or she learns to tolerate, and thus develops his or her own sense of self.

It seems to me a useful analogy for running a house. We have all perhaps come across the 'perfect' housekeeper, whose house is spotless, where every family need is anticipated and attended to before it has even been thought of, where nothing is allowed to disrupt the running of the house. To visitors, the house seems cold and lifeless, and they may be afraid to touch anything for fear of disturbing the pristine setting. To the family, it is often stifling, allowing for no spontaneity and creating an atmosphere in which nothing can ever change.

At the other end of the spectrum is the chaotic house, where no one can find anything, where physical discomfort is matched by the mental unease that lack of boundaries induces. This was the sort of house I grew up in, and ever since I have equated chaotic houses with unhappy families.

The most comfortable solution lies somewhere in between these two extremes. But within that there is a whole spectrum, and the trick is to find the happy mean that is 'good enough' for your family and the way you like to live.

291

The essentials

By scheduling cleaning as a job, you are more likely to get it done. You would not hire a cleaner who says that she will come to your house 'some day next week or next month when there is nothing else worth doing'. Set aside a reasonable amount of time for the job. To know how much time to allot, start by working out what has to be done daily, weekly, monthly or longer.

IN PRAISE OF TIDINESS

My sister Deborah took untidiness to heroic levels. To the day she died, she honestly did not notice the clutter that surrounded her. Because she was fun, if anyone noticed, they certainly didn't care. Quite the opposite of her was a school friend, whose house was so tidy that everyone was afraid to sit down for fear of disturbing its chilly perfection.

It has taken me years to develop the habit of neatness – and it took a disaster for it to become enshrined. I used to shove all my papers into plastic bags any old how – the important stuff along with the rubbish, which I used to throw out when it all got too much. One day, about a week before I was due to go to Italy to interview someone, I started rummaging through the bags for my passport. Of course, it had been thrown out.

Now I still accumulate piles of paper, but I know what is in them and make an effort to file them properly at least once a month.

Apart from anything else, a tidy house is easier to clean. You can't do the job if surfaces are covered with paper, toys, dirty washing up and general clutter. But at its most basic, getting into the habit of tidying up in the morning and at the end of the day keeps the house ticking over. This does not mean that one has to be obsessive about it. Leaving a book open at the page you were reading or a children's game at a crucial stage is what a home is all about.

TIPS FOR BEING TIDY

You can never be tidy without good storage, a particular problem with modern houses and with flats, so you will either have to buy furniture or build storage in – fitted wardrobes, shelving units, ample cupboard space. Built-in window seats, with storage underneath, are a neat solution.

292

And then there is the mysterious ability of possessions to migrate to any part of the house other than the one they are supposed to be in. Get into the habit of never going up or downstairs or leaving a room without carrying something. One good idea is stair baskets, which are designed to sit at the bottom of the stairs, to be filled with whatever and taken up when full. Ideally, have two – one for the top and one for the bottom of the stairs – because things need to be carried down too. A small financial incentive might induce children to get into the habit of carrying them up and down.

Instead of nagging other members of the family to keep their rooms tidy, accept that their space is their own. But you can make certain rules – nothing to be washed unless it is in the laundry basket is a good one. Use your imagination.

File all papers at least once a month.

CHILDREN AND HOUSEWORK

With children in the house, something has to give, and that has to be the housework. No one actually wants a perfect home. Perfection is undesirable, even it were attainable, which it is not. You have still got to live, however, so work out what is realistic.

When children are small, concentrate on the areas that matter – the kitchen, bathroom and the children's room(s). All they require is a lick and a promise. Tidy up no more than once a day. If a child is still at the stage of a daytime nap, use that time to do the chores (or use the time for a nap yourself).

The constant round of cooking for and feeding children makes a dishwasher – along with the washing machine – one of the best investments you can make. If you are worried about the dishwasher's green credentials, see the discussion on p. 32. Labour-saving devices are not called 'labour-saving' for nothing.

When children are very young, turn housework into a game with them. One kitchen game my mother used to play with me was Shop. What she was actually doing was turning out the kitchen cupboards. She took out all the food and put it on the kitchen table. I then turned it into a 'shop'. The table was my shop counter and my sister and I took it in turns to be shopkeeper and customer. In the meantime, my mother could get on and clean the cupboards.

Washing up can also be turned into a game with children. Put an apron on them and sit them on the kitchen floor with a bucket half-filled with lukewarm water and dish soap. Let the children 'wash up' any wooden or plastic (i.e. unbreakable) items while you get on with the real washing up. Never mind any spills – let the children have a go at mopping it all up with a paper towel.

The laundry is another endless task. Do the washing every day and avoid anything that needs to be washed by hand. Tumble-dryers may be energy-hungry, but are a godsend to parents. Invest in one, but use it judiciously. Save time and sanity by not ironing unless absolutely necessary. In the short term, if you can afford it, consider sending bedding and men's shirts to the laundry.

Again, you can turn the laundry into a game. While you are loading the washing machine, ask the children to help sort all the clothes into piles – all the red ones, say, or all the white shirts. Be lavish with praise when they get it right, and play games like peek-a-boo – hiding them in things like sheets.

Get help, if possible. Hire a cleaner or get together with another friend who has young children and take it in turns to watch each other's children while the other one gets on with her chores. This combines a playdate for the children with company for the mother and a chance to do weekly housekeeping jobs. Involve the children here, too. Children like dusting – get them to do this while you vacuum (not anything breakable, obviously, but table tops and window sills). Turn plumping up cushions into a game of catch.

Shop online if you can – for everything, not just for food. There is virtually nothing now that cannot be bought online – a shopping revolution that is particularly suited to parents because it can be done at any time: one amazingly efficient friend of mine has even been known to order online stocking-filler toys in August.

Make one room a child-free zone so that if the rest of the house is in chaos, there is a haven for adults at the end of the day. In order to do this, decent storage for children's toys is a necessity. For more on this, see 'Children's bedrooms', p. 87. Involve small children in tidying up at the end of the day, so that it becomes part of the play.

Older children need their space. Their rooms are their own and can be kept as tidy or as untidy as they like. But they can all learn that a family is a unit that works together. The least children can learn to do is make a bed (even if they choose not to do so), wash up, empty the rubbish bins and the dishwasher, put dirty laundry in the laundry basket if they want it washed and not leave their stuff lying round the house. Pocket money is a good incentive here.

Daily schedules

To keep the house running Monday to Friday, little and often is the key. Concentrate on the rooms that are used most frequently and that can make life seem most miserable when they are in disarray – the bedrooms, bathroom, kitchen and sitting-room. Just forget the rest. In an emergency, forget the sitting-room too. At the very, very least, make the beds, wash up, hang up clothes, put out the rubbish.

I admit that, written down, a daily schedule may seem ridiculously prescriptive. But – think about it – you will be in the kitchen, bathroom or wherever anyway, and it is a matter of minutes to whisk a few things away and wipe up. And the result is worth it. Which you would rather come home to: a tidy welcoming home, or cornflake-encrusted crockery and a stale, unmade bed? What would you rather see when you come down for breakfast in the morning: a clean kitchen, or last night's washing-up and a smelly bin?

IN THE MORNING

Many people say they have no time to worry about the house first thing in the morning, yet they manage to find time to get themselves properly dressed for work, to put on a suit and tie, or to do their hair and make-up; they manage to get their children ready for school. I probably would not go so far as the former colleague who used to get up at 6.30 to vacuum the entire house before work, but it is worthwhile trying to incorporate the following into the morning routine.

The bedroom: When you get up, open the bedroom windows wide, pull back the bedclothes and allow the beds to air while you are having breakfast or your bath. Make the beds.

The bathroom: Always clean the bath after using it. Apart from the horror of facing someone else's tidemark, the bath is much easier to clean when it has just been used. Tidy away make-up and wipe the basin. Hang up towels.

The kitchen: Unload the dishwasher if it is full from the night before. Either wash up the breakfast things by hand, or reload the dishwasher. Before you leave for work, remember to switch on the dishwasher so it can work while you are out.

(If the dishwasher is not full, leave it till the evening.) Wipe kitchen worktops and, if necessary, sweep the floor. If you have loaded the washing machine the evening before, switch it on now.

Keep the fridge clean and follow the advice given on what to put where – and why – in the section on fridges and freezers (see 'The Kitchen', p. 13).

IN THE EVENING

The evening is essentially a chance for a bit of leisure and to recover from the day, so while there is slightly more time in the evening to put the house in order, it should not be an end in itself – more an opportunity to sort out what is needed for the next day.

The bedroom: Hang up your work clothes and put any other dirty laundry in the laundry basket or in the washing machine, ready for the next wash.

If you're feeling really organised, sort out which clothes you and everyone else will be wearing next day, especially any special requirements (PE kit, swimming gear, gym kit) and put it out ready for the morning. It saves a lot of time and anxiety in the morning. I often put anything that I know I have to take out the following morning (such as an important letter that must be posted) on the mat by the front door, so that I don't forget it.

296

The bathroom: Wipe round bath and basin. Hang up towels and check whether clean ones are needed.

The kitchen: Take out the washing from the morning's wash and hang it out to dry or put in the tumble-dryer. Sort out a load of washing for next morning, but do not switch on the machine until the morning.

> *Note: If you live on your own or with just one other person, you will probably not need to put the washing machine on every day. See 'Weekly schedules', below.*

After supper, wash up or load the dishwasher and run it. Wash pets' dishes separately. Wipe down kitchen surfaces, including the stove if it got spattered, and the sink. Put out clean tea towels and/or dish cloths. Sweep or mop the kitchen floor. Put out the rubbish. Empty and clean out pets' litter trays.

The sitting-room: Tidy away books, empty waste-paper baskets and put newspapers/magazines in the recycling bin. Plump up cushions – for some reason, this always makes a room look as if it has been cleaned, even if it has not. Water plants and top up vases, or throw away any flowers that have had their day.

Weekly schedules

The idea of a weekly routine – six days of hard work with a day of rest on the Sabbath – may seem anachronistic and hardly in keeping with our free-form, busy, busy lifestyle – all play-days and school runs. But in order for the home to function well, establishing a routine allows you to see what needs doing and gives you time to do it.

Boiled down to basics, the three most important weekly tasks are: laundry, cleaning and food shopping.

There are several ways you can tackle these tasks. The deciding factor is the size of your family. Below is a list of suggested timetables for different sizes of household. I repeat, they are suggestions to be adapted, not hard and fast rules.

One-person and two-person households. It is easy to allot one task to each day.
> Monday: washing, including pets' bedding (wash separately); take clothes to the
> dry-cleaner.
> Tuesday: ironing (if any – see 'To reduce ironing', p. 190).
> Wednesday: do bills/household accounts/mending.
> Thursday: weekly food shop – or have it delivered.
> Friday: do nothing.
> Saturday: clean house
> Sunday: do nothing/any major seasonal chores such as cleaning the windows.

Small families. A bit more juggling will be required.
> Monday: washing, including pets' bedding if applicable; take clothes to the dry-
> cleaner.
> Tuesday: ironing (but see above).
> Wednesday: washing; mini-clean of house (this will probably include vacuuming
> some of the rooms and cleaning anywhere that has got particularly dirty,
> such as a hallway).
> Thursday: weekly food shop (or delivery); do ironing if necessary.
> Friday: do bills and household accounts.
> Saturday: clean house; do washing if necessary.
> Sunday: do nothing, or odd/seasonal jobs.

Large families. How many balls have you got in the air?
> Monday: washing (see pets, above); do bills; interim food shop; take clothes to
> dry-cleaner.
> Tuesday: washing; ironing from previous day (but see above).
> Wednesday: washing; ironing from previous day if necessary; mini-clean of house
> (see above).
> Thursday: washing and ironing as above; weekly food shop (or delivery).
> Friday: do nothing (washing and ironing only if absolutely necessary).
> Saturday: clean house.
> Sunday: do nothing/odd jobs

The bedroom: Change the bed linen (do this twice a week in very hot weather).
Dust all surfaces. Vacuum carpets, rugs, hard floors, blinds and/or curtains.

The bathroom: Clean all fixtures and fittings: bath, washbasin, shower cabinet. Clean and disinfect the toilet bowl. Clean all other surfaces, such as tiles, splashbacks, bathroom cabinets and mirrors. Wash the floor thoroughly. Wash and disinfect waste-bins, especially if they have been used for nappies/sanitary napkins. Disinfect the waste pipes if necessary.

The kitchen: Clean all surfaces, including tiles, splashbacks and faucets. Wipe over drawer and cupboard fronts, especially round doorknobs.

> Note: if you have been wiping the worktops and stovetop every day,
> as per the daily schedule above, this is all so much easier. Suddenly,
> it all makes sense.

Wipe down other appliances such as the washing machine and dishwasher. Clean the filter and powder dispenser drawer on the washing machine. Check salt levels in the dishwasher (if your dishwasher uses salt).

Clean the fridge inside and out (it makes sense to do this on the day you do your weekly shop, when the fridge will be empty).

Clean the oven (if you give it a quick wipe-over every time you use it, it does not become such a daunting task).

Wash the floor thoroughly (again, if you have swept every day, this will take a matter of minutes).

Wash and disinfect the rubbish bins. Clean and disinfect the sink and waste pipe.

Wipe down Venetian blinds. Wash all cleaning cloths, tea towels, dish cloths and dusters.

The sitting-room and the rest of the house: Dust all surfaces, including furniture, shelves and ornaments, light fittings, tops of books, televisions, hi-fi equipment and pictures.

Wash marks in any areas of heavy traffic – e.g. doorknobs in the hall, scuffed skirting boards, smears on woodwork.

Clean mirrors. Wipe the telephone and computer keyboards.

Vacuum all carpets, rugs, lampshades, upholstery and curtains and/or blinds. Wash all washable floors.

299

Monthly schedules

Unless you have a fridge or freezer that defrosts automatically, check once a month that there is no build-up of ice. Defrost when it needs it (see 'The fridge', p. 13, and 'The freezer', p. 19).

Clean the windows, or have them cleaned. If you live in the country or somewhere where the air is clean, then once a quarter will be more than enough (see 'Windows', p. 246).

File all papers and household accounts (see 'Paperwork', p. 202).

Turn the mattresses on all the beds, if necessary – many modern mattresses do not require turning. Vacuum the mattresses. Wash mattress covers and pillow protectors (see 'Bed accessories', p. 69).

Do maintenance washes to clean the interior of the washing machine and dishwasher (see 'Washing up', p. 35).

Wash hair and make-up brushes.

300

Spring cleaning

Spring cleaning is an ancient and noble tradition. In the days of coal fires and gaslight, it was a necessity. The soot and smuts they produced would have coated the entire house in a layer of grime. In the dark winter days, this would probably not have been noticeable. Even if it were, there would not have been the wherewithal to wash things such as blankets and rugs, and to get them properly dry (our ancestors had a horror of damp out of all proportion to its dangers). With the coming of spring, the longer days and warmer temperatures, the entire house had to be cleaned from top to bottom – every drawer and cupboard turned out and cleaned, every wall and surface washed, bedding washed, upholstery cleaned. It was a nightmare.

Electric lights and central heating have not rendered such a routine entirely obsolete. Do not dismiss it utterly. The quality of daylight changes in the spring and seems to highlight the grime, dust and cobwebs that have accumulated over the winter. The longer evenings make us feel we can do more in a day. In short, the change of seasons energises us at a deep, primitive level. Spring puts a spring in our step.

> Note: Although there is a psychological boost in spring cleaning, annual deep-cleaning doesn't have to be done in the spring. In Scotland, the tradition is to clean the house from top to bottom after Christmas, so the New Year begins with a clean slate. You might, for example, like to do early autumn cleaning instead, when the days are still long and the temperatures still warm. That way, the house will be super-clean for Christmas.

An annual spring clean has many practical benefits for the house, including the following:

CLUTTER

Spring cleaning is an opportunity to go through stuff, to find out exactly what you have got and discard what you do not need. Of course, this does not mean that you have to throw things away. You can sell your stuff via a garage sale or online auction, or give it to charity.

Things you might consider selling/giving away: books, CDs, videos/DVDs, bric-à-brac, clothes, unwanted presents.

BEDDING

Winter bedding – blankets, quilts, heavier duvets, pillows, bedspreads, decorative throws and eiderdowns – should be washed or dry-cleaned before being stored. Apart from the basic requirements of hygiene, if they are stored when dirty, they are likely to be attacked by moths.

WINTER CLOTHES

All your winter coats and other clothes need cleaning and mending before being put away for the summer. Before you go to the trouble and expense of doing this, go through your clothes and decide whether each item has had its day or is worth keeping for another year (see 'Seasonal storage', p. 76).

Emptying out and cleaning wardrobes and chests of drawers will also help keep clothes moths at bay. Moths lay their eggs at any time of year, but are

301

particularly active in spring and summer. It is their larvae that chomp their way through your best coat. They prefer dark, dusty, warm places – the wardrobe is ideal. Cleaning out cupboards and drawers and the clothes they contain is therefore vital if you want to control this voracious pest (see 'Household pests', p. 322).

FURNITURE

Spring cleaning gives you a chance to examine your furniture properly. Do you see new woodworm holes? New woodworm holes have sharp edges, and if woodworm is active, a powdery dust (called frass) will fall out of them. If you think woodworm is active, seek professional help. For more on woodworm, see 'To prevent woodworm', p. 277.

Like moths, woodworm likes dark, dusty places. You can lessen the likelihood of attack by good housekeeping. The insides of all wooden cupboards and drawers should be vacuumed once a year.

OTHER SPRING CLEANING TASKS:

Polish the furniture
Wash ornaments
Dust or vacuum books (send those you will never read again to charity)
Clean lampshades, light fittings and chandeliers

Have carpets, upholstery and curtains and/or fabric blinds such as Roman
   blinds cleaned

Wash Venetian blinds

Send rugs to the cleaners

If you think the walls need washing, it is usually simpler and quicker to give
   them a fresh coat of paint instead

Turn out and clean the loft

Clean out the garage

Clean out cupboard under the stairs and any other cluttered storage area

Check outside gutters and drains for blockages or damage

Have the furnace or boiler and other appliances serviced

Empty and clean out all rarely used cupboards

Have the chimney(s) swept

Appendix A: Stains

Fabric stains

A stain on a fabric is something that has not been removed by normal washing. A stain is not dirt – what you have done is dye the fabric – so something can be stained but still clean. That said, most 'stains' will respond to a soak and wash.

The garment may have to be washed more than once; you may have to try stronger remedies; but if you are patient, do not panic and tackle the mark in an orderly way, it will disappear in the end.

> Note: The following applies only to washable fabrics. Do not attempt on fabrics that need to be dry-cleaned.

FABRIC STAIN REMOVAL PRODUCTS

There are plenty of commercial spot and stain removers on the market, and many of them are very good, but the basic household chemicals already to hand do the job just as well. Most common household stains can be tackled with one of the following:

> Enzymes – as found in biological pre-soak products and washing detergents
> Acids – lemon juice and white vinegar
> Alcohol – rubbing alcohol or any other pure colourless spirit, such as vodka
> Bleach – oxygen fabric bleach for preference. Use chlorine bleach only when absolutely necessary

To these, add a commercial stain removal product, such as White Wizard; a solvent spot remover, such as De-Solv-It, for ink stains; Wine Away for fruit and wine stains; and glycerine, which is available from pharmacies. A dry-stick spot remover is also useful for grease. (The only one as far as I know that is available in the UK is an American brand, called Janie.)

Of all these products, the most useful and gentlest are ordinary detergents and pre-wash products – especially on grease marks, food spots and oil marks.

TO TACKLE A LIQUID SPILL

Most liquid spills only become a problem when the substance has dried in. To prevent a spill becoming a stain, treat it as quickly as possible. Blot the spill with a white cloth or white paper towels. Do not rub it because you may spread the spill and damage the fabric. Work from the outside to the middle of the spill and be patient. Thorough blotting followed by normal washing to get rid of the final marks will prevent permanent staining in most cases.

TO TACKLE A SOLID SPILL

Solid substances, such as tar, mayonnaise, curry or vomit should be scraped off first. Use a knife or a spatula or, failing that, a piece of sturdy cardboard. Work from the outside in, to avoid spreading the substance. Once the residue has been removed, lift any remaining marks either by washing or with one of the remedies given in 'An A–Z of fabric stains', below.

TO TACKLE A DRIED-IN STAIN

This is the technique to use on all the stains mentioned below. Apply stain removers from the wrong side of the fabric. Applying them on the right side means the stain is merely pushed further into the fabric.

Make a pad of clean white cloth and place it over the stain on the right side of the fabric. On the underside, apply an appropriate stain remover. Work from the outside in, to avoid spreading it. Dab the stain rather than rubbing the fabric, which may damage its structure.

Use plenty of remover, but do not saturate the fabric in one go – use several small, repeated applications. As the pad underneath becomes wet, replace it. Be patient and keep reapplying until the stain disappears.

When the stain has been removed, rinse the entire garment in cold water, to remove all traces of remover, then wash as usual.

> *Note: Approach stain removal with caution. Many stain removal products cannot be used on wool, silk, leather or suede. Solvents may damage acetate and similar synthetic fibres, while bleaches should not generally be used on nylon and Lycra. Be guided by the care label, and if a fabric says 'Dry-clean only', do not attempt to remove the stain, but take the garment to the cleaners.*

HOW NOT TO TACKLE A STAIN

Do not try to remove stains with hot water. Hot water will set any stain containing protein, such as blood, milk, egg, urine and faeces. Heat has the same effect on the toner powder used in photocopiers and printers, because the machines use heat to set the ink. Do not try to remove grease-based stains, such as mayonnaise, with water alone. Water does not dissolve the grease and also seems to set the stain.

Do not use soap to remove stains. Soap sets stains containing tannins. These include tea and coffee; some berries, including cranberries and blackcurrants; felt-tip pen; ink; fizzy drinks.

If the stain remains after washing, do not dry the clothes or iron them. The heat in an iron or a tumble-dryer will probably set the stain. Wash again while still wet and repeat until the stain disappears. You may need to do this several times. Only dry and/or iron once it has gone.

AN A–Z OF FABRIC STAINS

Try these methods on dried-in stains or stains that have not been removed by normal washing. Before trying any of them, test the stain remover on an inconspicuous part of the fabric first: what removes the stain may also remove the dye on coloured fabrics.

Anti-perspirant/deodorant: Rub undiluted liquid biological detergent into the stain (or mix powder detergent to a paste with water). Leave for an hour or so. Rinse, then wash as usual.

Ballpoint pens: Spot-treat using a solution of an oxygen bleach (e.g. Oxi-Clean). Or use a commercial stain remover designed for ballpoint pens. You can also try plain alcohol – rubbing alcohol or vodka. Rinse, then wash as usual.

> *Tip: Some people recommend hairspray, but it can potentially cause staining in its own right.*

Beetroot: Rinse with cold water to loosen the stain, then wash as usual using biological detergent. Check that the stain has gone before drying. If not, repeat, using oxygen bleach.

Bird droppings: Scrape off the dropping, then wash as usual. If marks remain, soak in a solution of oxygen bleach (following instructions on the bottle), then wash again.

Blackcurrant juice: Rinse thoroughly with cold water to loosen the stain, then soak in a solution of biological detergent. If marks remain, treat with Wine Away (or similar), then wash with biological detergent. Do not dry until you are satisfied the stain has gone.

Blood: Soak in cold water only – hot water will set the stain. Wash, using biological detergent. Check that the stain has gone before drying or ironing. The heat of the tumble-dryer or iron will set the stain.

Candle wax: Rub ice cubes over the wax to harden. Even better is to put the item into a plastic bag in the freezer. Scrape off the hardened wax. To remove the waxy stain left on the fabric, place white paper towels on either side of the stain and press with a warm iron. Iron from the reverse side, so that the stain is not pushed further into the fabric. If there is still a mark, for example from coloured candles, try again, or use a spot stain remover such as De-Solv-It. Rinse, then wash as usual.

308

Chewing gum: Freeze as for candle wax, above. Once it is completely brittle, pick or scrape it off. Remove any greasy marks with White Wizard and wash.

Chocolate and cocoa: Scrape off, then soak in biological detergent or enzyme pre-wash. Rinse, then wash as usual, using biological detergent and oxygen bleach. If the stain has not gone, wash again while the garment is still wet.

Coffee: Soak in cold water. If the stain is still there, soak again in a solution of cold water and biological detergent or enzyme pre-wash. Rinse, then wash as usual, using oxygen bleach if necessary.

Colour runs: For full instructions, see 'Doing the laundry', p. 17.

Crayon: Treat exactly as candle wax. You will be left with a coloured stain. Treat with a spot stain-removerm such as De-Solv-It, then wash using oxygen bleach if necessary.

Curry: Scrape off curry. Soak in biological detergent, then wash as usual using oxygen bleach if necessary.

Yellow curry stains, usually caused by turmeric, can be removed from white fabrics by bleaching them in bright sunlight.

> Tip: If you are going out for curry and are worried about spillage, wear white clothes. White fabrics are, paradoxically, easier to clean than coloured ones because there is no chance of the dye fading.

Dyes: Dyes are very difficult to remove, because their raison d'être is to alter colour permanently. Hair dye is particularly recalcitrant – hence the reason that most hair salons use dark towels. Hair dye marks usually appear on pillowcases. Soak overnight in a solution of biological washing powder and wash, using oxygen bleach. Much depends on the fabric that has been stained. Poly-cotton tends to hold stains, whereas cotton can take harder laundering. If the stains have not come out of white cotton pillowcases, you may have to resort to chlorine bleach (see 'Bleach', p. 161).

Although the stains will look worse on white pillowcases than on coloured ones, white is easier to deal with because it can be washed at hot temperatures and can withstand bleaching.

309

Felt-tip pen: Soak to loosen the stain, then blot as much as possible using white paper towel. Wash using oxygen bleach. Check that the stain has gone before drying. If not, you may have to use a proprietary stain remover designed for felt-tip pen, such as the ink-removal formula of Dylon Stain Remover.

Fruit and fruit juices: As for beetroot (see above): rinse, soak, machine-wash. Repeat with oxygen bleach if the stains remain.

> Tip: Most fruit stains respond well to biological detergents.

Glue (all-purpose): On natural fibres, blot with acetone, i.e. nail polish remover, until the glue dissolves, rinse very well and then wash as usual. Do not use acetone on man-made fibres, particularly acetates, because it will dissolve them along with the glue. Work quickly before the glue has a chance to harden.

Glue (*paper*): Paper glues include Pritt and Copydex. Pick off any residue and wash as usual. These glues normally come out fairly easily.

Glue (*super*): Soak in hot soapy water to soften the glue before washing. Or use a proprietary glue remover.

Grass: Soak using an enzyme pre-wash. If the stains remain, blot with alcohol. Use undiluted on natural fibres; on synthetics, dilute with two parts of water, but go easy. Rinse and wash using a biological detergent and oxygen bleach.

> *Tip: A grass stain can be removed by rubbing a small amount of golden syrup (similar to corn syrup) on to it with your finger. You have to work away at it, and a brownish mark will remain, but this will come out with normal laundering.*

Grease, fats and oils: Grease stains always look worse than they are, but respond well to treatment.

Sprinkle the stain liberally with talcum powder, roll up the garment and leave overnight. The powder will soak up the grease, and all you have to do next day is brush it off. You may still have to wash it, but most of the grease will have gone.

Working on the same principle, use a dry-stick spot remover. Rub well into the stain and then brush off.

Alternatively, place the garment face down on a pad of white cloth or white paper towel and treat with a solvent stain remover such as De-Solv-It, applying it to the back of the stain and replacing the paper towels as they become saturated. Rinse with cold water and wash as normal, using a biological detergent.

Grime on collars and cuffs: Rub grimy areas with a little dish soap and leave for half an hour before washing as normal.

Ink: Soak in cold water to loosen the stain. Then place the garment face down on white cloths or white paper towels and apply White Wizard or a proprietary ink stain remover to the underside. Rinse thoroughly and then wash as usual.

> *Note: Detergent will set ink stains, so do not wash until you feel you have removed as much of the stain as is feasible.*

310

Ketchup: Soak in biological detergent, then wash as usual.

Lipstick and other cosmetics: Place the garment face down on a white cotton pad or white paper towels and blot with De-Solv-It. Keep blotting until the stain has softened, then wash as usual. Lipstick is notoriously difficult to remove. For make-up stains on pillowcases, see 'Dyes', above.

Mayonnaise: Sponge with lukewarm water. Hot water will set the stain. Soak and wash as normal, using a biological detergent.

Mildew and mould: Moulds attack and weaken fabric, so treat as soon as possible. Treat light mildew by washing using biological washing powder, and dry whites (not nylons) in bright sunlight for its bleaching effect.

Treat older stains on white fabrics (not nylon) with a solution of chlorine bleach (4 tbs to 5 quarts). Leave to soak for half an hour or so, then rinse thoroughly in water before washing as usual on a high temperature. Dry in sunlight if possible. Coloured fabrics can be treated with oxygen bleach.

311

Mud: Do not try to remove wet mud. Let it dry, then brush off as much as possible with a stiff brush. Rub undiluted liquid detergent into the stains (or make a paste of powder detergent and water) and leave for half an hour or so. Wash, using a pre-wash programme. If the stain has not gone, wash again.

Mustard: Dampen the stain and rub with liquid detergent (or make a paste of powder detergent and water). Wash as usual. Dry white items (not nylon) in bright sunlight to fade the stain.

Nail polish: Try using a nail polish remover that contains acetone to soften the polish and fade the stain, but test it on a hidden part of the garment first. Do not use on synthetic fabrics, particularly acetate, because it will melt them. The fact is that nail polish is virtually impossible to remove.

> Counsel of desperation: Place the stain face down on a pad of white
> paper towels and blot with a white cotton wool swab saturated with
> nail polish remover.

Paint: For water-based paints such as latex, sluice the garment in plenty of warm water, then wash as usual. Oil-based paints pose more of a problem. If the fabric can stand it, try using paint removers or turpentine. Rinse thoroughly, before washing.

Perfume: Soften dried-in perfume stains with a solution made of equal parts of glycerine (available from pharmacies) and water. Leave for an hour or so, then wash as usual.

Pollen: Do not rub pollen into fabrics, or it will make an indelible stain. Vacuum off using the lowest setting. Use a piece of sticky tape to remove any pollen that is left, then wash as usual, using bleach if necessary.

Red wine: Apply a proprietary stain remover designed for wine and fruit juices, such as Wine Away. It turns the stain an alarming shade of blue, which then just washes out.

> Tip: Never put salt on red wine spills. It will set the mark, making an indelible blue stain.

Rust: Apply lemon juice or white vinegar to the stain, rinse and wash as usual.
Or:
Crush a vitamin C tablet, moisten the rust mark and rub the crushed tablet into it. Leave overnight, not allowing the fabric to dry out. Next day, the rust stain will have gone, leaving a grey, muddy-looking mark, which will just wash out.

> Note: Never try to remove rust marks with chlorine bleach. It will set them for ever.

Scorch marks: Scorching is not really a stain. The heat has damaged the fabric. Bad scorch marks are impossible to remove; light marks may wash out (use bleach if appropriate).

Shoe polish: Scrape off shoe polish, place the garment face down on a white cloth or white paper towels and treat the stain from the underside, using a solvent stain remover such as De-Solv-It. Rinse thoroughly and then wash as usual. Use the same techniques to remove red polish from cricket whites.

Soot: As with pollen, avoid rubbing soot into the fabric. Dust with talcum powder and then vacuum that off. Wash as usual. It may take more than one wash to remove the soot marks, but repeated washings will gradually fade the stains.

Sweat: Make a solution of white vinegar and water (I tbsp vinegar to I cup water) and blot the stain, to clean and deodorise. Then soak white or colourfast garments overnight in biological detergent. Fabrics that can stand tough handling can be scrubbed with more biological detergent before washing as usual, again using biological detergent. The problem is that, without such tough measures, sweat seems to set indelibly into fabrics – silk and wool seem particularly prone to sweat staining, but will not withstand much soaking and scrubbing.

On delicate fabrics, try the vinegar solution mentioned above. Or soften old stains with glycerine (available from pharmacies). Pour on a small amount, work in gently (do not rub the fabric, especially if it is delicate), then wash as usual.

Tar: Scrape off as much as possible, then place the stain face down on a pad of white cloth or white paper towels and use a solvent stain remover, such as De-Solv-It. Rinse thoroughly and launder the garment using the hottest wash suitable for the fabric.

313

Tea: Treat as coffee.

Urine: Soak overnight using biological detergent in lukewarm water. Wash as usual, again using biological detergent.

Vomit and faeces: Remove any residue and rinse thoroughly in cold water. Soak overnight using biological detergent. Wash again, using biological detergent.

Carpet stains

Dealing with stains on clothes is relatively easy because they are small and portable. It is one thing to spill red wine on a shirt, quite another to spill it on a carpet, which you cannot just fling in the washing machine. But carpets, by their very nature, are tough and can withstand fairly vigorous cleaning. The main point is not to let the carpet get so wet that the backing becomes saturated, which could cause it to rot.

Before rushing for the stain removers, bear in mind that when you stain something, you are inadvertently dyeing it. Removing the stain from a carpet might make it look worse than leaving it and living with it. If the spill is on a dark or patterned carpet, the stain can often merge into the background so that it can barely be seen, if at all.

CARPET-CLEANING PRODUCTS

Before using any stain remover, check that it is suitable for use on carpets. Many fabric stain removers cannot be used on carpets; others cannot be used on foam-backed carpets. It is always better to start with the gentlest detergent and then if necessary move up, rather than risk damaging the carpet. The most useful products are:

White paper towels and white cotton cloths. Coloured towels and cloths can transfer dye on to the carpet, creating more stains

Mild, uncoloured, unperfumed detergent for washing woollens, such as Woolite, and/or mild, uncoloured, unperfumed dish soap

Soda water

White vinegar

A couple of proprietary carpet stain removers, such as White Wizard, or a dry-stick spot remover

For wine, fruit and other red stains: Wine Away

Glycerine (for dried-in stains)

For homes with pets, a special pet stain remover suitable for carpets, available from pet shops

See also p. 237 for a couple of home-made carpet cleaners, which are useful to know about in an emergency and in the absence of any of the above.

Note: Badly stained carpets should be professionally cleaned.

TO TACKLE A LIQUID SPILL

Blot the spill with white paper towels. Blot for at least five minutes, because the more of the substance you get out at this stage, the better your chances of it not staining the carpet. Do not rub, because that will spread the stain.

Extremely thorough blotting at this stage could remove most of the spill. If not, squirt the remaining mark with soda water. The idea is that the bubbles lift the stains to the surface and the alkali in the water will also help in the cleaning process. Do not saturate a large area of the carpet; put the water on the spill. Continue to blot, changing the paper towels often.

If a mark requires further treatment, try a proprietary carpet cleaner. Typically, these form a foam, which is worked into the spill to remove it. Use a white cloth to work the foam in gently. Work from the outside in so as not to spread the mark. Blot the excess with white paper towels and apply a second time if necessary. Once you are satisfied that the mark has disappeared, sponge-rinse with plain water to remove the detergent. Although it is important not to get a carpet too wet, because the backing could be damaged, it is equally important to remove all the detergent. Leaving in the detergent creates a permanently greasy patch that will attract more dirt. After rinsing, place plenty of white paper towels on the carpet, weigh down and allow the carpet to dry. Once the carpet is completely dry, vacuum to bring up the pile.

315

TO TACKLE A SOLID SPILL

By solid spills, I mean things like chocolate or vomit. With the exception of mud, all these stains will be much easier to deal with if they are not allowed to dry. Carefully scrape up any solid bits with the back of a knife, trying not to spread the stain further. Remove any residual stain on the carpet using one of the cleaners above. Once you are satisfied the stain has gone, rinse and blot well. Finally, place plenty of white paper towels on top of the stain, weight it down and leave to dry. Once dry, vacuum or brush the carpet to bring up the pile.

The exception to this rule is mud, which should be allowed to dry completely. Brush it off the carpet with a stiff brush and vacuum. Remove any residual marks with a solution of 1 tsp mild detergent to ½ pint warm water. Rinse and dry as above.

TO TACKLE A DRIED-IN STAIN

Pour half a pint of cold water slowly into the middle of the stain so that it spreads all over it. Immediately cover with white paper towel. Use at least one whole roll, to make a thick blanket of paper. Place a plastic tea tray or similar on the paper and put a couple of bricks on top. Leave for 12 hours. The water (and stain) should be drawn out of the carpet by capillary action.

If it has not all gone, tackle with carpet cleaner or foam, as above. It will be much easier to deal with when damp. This method works extremely well.

AN A–Z OF CARPET STAINS

As with any stain, the quicker you deal with it, the better the results. With two exceptions, mud and pollen, a spill is much easier to deal with while it is still wet.

After removing all stains, put a thick layer of white paper towels on the wet mark, weight it down and leave to dry. As well as drawing out any moisture that may be left in the carpet, it is an obvious reminder to everyone in the house not to walk on that part of the floor until the carpet is dry.

Blood: Use 1 tsp mild detergent to ½ pint cold water. Hot water will set the stain. Blot with a white cloth until the stain disappears. If not, try the same thing with a solution of mild oxygen bleach, such as Oxi-Clean (test on an inconspicuous part of the carpet first). Sponge-rinse with plain water. Dry as above.

316

> Tip: If it is your own blood, small amounts can be removed with your
> saliva. Work it into the stain, then rinse with plain cold water.

Candle wax: Pick off as much wax as possible from the carpet. It is easier to do this when it is hard, so fill a plastic bag with ice cubes and hold it over the wax. To remove any that is left, put a piece of white paper towel over the mark and iron gently on a low setting. Iron the paper, not the carpet, or you may scorch or flatten the pile. Once the wax has been absorbed, remove any residue with carpet shampoo. Or use a dry-stick spot remover.

Chewing gum: Hold a plastic bag of ice cubes on the gum until it becomes brittle enough to be picked off the carpet. Blot with a grease remover such as White Wizard, then blot with plain water to remove the detergent residue. Dry as above.

Chocolate: Scrape off residue with the back of a knife. Blot with spray carpet cleaner. Rinse with plain water. Dry as above.

Coffee: Dilute with soda water. Blot. Remove any other staining with a solution of 1 tsp mild detergent to ½ pint lukewarm water. Sponge-rinse with clean water. Dry as above.

Felt-tip pen: Do not allow to dry. Blot as much as you can with white paper towel before using a proprietary cleaner as above. If the stain has dried, try diluting with soda water first to loosen it.

Fruit juice: Blot up as much of the spill as possible with white paper towels before it has had a chance to dry. Treat with 1 tsp mild detergent in ½ pint lukewarm water. Rinse and dry as above. For dark fruit stains such as cranberry, use Wine Away (see 'Dried-in wine stains', p. 318).

Grease: Blot up as much as possible using white paper towel. Use a dry-stick spot remover. Work the stick into the stain, then vacuum out.

Ketchup: Scrape off excess, taking care not to spread the stain. Flush with soda water. Blot to remove as much of the stain as possible. Remove any final marks with a carpet shampoo.

317

> Note: Dried-in stains can be softened with a solution of equal parts
> of glycerine and water. Apply the solution, then leave it for an hour
> or so, covered with a white paper towel. When the ketchup has
> softened, proceed as above.

Mud: Allow the mud to dry completely, then remove with a stiff brush and vacuum. Remove any residual stain with a solution of 1 tsp mild detergent to ½ pint warm water. Rinse and dry as above.

Pet messes: See 'Pets', p. 330.

Pollen: Vacuum up immediately or use sticky tape to remove pollen from carpet. Do not rub.

Red wine: Red wine has a mythical status as the hardest stain to get out of carpets. In fact, it is not difficult to remove. It is what we do to the stains that causes the problems:

Do not pour salt on to a red wine stain. First, salt is used to set dyes, so even if you tackle the stain later, you are likely to be left with a blue mark on the carpet, which is difficult to get out. Second, the salt seems to make the carpet permanently damp. So even if the stain appears to have gone, the area of the carpet that was stained will tend to attract dirt. By the same token, do not pour white wine on the stain; another traditional remedy. The idea behind it is that the white wine 'neutralises' the red. How can this be? White wine may dissipate the red colour, but you still have a wine-stained carpet.

What you should do instead is the following:

Act quickly: Ideally, all stains should be tackled as soon as they happen. However, red wine is usually spilt during a social event, and it is not good manners to get out the carpet cleaner and be fretting about stains when guests are still there (see 'Dried-in wine stains', below).

Blot: There was a certain logic to the salt remedy, in that it was supposed to soak up the spill. Squirt the stain with soda water (its alkaline properties and bubbles lift the stain). Blot well (do not rub). Once the mark has disappeared, put a thick layer of white paper towel on top and weight it down to help draw out the stain. Leave overnight.

Dried-in wine stains: Soften dried-in stains with a solution of half and half glycerine and water. Dab it on, leave for an hour and then treat using one of the following:

Mix I tsp of mild detergent for washing woollens in ½ pint barely lukewarm water. Blot the stain with a white cloth until it disappears. Spray with a solution of four parts water to one part white vinegar. Blot. Repeat until the stain disappears. Finally, sponge-rinse with plain water. Put white paper towel on top, weight it down and leave to soak up the water.

Or use Wine Away, which removes not only red wine but cranberry juice and other red fruit stains and works very well. To use, follow instructions.

Tar: Scrape up as much as possible. Treat with a proprietary solvent stain remover, such as De-Solv-It (but note: do not use on foam-backed carpets), following instructions. Rinse. Any residual marks may need treating with proprietary carpet shampoo (see above).

Vomit: Scrape up as much as possible and treat with a solution of biological detergent. Rinse with plain water. Dry as above.

Upholstery stains

Before rushing to treat a stain, remember that if the upholstery is generally grimy, you may be left with a lighter patch, which will be as noticeable as the stain.

In case of very bad staining, call in the professionals.

UPHOLSTERY-CLEANING PRODUCTS

White paper towels and white cotton cloths.

Proprietary upholstery shampoo. To save doubling up on chemicals, look for a shampoo that can also be used to treat carpets

White Wizard spot stain remover

Dry-stick spot remover

For homes with pets, a special pet stain remover suitable for upholstery, available from pet shops

See also p. 237 for a home-made upholstery cleaner, which is useful in an emergency or in the absence of any of the above.

TACKLING LIQUID SPILLS ON FIXED UPHOLSTERY

Scrape off any solids, or blot spills over and over with white paper towels to remove as much as possible. To remove any remaining stain, use an upholstery shampoo. Apply the shampoo to the mark, work in with a white cloth, working into the centre, to avoid spreading the stain. It is important to work quickly so that the upholstery does not get too wet. At worst, it could rot or develop mildew; at best, it leaves your house smelling of wet dog.

Once you are satisfied that the mark has gone, sponge-rinse with clean water to remove detergent. Dry rapidly (try a hairdryer on a low setting). Do not sit on the furniture until it is completely dry because it is likely to get dirty again.

If the furniture is badly stained, call in the professionals.

To tackle a stain on slipcovers: Remove slipcovers and turn inside out. Place the stain face down on white paper towels or white cloth and treat from the wrong side.

319

The aim is to push the stain out, rather than pushing it further into the fabric. Once the stain has been treated, slipcovers can be dry-cleaned or washed according to instructions. Sometimes, with removable cushion covers, the advice is to treat stains without taking them off the cushions, which seems to defeat the point of having them. Treat the stain and then put the cover back immediately on the cushion. If you decide that the cushion cover then needs cleaning, have any other covers (for example, on a sofa) cleaned at the same time so they fade evenly.

> Tip: If washing slipcovers, put them back on the chair or sofa when still slightly damp so they dry in shape. But do not allow anyone to sit on them until completely dry. Apart from being uncomfortable, sitting on wet fabric can make it dirty.

To remove a fresh, water-soluble stain: The following also works with removable cushion covers. Take off the cover and wrap a rubber band round the stained area to isolate it from the rest of the fabric. Rinse the stained area very quickly with cold water until the stain has gone. Squeeze out any excess and immediately put the covers back on the furniture. Allow to dry.

This method works only on fresh water-soluble stains on washable fabrics. On dry-clean only fabrics, proceed with caution, because although the stain has gone, you may be left with a water mark.

AN A–Z OF UPHOLSTERY STAINS

Before trying any of these methods, test the stain remover on an inconspicuous part of the fabric first: what removes the stain may also remove the dye on coloured fabrics.

Ballpoint pen, felt-tip pens, ink: Sponge immediately with White Wizard. Rinse with clean water and dry.

> Tip: Allow only washable felt-tips and ink into the house.

Blackcurrant: Sponge immediately with cold water. Blot dry. To remove residual stains, dab with upholstery shampoo. Rinse and dry.

Blood: Sponge immediately with cold water to remove as much as possible. Treat any remaining stain with carpet/upholstery shampoo. Rinse and dry.

Candle wax: Pick off any obvious residue. To remove the rest, place a sheet of white paper towel over the stain and iron with a warm iron. Remove any remaining colour with upholstery shampoo.

> *Tip: White candles stain less than coloured ones.*

Chocolate: Scrape off solid chocolate. Apply a stain remover, such as White Wizard, following instructions. Rinse and dry.

Coffee: Sponge immediately with cold water. Treat with White Wizard. Rinse and dry.

Grease and oil: Sprinkle liberally with talcum powder. Leave for several hours, then vacuum off. Treat any remaining marks with a proprietary carpet/upholstery shampoo.
  Or:
  Use a dry-stick spot remover.

Ice cream: Sponge with lukewarm water, then treat any remaining marks with a proprietary upholstery shampoo. Rinse and dry.

Pet messes: See 'Pets', p. 330. Note that upholstery is more difficult to clean than carpet, and the smell from pet messes may linger. If so, have the furniture professionally cleaned.

Red wine: Do not pour salt on to the stain. Sponge with lukewarm water and blot to remove excess. Treat with Wine Away. Rinse and dry.

Shoe polish: Marks from the backs of people's shoes often appear at the base of a sofa or armchair. Spray a solvent stain remover such as De-Solv-It on to a white cloth and use to remove stain (check that it is suitable for the fabric first). Spraying on to a cloth avoids over-wetting the upholstery. Once the stain has gone, rinse and dry.

Tea: Treat as coffee.

Vomit: Scrape away the residue and sponge the area with warm water and a solution of biological washing powder. Rinse and blot dry. If the stain persists, try upholstery shampoo. As with pet messes, the smell of vomit can linger even when the mark has gone. If so, have the furniture professionally cleaned.

Appendix B: Household Pests

We live in a sanitised age, but we still share our homes with uninvited creatures that can have an impact on our health and comfort. Some are merely a nuisance, but other pests are really destructive, or positively dangerous – such as the squirrel that chewed its way through the electric wiring of a friend's house and caused a major fire. Some, such as rats, spread disease, particularly food poisoning, and cause acute embarrassment.

Luckily, with one or two exceptions, they are relatively easy to deal with.

ANTS

The familiar black garden ant is in many ways an attractive creature – industrious, robust, prolific, community-minded, even clean. Ants do not spread diseases, but they become a nuisance because of their tendency to invade houses in search of food.

TO DEAL WITH ANTS

Stop ants coming into the house. Check for points of access, such as holes at the junctions of walls and floors, gaps under doors and in window frames, and repair where necessary. In late spring cut back vegetation near to the house and check for ant nests. Fit special sticky tape across thresholds to deter ants from entering the house.

Sweep kitchen floors every day to get rid of crumbs that might attract ants, and ensure contents of kitchen cupboards are kept in airtight tins.

If ants invade the house, dust the ant runs with a proprietary ant powder (widely available). The powder tastes nice to the ants, which carry it back to the nest and poison the entire colony. If you find a nest, pour a kettleful of boiling water on it and dust with more ant powder.

Tip: A green option is to spray the ants with full-strength white vinegar. Use vinegar also to wipe round their entry points to the house. This is particularly suitable if you think children or animals might eat any poison lying around.

BEDBUGS

Bedbugs are increasing in number. This may be something to do with our love of travel to less developed parts of the world. A bug can easily be brought home in luggage. Infestations in this country often occur in hotels. Bedbugs can also get into the home via second-hand furniture or other hosts, such as bats and chickens.

The adult bedbug is wingless, measures 4–5 mm, and is thin, flat and oval in shape. It is dark brown in colour, unless it has just fed, when it becomes fatter and turns dark red. In very bad infestations, the room will have a characteristic foul, sweetish-smelling odour, similar to blackcurrants.

Bedbugs hide in the cracks and crevices of bedsteads, around the buttons on mattresses and in bedclothes. They come out at night to feed, and the saliva in their bites causes extreme irritation. It is the bites that usually betray the presence of bugs, along with tiny spots of blood appearing on bedding.

TO DEAL WITH BEDBUGS

An infestation should be dealt with by professional pest controllers, who will spray or dust the infested property with a broad-spectrum insecticide. All bedding should be washed on a very hot wash. Mattresses can be treated, but it is probably a better idea to buy a new one.

CARPET BEETLES

The carpet beetle measures 2–4 mm long, and has a brown or black body mottled with yellow or white scales, and looks similar to a ladybug.

Carpet beetles like to be warm, dry and undisturbed. Thanks to central heating and fitted carpets their numbers have risen hugely and they are now a major pest. The adult beetles live outdoors in summer, feeding on pollen and nectar. They move indoors in autumn to mate and hibernate.

It is the carpet beetles' larvae that cause the damage. These are sometimes called woolly bears, a cosy name that belies their destructiveness. They attack textiles of animal origin – in particular, wool, fur, leather and silk. Look for irregular holes and grazed areas on the surface of the fabric. Sometimes the short, hairy cast-off skins of the larvae can be seen lying nearby.

TO DEAL WITH CARPET BEETLES

Carpet beetles thrive in secluded situations, for example beneath carpets, around baseboards and in wardrobes and airing cupboards, so the best way to combat them is with regular, vigorous cleaning. Vacuum right to the edges of carpets and into all nooks and crannies. Lift rugs and vacuum under them. Remove all the contents from infested cupboards and clean or wash them, and then thoroughly vacuum the cupboard.

To prevent carpet beetle attack, spray the cupboard with insecticide or – the green option – set pheromone traps. These attract the adult beetles, allowing you to catch them before they mate.

COCKROACHES

Few household pests cause as much embarrassment and revulsion as cockroaches.

TO DEAL WITH COCKROACHES

Good hygiene practices should keep cockroaches at bay. Wash and dry dishes after eating – do not leave washing up soaking overnight. After washing up, wipe the sink dry and do not leave damp cloths lying around. Wipe up all crumbs and food debris and do not leave food out (this includes pet food: empty and wash animal food bowls).

Store all food in airtight containers. Use a rubbish bin with a tightly fitting lid and put the rubbish out every night.

In cases of serious infestation, call an exterminator.

DUST MITES

Dust mites are tiny arachnids that live in vast numbers in the dust in our houses. The mites feed off human skin. They are not parasites and do no damage unless someone in the house is allergic to them – or rather their droppings. These allergens have been identified as a major cause of asthma.

The mites are found in great concentrations in carpets and upholstered furniture. However, their favoured location is bedrooms, especially bedding.

To deal with dust mites:

Dust mites are in every home and are impossible to eradicate. Even if you were able to get rid of them all, they would quickly recolonise the house, floating in on the air as soon as a window was opened. If you or a member of your family has asthma, ask your doctor or specialist for advice on controlling dust mites. Health advice is beyond the scope of this book, but the following may help.

Air the bed. Sunlight and dry air reduce dust mite numbers. Every morning, open the windows, pull back the bedclothes and leave for as long as possible – up to an hour if you can; if not, for at least 20 minutes. To get the bed as dry as possible, use an electric blanket.

Wash bedding at high temperatures. Mites are killed by temperatures of 125°F and above, so buy bedding that can be washed at high temperatures (usually, this means a hot wash). Dry-cleaning will also kill dust mites.

Use mite-proof mattress and pillow covers. There are many different types, including micro-porous synthetic covers, which contain tiny holes that let water vapour through. Best of all are anti-mite covers made from high-quality Egyptian cotton, whose weave is so tight that dust mites cannot get through. They are expensive but last a lifetime and can be washed at high temperatures. Whichever you choose, the covers must enclose the mattress and pillows completely.

Keep the house as dry and well ventilated as possible. Open windows every day to let in air and sunlight. If the bathroom is carpeted, take up the carpet and replace with tiles or vinyl flooring. When vacuuming the bedroom, cover the bed with a clean dustsheet and leave the windows open for an hour afterwards to let the dust settle. When dusting, use a damp cloth to prevent dust flying about.

FLEAS

The cat flea and the dog flea are the two most common forms of flea found in houses. Fleas do not live on pets. They live deep in the pile of carpets, hopping on to the household pet for a quick meal and then hopping back on to the carpet. This is the reason that fleas seem to be at their most voracious when the house has been empty for a while. The starved fleas will launch themselves on to the first warm-blooded creatures they encounter.

By and large, fleas bite humans only when there is nothing else to hand, much preferring cats or dogs. If there is no animal in the house, they will eventually die of old age, but this can take several months.

To prevent fleas: Try to prevent pets from getting fleas. If they develop a flea allergy they can suffer terribly, literally scratching their skin raw.

If you suspect flea infestation in a dog, you can just give it a bath. With cats, flea powder used to be the only remedy, involving a harrowing half-hour of yowls, desperate bids for freedom, blood-letting and loss of dignity (it was horrible for the cats, too). Nowadays, all sorts of anti-flea magic is available, including injections, pills and drops of lotion applied to the back of the animal's neck. Consult a vet as to which is the most suitable.

To rid the house of fleas: Seeing fleas on your pet or on you is an obvious sign of infestation. Another sign is grey and white dust over your pet's bed. This is a mixture of grey flea larvae and white eggs, and is a sign of serious infestation.

First, attend to the pet's bed. If the infestation is very bad, you may have to burn the bedding. If not, wash it on a very hot wash using biological washing powder. If the pet has been used to sleeping in people's beds, remove all bedding, including the mattress cover, and wash on a hot wash. Tumble-dry the pillows on high for 15 minutes and vacuum the mattress. Turn and vacuum the other side before putting bedding back.

From then on, the best remedy is meticulous vacuuming. Pay particular attention to the area around your pet's bed and any other places where it likes to sleep. Vacuum these areas every day, along with all other carpets and upholstery, including the edges of carpets and down the backs and sides of chairs and sofas. Use the crevice tool to get into all the nooks and crannies.

Once you have finished, remove and throw away the vacuum cleaner bag immediately because the fleas will live inside it.

Do this every day until the problem disappears, remembering to change the vacuum cleaner bag every time.

FLIES

The house fly is associated with more than 100 pathogens that cause disease in humans, including typhoid, cholera and food poisoning, particularly salmonella.

Fruit flies are attracted to ripe fruit and vegetables in the kitchen, but will also breed in drains, waste disposals, empty bottles and cans, rubbish bins, mops and cleaning rags. They are primarily nuisance pests, but they too can contaminate food with bacteria.

Cluster flies emerge at the end of summer seeking a warm place for the winter – often in the walls, attics and basements of houses. Crawling over windows and congregating in unused rooms, they can be a real nuisance.

To deal with houseflies: Keep the kitchen scrupulously clean. Do not leave scraps of food or dirty dishes lying around. Wash up and wipe all worktops and other surfaces after use. Keep food covered or refrigerated. Invest in food nets to cover food that is not being refrigerated. Buy a rubbish bin with a tight-fitting lid and take the rubbish out every night. Clean the bin regularly (once a week).

If flies are a real problem, the green choice is a flypaper or strip rather than insecticide. Flypapers are covered with a sticky substance containing pheromones that attract the flies. They settle on the paper and become stuck fast.

To deal with fruit flies: Do not leave fruit out in the open. Cover or refrigerate it. Keep vegetable racks clean and throw away any overripe vegetables. Wipe up all spillages and keep worktops and other surfaces clean. Clean waste disposal units regularly (see 'Waste', p. 51).

327

> *Tip: To check whether waste disposal units are breeding sites for fruit flies, tape a plastic bag over the opening overnight. If flies are breeding, the adults will emerge and be trapped in the bag.*

To deal with cluster flies: For small infestations, you will have to treat with insecticide. Pay particular attention to points of access – look for any small holes and around the baseboards. For large infestations, call in the experts.

MOTHS

The creature that chomped its way through your best cashmere jumper was probably the common clothes moth. Clothes moths are silvery yellow in colour and, unlike other moths, do not fly to lights at night, but prefer warm, dark, dusty places such as cupboards and wardrobes.

Clothes moths used to be a summer hazard only, but thanks to central heating they now lay their eggs all year round. The eggs can take up to three weeks to hatch in winter (four to ten days in summer). It is these larvae that eat your clothes. They prefer natural fibres, and wool, silk, cotton, leather, fur and feathers are most at risk. A sign of a heavy infestation is a mess of debris (called frass) along with the characteristic ragged holes.

Other types of moth infest other rooms in the house, particularly the kitchen. In this case, the culprit is probably the brown house moth.

TO DEAL WITH CLOTHES MOTHS

Prevent the moths getting a toehold in the first place by thorough spring cleaning (see 'Schedules', p. 301). Once or twice a year, empty out all cupboards, wardrobes and chests of drawers. Vacuum thoroughly, making sure you get into all nooks, crannies and crevices. Now, wash down the shelves and the interiors of drawers, rinse and allow to dry before replacing clothes. Reline drawers and shelves with fresh paper. Lightly spray the interiors of wardrobes with an insecticide spray. Look for a spray based on natural products. If someone gives you a present of a second-hand piece of clothing, wash or dry-clean before putting it in your wardrobe. Any clothes that are stored for a long time should be dry-cleaned or washed first. Moth larvae prefer dirty clothes to clean ones.

328

Small items such as cashmere jumpers can be frozen to kill moth larvae. Wrap the jumper in acid-free tissue paper and then in a plastic bag. Place the bag in the freezer for at least seven days. Remove from the freezer and allow to defrost slowly before drying completely and putting away.

Moths can be discouraged from attacking carpets by thorough, regular vacuuming. Use the crevice tool to get into the corners and edges of fitted carpets. Move rugs and vacuum the carpet underneath and the underside of the rug. Dry-clean rugs and shampoo carpets and upholstery once a year.

Hang moth-deterrent strips based on permethrin (widely available) in the wardrobe along with your clothes.

> *Note: Do not put moth deterrents in a wardrobe that is already infested. Clean out and clean clothes as above first.*

TO DEAL WITH HOUSE MOTHS

If moths get into kitchen cupboards, empty the cupboards out and throw away all the food (the larvae can even get into closed packets). Thoroughly clean out the cupboards, making sure you get into all the corners and cracks. There are some insecticides that are suitable for food cupboards, but check beforehand. Spray the interior of the cupboard lightly and allow to dry completely before replacing the food. To guard against the moths returning, do not buy more food than is necessary and keep an eye on use-by dates. Do not leave opened packets of food in cupboards, but transfer to airtight containers.

Once the moths have been eradicated, place pheromone traps to catch any more. The traps attract male moths, leaving no mates for the females.

RODENTS (MICE, RATS, SQUIRRELS)

Mice enjoy the warmth and shelter of buildings and can get into houses through a hole as little as ³/₈ in wide. They can damage the structure of a house, nibbling through electric cables and gas and water pipes. They contaminate food with their droppings and urine and carry a number of diseases, including food poisoning. Rats are rarely seen in houses; they prefer sewers and rubbish dumps.

TO DEAL WITH RODENTS

Stop mice coming into the house. Check for points of access, such as holes at the junctions of walls and floors, gaps under doors and in window frames, ducts and drains, and repair where necessary.

If it is just one or two mice, they can often be caught in a humane trap and removed to woodland. If that fails, even the traditional mousetrap is preferable to poison, as it is a quicker and less painful end. Also, a poisoned mouse will go away to die, but possibly not far, and the smell of decomposing mouse is quite astounding.

A large infestation of mice and all infestations of rats and squirrels should be dealt with by experts. After the rodents have gone, stop up any access holes to prevent them coming back.

WOODWORM

For details on dealing with woodworm, see 'Wood furniture', p. 272.

Appendix C: Pets

I think every family should have a pet. Pets teach us to think about something other than ourselves, to recognise that in return for all that unconditional devotion it is our responsibility to look after them properly. Pets are warm, companionable and fun, and they depend on us.

This section deals with furred pets, specifically cats, dogs and things like hamsters and gerbils. Birds and reptiles need specialist care that is beyond the scope of this book.

HOW TO LIVE WITH YOUR PET

Pets are pets – they are not little furry people, and they can pass on some unpleasant things, including intestinal worms, campylobacter, toxoplasmosis and salmonella. Their fleas will not make you ill, but their bites can cause discomfort and embarrassment.

It is therefore imperative to follow basic rules of hygiene. Always wash your hands after stroking or handling a pet, especially before eating or preparing a meal. Children should have this principle drummed into them. Do not let pets sleep on beds. This is easier with dogs, which can be trained not to go into certain rooms. With cats, you just have to be disciplined about shutting bedroom doors. Keeping cats off chairs is also virtually impossible, but a dog can be trained to use its own bed or basket.

Do not let cats walk on tables or work surfaces, especially where food is prepared.

Do not allow children to keep hamsters, gerbils, mice and the like in cages in their bedrooms.

KITCHEN HYGIENE AND PETS

Do not let pets eat off the same plates as the family, or allow them to lick plates. Do not let pets beg at the table or feed them titbits during the meal. Keep special water and food dishes for pets. Try not to feed animals in the same place that the family's food is prepared. A utility room or a garage is a better proposition. You can keep all their food near the bowls, too, but opened tins need to be refrigerated.

If pets absolutely have to be fed in the kitchen, keep their feeding bowls as far away from food preparation areas as possible. Wash them up separately as soon as possible after use. This is sometimes difficult with cats, which have a maddening habit of leaving food, so they can come back to it for a little snack later. Try to break the habit by removing the dish and washing it up. The cat will eventually get the idea (always make sure there is a bowl of water available, though). Use hot, soapy water for the dishes, then rinse and dry with a paper towel.

HOUSEKEEPING AND PETS

Keep the house well ventilated and let your pet go outside as much as possible.

Frequently vacuum areas of the house where the pet goes – daily if necessary. Pay particular attention to carpets and upholstery (some vacuum cleaners are designed to deal with pet hair).

If the hairs persist, try using a clothes brush designed to pick up hairs or a lint-attracting clothes roller that picks up hair and can then be rinsed under the faucet. Keep all brushes and rollers specifically for this purpose.

Air and shake out pets' bedding daily and wash it once a week on a hot wash.

Clean up messes immediately and scrupulously.

TO DEAL WITH LITTER TRAYS

Keep litter trays in areas with good ventilation and away from food preparation areas. A utility room, garage, porch or balcony is preferable to a bathroom, although many people like the convenience of being able to flush the animal's faeces away easily. Unless it is impossible to do otherwise, never keep a litter tray in the kitchen.

Change and clean the tray every other day, or daily if the weather is very hot. If you use litter tray liners, this is just a matter of lifting it out, tying it and throwing it away. Try to change it outside if you can.

Wash the box thoroughly with hot, soapy water and then disinfect with bleach or disinfectant.

TO DEAL WITH PETS' CAGES

Clean cages at least once a week, outside if possible to prevent the smell pervading the house. Some animals are sensitive to certain disinfectants, so get advice from your vet before using them to disinfect cages.

TO DEAL WITH CATS THAT SPRAY

Cat urine is one of the world's most uncompromising bad smells. The spraying can have many causes and if your cat persists, consult a vet before it becomes chronic.

Deal with the problem as quickly as possible.

TO REMOVE CAT URINE FROM CARPETS AND UPHOLSTERY

Blot up as much as possible, using copious quantities of paper towels.

Small rugs can be taken to the cleaner after blotting. For fitted carpets and upholstery, use one of the enzyme cleaners available from pet shops. If this is not available, make a solution of biological washing powder and warm water. Using paper towels, blot the stain with this solution until the stain has gone. This will take time, so be patient. Rinse thoroughly with plain water. Repeat as necessary until all trace has gone.

Either allow to dry or, if practicable, put a large wad of paper towel (an entire roll's worth) on top of the stain. Place a board on top and then a couple of bricks on top of that. Leave overnight. Capillary action will draw out the moisture.

The next day, apply an enzyme odour remover (available from pet shops). Allow the area to dry completely.

> *Note: Vinegar and ammonia will not work on cat stains. Neither will bleach, disinfectant or anything pine-, rose- or lemon-scented. They all smell like urine to a cat.*

TO PREVENT YOUR CAT SPRAYING AGAIN

'Mark' the area that has been sprayed for the cat. Either take a piece of white cloth and rub it on the cat's cheeks before rubbing the spot where it has sprayed, or use Feliway spray (available from vets). This is a pheromone spray that mimics the effects of cats' facial marking (this is what they are doing when they rub against things). The effect of both is to calm the cat, making it less likely to spray. Both are effective, but the white cloth technique is cheaper.

TO DEAL WITH FLEAS

See 'Household pests', p. 322.

PETS AND ALLERGIES

Cats, dogs, mice and rats, birds and horses can all induce allergic reactions. The good news is that people are generally allergic only to one species. Cats seem to be a particular culprit because the allergens they produce are especially potent.

Cat allergens come not from their fur but from a protein in their sweat and saliva. Cats' constant grooming carries the saliva to their skin and fur, and the allergens are then deposited anywhere that the cat lies or sits. The allergens stick to tiny particles of skin (known as dander) and also float around in the air in the form of microscopic particles. They float around for a long time and when they do settle, are easily wafted up into the air again. Allergens are also present in urine. Once it dries, they are released into the atmosphere. This creates a problem with mice and other small rodents, whose cages can be a potent allergen producer. In really bad cases, the only solution may be not to keep pets at all.

TO REDUCE PET ALLERGENS

It is impossible to eliminate allergens, because the animal is constantly producing them. But you can reduce them to some extent by grooming the animal daily — something animals enjoy very much. Do it outside, removing fur from brushes and throwing it away. Give the animal regular baths. This is easier with dogs than cats, but cats can be bathed if you get them used to it when they are young. Ask your vet about appropriate products for both.

Keep the house well ventilated and let the pet go outside as often as possible. If you can make a warm, comfortable bed for it outside the main part of the house (for example, in a utility room), so much the better. It is obviously imperative that animals must not be allowed to sleep on beds where there is an allergy sufferer in the house.

Keep the pet's bedding clean and keep pets out of all bedrooms and off the beds. Keep the bedroom doors shut at all times. If the animal gets on the bed, strip it and wash the bedding.

Vacuum thoroughly several times a week — this means curtains and upholstery as well as carpets and hard floors. Invest in a vacuum cleaner with a HEPA filter, or one that is designed for allergy sufferers. Empty the vacuum cleaner bag or dust container outside after cleaning.

Appendix D: Self-Storage

De-cluttering is the buzz-word, but what are you supposed to do with the things that are left over, the things that you may use only once a year, but still need to find room for – such as the Christmas decorations, walking gear, ski gear, the barbecue and so on?

In the absence of a garage or an attic, the modern solution is to hire a unit in a self-storage facility.

Self-storage is particularly popular in the south-east and in cities, as flats do not have much storage space.

CHOOSING SELF-STORAGE

Try to work out how much space you need. It is probably less than you think, because things will be stacked on top of each other. Ask for advice. Also consider how far you want to travel each time you need to get something out of storage – if you are not planning to visit the storage facility often, it will probably be cheaper to find one out of town. Make sure the storage room is secure, clean and dry, and that there are adequate fire precautions; and check the insurance requirements.

TIPS FOR LONG-TERM STORAGE

Put down dust cloths, so that items such as furniture are not in contact with concrete floors. Wrap pictures and china in bubble wrap. Cover anything that will get impregnated with dust, such as mattresses, with a dustsheet. Put the stuff you will need most often at the front of the storage facility. Make an inventory, so that you know what you are storing and where it is.

Appendix E: Employing a Cleaner

You might come to the conclusion that the best way to clean your house is to get someone else to do it. One in ten British households now employ domestic help.

Many people feel awkward about employing a cleaner. This is partly because cleaners are virtually invisible, coming into houses when their employers are at work and leaving before they return home. The only evidence that they have been in the house at all is a sparkling sink and a pile of ironing. The following guidelines should help both cleaner and client.

CHECKING REFERENCES

Four-fifths of cleaners are found by word-of-mouth recommendation. Before employing a cleaner, ask for references and follow them up (ask for more than one reference). If they are reluctant to supply them, go elsewhere. If your cleaner is going to have a set of house keys, ask for a deposit ($30 is about right), which will be returned when they stop working for you. If they do disappear, have the locks changed.

PAY AND CONDITIONS

A cleaner is entitled to fair pay. The current hourly wage for housekeepers or maids in the US is between $10 and $15. Check with your local tax office about your obligations to pay Social Security. (However, it must be admitted that many cleaners prefer to work cash in hand and will not thank you for alerting the tax man to their presence.)

Check with your household insurance policy about your coverage for accidents or breakages. If a cleaner is employed via an agency, which will sort out things such as Social Security, check that they get a fair proportion of the overall fee.

If, like many people, you are paying your cleaner cash in hand, it is decent and fair to pay them when you are on holiday. Why should they lose their income, just because you have decided to go away? A good employer gives a cleaner a

Christmas bonus – a week's pay is about right. A decent Christmas present would not go amiss either; neither would a birthday card.

TREAT YOUR CLEANER WITH RESPECT

Just because your cleaner does housework (work that you choose not to do yourself), do not dismiss their job as menial. It enables you to combine a career and family and keep the show on the road. Most cleaners view themselves as professionals, take pride in their job and know their value. Many stay with the same family for years and become friends.

If the cleaner breaks something, you may be able to make an insurance claim, which is why it is important to check the conditions of coverage. You can ask a cleaner to be more careful, and have the right to expect an apology, but to ask them to pay for the broken object is bad form.

TIDY UP BEFOREHAND

To clean an average-sized, averagely dirty three-bedroom house will take a good cleaner four hours a week. If they are expected to do the ironing as well, allow another couple of hours. Cleaners are not superhuman. If 4–6 hours seems a lot, try cleaning the house and doing the ironing all in one go yourself and see how long it takes.

A cleaner's job is to clean, and their job will be much more difficult if they are expected to clean round clutter. On the day the cleaner is due, wash up, clear away clutter, put clothes away, empty bins. If teenagers' rooms are health hazards, tell the cleaner to leave them.

EQUIPMENT

Most cleaners will say which equipment and cleaning products they prefer. It might be your home, but it is your cleaner's place of work, so consider health and safety standards. Minimise the cleaner's exposure to toxic chemicals by using greener brands and keeping use of chemicals to a minimum (see 'Household chemicals', p. 225). That said, if your cleaner insists that they will not work without bleach or whatever, give in gracefully.

Keep equipment clean and in good order. Change the bag and filter in the vacuum cleaner regularly; ditto the mop head. Make sure there are plenty of clean cloths and dusters. Ask the cleaner to leave used cloths out, and wash them ready for next time.

Make it clear what you expect from a cleaner at the outset. If you are not satisfied with their work, talk to them about it – preferably in person, or on the phone.

Do not ask a cleaner to do any job you would not tackle yourself, such as cleaning the outsides of upstairs windows. You are within your rights to ask them to clean the oven, but if it is really filthy, you cannot expect them to do the routine cleaning as well. If you have antiques or anything old or valuable, you might want to look after them yourself.

Index

347

Acknowledgements

A large number of people generously shared their time and knowledge with me in the making of this book. I would like to thank Sarah Staniforth, Historic Properties Director, Helen Lloyd, deputy head conservator and preventive conservation adviser, at the National Trust for all their information on conservation techniques and the care of fine china and glass; David Burton, House Manager of Chirk Castle for all the information about the workings of the castle's laundries in the 1930s; Trevor Proudfoot, Cliveden Conservation, for his help on the care of stone; conservators at the Stableyard Workshop at Burghley, including Barry Witmond (silver), Anthony Beech (wood) and Sheila Landi (textiles); John Wilkie of Wilkie Furniture Design for more advice on the care of wood; Bob Cry of Pest Control Direct who knows all there it to know about pests and how to get rid of them; Mark Sargeant, head chef at Gordon Ramsay's Claridge's for his kitchen wisdom; the tireless Lisa Balliache of the John Lewis PR department; John Murphy, assistant buyer, electrical services at John Lewis for his encyclopaedic knowledge of kitchen appliances; Dr Imtiaz Ahmad, APU, Department of Forensic Science and Chemistry, Cambridge, for her fascinating information on the danger of household chemicals; Tony Luke, 'the best dry cleaner in Europe'; Hilary Bennett of Thames Water for advice on water usage; Mr Cliff Walby of Furs of Mayfair for advice on how to look after and store furs; Jenny Catlin of Mintel; Michaeljohn hair salon for advice on caring for hair brushes and make-up brushes; numerous friends, acquaintances and correspondents, who lent me books and happily shared their household tips, including Rebecca Abrams; Sarah Crompton; Tiffany Daneff; Jocelyn James; Jo Barnes; Christine Lampier; Belinda Richardson; Sinclair McKay; Liz Grice; Miranda Worsley; Mrs Pamela Davison; Eva Goodhew; Sally Gritten; Mrs C. Tate; Mrs Lesley Humphries; Josephine Spiegel; Brenda Hayward; Saskia Daniel; Maureen Brindley; G.P. Hamilton.

This book had a long gestation and the fact that it has appeared at all is thanks to Richard Atkinson and Erica Jarnes of Bloomsbury, who imposed order on chaos. Thanks also to Rosemary Davidson, who championed it in the first place, my agent Lizzy Kremer, who was bossy when it was necessary, and Sarah Sands, who encouraged me to think that people might actually want to read about housework.

A NOTE ON THE AUTHOR

Rachel Simhon is a newspaper journalist, and until recently wrote a successful column on housekeeping for the *Daily Telegraph*. She lives in London.